Oracle Primavera P6 Version 8: Project and Portfolio Management

A comprehensive guide to managing projects, resources, and portfolios using Primavera P6, through version 8.2.

Daniel L. Williams, PhD

Elaine Britt Krazer, PMP

BIRMINGHAM - MUMBAI

Oracle Primavera P6 Version 8: Project and Portfolio Management

First published: August 2012

Production Reference: 1140812

Published by Packt Publishing Ltd.
Livery Place
35 Livery Street
Birmingham B3 2PB, UK.

ISBN 978-1-84968-468-2

www.packtpub.com

Cover Image by David Gutierrez (bilbaorocker@yahoo.co.uk)

Credits

Authors

Daniel L. Williams, PhD

Elaine Britt Krazer, PMP

Reviewers

Denitsa Banova

Robert W. Self, PMP

Deepak Vohra

Acquisition Editor

Rukshana Khambatta

Lead Technical Editors

Shreerang Deshpande

Sonali Tharwani

Technical Editors

Apoorva Bolar

Madhuri Das

Project Coordinator

Joel Goveya

Proofreader

Cecere Mario

Indexers

Hemangini Bairi

Tejal R. Soni

Graphics

Manu Joseph

Production Coordinator

Prachali Bhiwandkar

Cover Work

Prachali Bhiwandkar

About the Authors

Daniel L. Williams, PhD first began working with Primavera in 2001 as part of an integration project with JD Edwards World. Since then, he has helped clients integrate Primavera with many other systems, such as PeopleSoft, Timberline, and Oracle EBS. His work centers around helping people make best use of Primavera and other software investments. Sometimes this involves heavy integration; sometimes it involves customization and automation of business processes. Sometimes it simply involves listening to people talk through their business goals and helping them come up with workable solutions. Daniel's background includes a Ph.D. in Physics from Caltech, many years of programming in C, C++, C#, and Java, and for the past decade, leading numerous software development projects oriented around Primavera

I would first like to thank my wife Heather for being the cornerstone of our family and allowing me to pursue a career I enjoy. I would also like to thank Justin Cohen for his years as a friend and business partner, and Patrick Martin for his long-term friendship, advice, and support. This book would have not been possible without all of the clients I have worked for over the years—Wendy Kaszycki, David Myers, Sandy Kayser, Sally Rau, Beth Maclean, Cathy Rosczewski, and many others. Their guidance is what drives me to learn and improve every day, and their thanks is the greatest reward for my labors.

Elaine Britt Krazer, PMP began working with Primavera products as a project manager for a government contractor in a top secret environment in 2003. Having managed projects since 1986, she embraces Primavera as her tool of choice. She has written training materials and published materials that combine best practices (as defined by the Project Management Institute® and from experience) and the appropriate use of Primavera within client organizations. Her philosophy is that understanding an organization's strategic goals for projects are the foundation for project management excellence and Primavera is the tool of choice. She has a master's certificate from George Washington University 2002, and Project Management Professional (PMP®) and ITIL Foundations certifications. She is an Oracle Certified Primavera Implementation Specialist and is Primavera Training Authorized. Elaine has worked in most major industries implementing Primavera. Her past includes technical change management, business process redesign, data center management, and PMO creation.

I would like to thank Daniel, the team at Packt Publishing, and my family for their constant support during the writing of this book. I am blessed.

About the Reviewers

Denitsa Banova works as a Primavera implementation consultant. She has extensive experience in Portfolio/Program/Project Management gained in more than five years of work as a team leader, consultant, and trainer in Primavera implementation projects in various IT companies, construction and manufacturing sectors, and also as project manager in different software implementation projects. Her specialties are Primavera P6 EPPM and Primavera P6 Professional.

> I would like to thank Joel Goveya for being such a cooperative and an understanding project coordinator.

Robert W. Self, PMP has over 20 years experience in training, implementation and use of Primavera products with expertise in Primavera Project Manager (P6), Contract Manager (Expedition), and Project Risk Manager (PertMaster).

He has written multiple training manuals to help students become power users of P3 and P6. These manuals range from basic concepts through advanced topics, such as reporting, resource management, and use of Risk in P6.

Currently, Robert is a part of the project controls team at the DFW International Airport, working directly with civil and facility project managers on a variety of projects ($1M – $20M each project) throughout the entire project lifecycle. These projects include basic renovation to Greenfield projects, even the occasional LEED project. His daily duties include performing frontline evaluation of programmatic (internal), as well as contractor schedules. In addition to his regular duties, he provides mentoring to DFW colleges and contractors in terms of schedules and project controls.

I would like to thank my wife, Sharon, for her patience and understanding. She has been and remains my inspiration. She has long suffered as a road warrior's wife.

I would also like to thank Mike Stone for giving me the opportunity to get into the training and consulting business by working with the Houston Primavera dealer. The variety of industries and clientele proved an excellent crucible to focus my understanding and appreciation of quality project management tools and techniques.

Deepak Vohra is a consultant and a principal member of the NuBean.com software company. Deepak is a Sun certified Java programmer and web component developer, and has worked in the fields of XML and Java programming and J2EE for over five years. Deepak is the co-author of the Apress book Pro XML Development with Java Technology and was the technical reviewer for the O'Reilly book WebLogic: The Definitive Guide. Deepak was also the technical reviewer for the Course Technology PTR book Ruby Programming for the Absolute Beginner, and a technical editor for the Manning Publications book Prototype and Scriptaculous in Action. Deepak is also the author of the Packt Publishing books JDBC 4.0 and Oracle JDeveloper for J2EE Development, Processing XML Documents with Oracle JDeveloper 11g, and EJB 3.0 Database Persistence with Oracle Fusion Middleware 11g.

www.PacktPub.com

Support files, eBooks, discount offers and more

You might want to visit www.PacktPub.com for support files and downloads related to your book.

Did you know that Packt offers eBook versions of every book published, with PDF and ePub files available? You can upgrade to the eBook version at www.PacktPub.com and as a print book customer, you are entitled to a discount on the eBook copy. Get in touch with us at service@packtpub.com for more details.

At www.PacktPub.com, you can also read a collection of free technical articles, sign up for a range of free newsletters and receive exclusive discounts and offers on Packt books and eBooks.

http://PacktLib.PacktPub.com

Do you need instant solutions to your IT questions? PacktLib is Packt's online digital book library. Here, you can access, read and search across Packt's entire library of books.

Why Subscribe?

- Fully searchable across every book published by Packt
- Copy and paste, print and bookmark content
- On demand and accessible via web browser

Free Access for Packt account holders

If you have an account with Packt at www.PacktPub.com, you can use this to access PacktLib today and view nine entirely free books. Simply use your login credentials for immediate access.

Instant Updates on New Packt Books

Get notified! Find out when new books are published by following @PacktEnterprise on Twitter, or the *Packt Enterprise* Facebook page.

Table of Contents

Preface

Oracle Primavera P6 is the most sophisticated and widely-used project portfolio management software in the world today. Some people think of P6 as simply a tool for scheduling projects, such as Microsoft Project, but on steroids. But while P6 can be used to plan a project a simple as writing one book, it can also be used to plan and manage a multi-year, globally-distributed set of engineering projects involving tens of thousands of workers, machines, and materials. When used to its fullest, it can give an organization the ability to manage current projects, plan future projects, and make key metrics to improve processes and ensure future success.

Primavera P6 is a vast product, with so many parts and features that it can seem overwhelming to the new user. And there are many aspects to discuss under the topic P6, such as the system architecture and database models, the various APIs and how they work, and fine-tuning P6 for optimal performance under varying conditions. There are also many books on project management and scheduling, centered around the principles set forth in the Project Management Body of Knowledge (PMBOK).

This book is designed to be a gentle introduction to P6, covering all of the main aspects of the product from a user's point of view. Novices to P6 may read this book from end to end, trying out the features and working through the examples as they read along. For those who already know P6, or perhaps P3, OpenPlan, or some similar product, this book serves as a refresher and shows the capabilities of P6 in its current release, what features there are, what they are for, and how to use them. Each chapter of this book covers one or more core features, and each of these features can be explored at a much greater depth than can be contained in these pages. It is the sincere hope of the authors that this book will serve your needs as you and your team use Primavera P6 to manage your projects and to continually improve your project management expertise.

What this book covers

Chapter 1, Getting Started with Oracle Primavera P6, reviews the history and core concepts of P6 and introduces the new features in version 8.

Chapter 2, Getting Around: Understanding and Customizing the P6 Interface, walks you through logging into P6 Professional and P6 web, and gives an overview of the key menus and screens in both applications. Users will also be shown how to customize the screens to best meet their needs.

Chapter 3, Organizing your Projects with EPS, OBS, and WBS, introduces the organizational elements of P6. The Enterprise Project Structure (EPS) organizes projects, and the Organizational Breakdown Structure (OBS) organizes people. Traditionally, EPS matches internal divisions within a company, and OBS matches the employee hierarchy. We also show how the WBS is used to organize work within a project. This chapter also covers how OBS relates to project access and security.

Chapter 4, Creating a New Project and Work Breakdown Structure, takes readers through setting up a new project, detailing all of the decision points including how to enter WBS according to best practices. We also discuss creating project codes and show how codes are used for other P6 entities as well. The chapter closes with a discussion of importing projects into P6 from other sources.

Chapter 5, Adding Activities and Relationships, shows the many types of activities and explains the relationships that can be created between them.

Chapter 6, Resources, discusses resources and roles, how they are created, organized, and used globally and within projects. This chapter will also cover how costs are associated with roles and resources.

Chapter 7, Scheduling and Constraints, zeros in on the heart of P6 scheduling. It will discuss the algorithms used and how to run schedule calculations. It also explains the many different settings in P6 that affect the scheduling algorithm.

Chapter 8, Issues and Risks, illustrates how to keep projects on track using issues and risks. Readers will learn to create, manage, and report on issues. Readers will also learn how to create project risks and how to track, manage, and report on risks.

Chapter 9, Baselines and Statusing, describes how to manage changes in a project schedule using baselines. We also discuss updating project status and entering actuals.

Chapter 10, Project Templates, illustrates the concept of project templates, which can be used to quickly generate new projects in a consistent manner.

Chapter 11, Portfolios, steps above the project level and discusses portfolios, how to coherently manage and analyze sets of projects. In this chapter, we show how to collect projects into static and dynamic portfolios. Readers will learn about key built-in project-level fields and how to group data for Portfolio Analysis. We also discuss user-defined fields (UDFs) and how to use these when creating portfolios.

Chapter 12, Portfolio Analysis, introduces the tools of portfolio analysis, such as scorecards and graphs, and shows how to use these to compare portfolio data.

Chapter 13, Measuring and Scoring Projects, discusses creating portfolio scenarios, scoring projects, and using waterline analysis.

Chapter 14, Capacity Planning and ROI, shows how to use P6 to plan out resource usage across projects. We also discuss how P6 calculates Return on Investment (ROI).

Chapter 15, Dashboards, presents real-time reporting using dashboards. These allow users to focus on the data they need the most. We show the wide variety of dashboards available, and how to customize and make your own dashboards.

Chapter 16, Resource Management, discusses the features of P6 that allow you to manage resources across the enterprise by analyzing resource requirements, requesting resources for projects, and committing resources to projects.

Appendix A, Integrations, gives a high-level overview of the key integrations provided by Oracle that tie data between P6 and each of Oracle's three key ERP systems—E-Business Suite, PeopleSoft, and JD Edwards.

Appendix B, Reporting, discusses the many ways to obtain and view data from P6, including screen printing and the built-in reporting engine in P6 Professional, and using BI Publisher in P6 EPPM.

What you need for this book

In order to get the most out of this book it is helpful to have a copy of P6 at hand so that you may try out the concepts for yourself. It is also very helpful to have one or more actual projects to work with, so that you can apply what you learn as you read along.

The easiest way to obtain P6 is to visit `edelivery.oracle.com`. If you do not already have an Oracle account, go ahead and make one, as it costs nothing and gives you access to a wide variety of resources, such as `forums.oracle.com` and `support.oracle.com`, which contains a rich variety of knowledge articles and allows you to communicate with other Primavera users and the Oracle support team.

Once you have logged-in and read and accepted the licensing terms and restrictions, you may search for and download many Oracle products. Choose the Product Pack called Primavera Applications and then choose the proper platform that you need.

Note that the screen will show many Primavera products besides P6, and will show many versions of P6 as well. By default, the products are arranged by release number. It is helpful to click on the **Updated** column twice so that the products are sorted by the one most recently updated. In the following screenshot we have highlighted P6 Enterprise version 8.2:

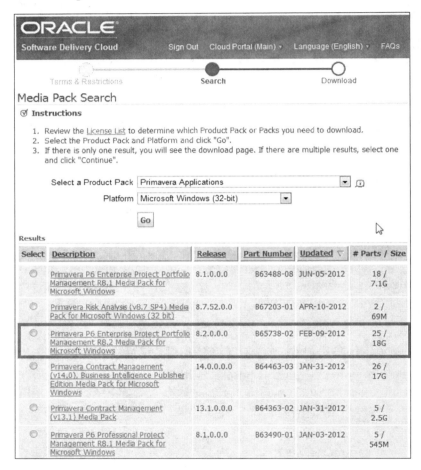

P6 Professional is in general much easier to install on your own system. P6 Enterprise (the web version) will require a greater deal of technical know-how, as you will be installing WebLogic and BI Publisher as well as P6.

If your company already has an installation of P6, then see if you can have someone create a database instance just for you to work with as you go through the book. This will allow you to try out all of the functionality of P6 without the risk of altering the production-level system.

Who this book is for

This book is for people who are new to P6 and who want an overview of the full product, and for people who are familiar with P6 or similar products, who want to understand the features available in version 8. It is a broad outline of P6, covering all of the aspects of the product. The reader is expected to have some basic understanding of scheduling concepts, as this book is by no means a stand-alone introduction to that vast topic!

While reading this book, the reader is encouraged to follow along and try out the ideas presented in each chapter. Hands-on experience, using real-world projects, is the best way to master P6.

Conventions

In this book, you will find a number of styles of text that distinguish between different kinds of information. Here are some examples of these styles, and an explanation of their meaning.

New terms and **important words** are shown in bold. Words that you see on the screen, in menus or dialog boxes for example, appear in the text like this: The **Role Limit** may be selected from either the resource limit of the **Primary Resource** or the custom limit assigned to the **Role**.

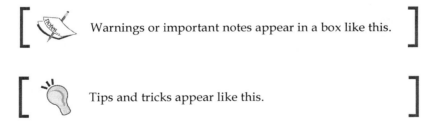

Warnings or important notes appear in a box like this.

Tips and tricks appear like this.

Reader feedback

Feedback from our readers is always welcome. Let us know what you think about this book—what you liked or may have disliked. Reader feedback is important for us to develop titles that you really get the most out of.

To send us general feedback, simply send an e-mail to feedback@packtpub.com, and mention the book title through the subject of your message.

If there is a topic that you have expertise in and you are interested in either writing or contributing to a book, see our author guide on www.packtpub.com/authors.

Customer support

Now that you are the proud owner of a Packt book, we have a number of things to help you to get the most from your purchase.

Errata

Although we have taken every care to ensure the accuracy of our content, mistakes do happen. If you find a mistake in one of our books—maybe a mistake in the text or the code—we would be grateful if you would report this to us. By doing so, you can save other readers from frustration and help us improve subsequent versions of this book. If you find any errata, please report them by visiting http://www.packtpub.com/support, selecting your book, clicking on the **errata submission form** link, and entering the details of your errata. Once your errata are verified, your submission will be accepted and the errata will be uploaded to our website, or added to any list of existing errata, under the Errata section of that title.

Piracy

Piracy of copyright material on the Internet is an ongoing problem across all media. At Packt, we take the protection of our copyright and licenses very seriously. If you come across any illegal copies of our works, in any form, on the Internet, please provide us with the location address or website name immediately so that we can pursue a remedy.

Please contact us at copyright@packtpub.com with a link to the suspected pirated material.

We appreciate your help in protecting our authors, and our ability to bring you valuable content.

Questions

You can contact us at questions@packtpub.com if you are having a problem with any aspect of the book, and we will do our best to address it.

1
Getting Started with Oracle Primavera P6

In this chapter, we introduce Oracle Primavera P6 Enterprise Project Portfolio Management or P6 for short. P6 is used worldwide to schedule projects in a range of industries, including construction, energy, aerospace, pharmaceuticals, IT, and finance, to name a few. At first glance, the program may appear daunting in the scope of its capabilities. It is the hope of the authors that this book will establish for our readers a strong foundation in P6 that will allow them to use P6 with confidence on a daily basis.

In this chapter we will cover:

- Product history
- What's in the Name?
- P6 Core Concepts
- What's New in P6 Release 8

Product history

The core concepts of project scheduling were laid down in the years following World War II, as construction projects in the United States became larger and more complex. By the 1960s, these concepts were being implemented in mainframe computers by such entities as DuPont, IBM, and the U.S. military.

In 1983, Joel Koppelman and Dick Faris founded Primavera Systems in Philadelphia. Their vision was that these same principles of project management could be implemented on desktop PCs, which were then just making their way into common use. The first product went on sale in 1983, available on a set of 5¼-inch floppy disks that held a whopping 360 KB of data each. The application required 256 KB of RAM to run, which was quite a lot at the time.

And so **Primavera Project Planner (P3)** was born. The company was quite successful and eventually P3 became the leading scheduling product in the engineering and construction industries. In fact, it soon became a *requirement* for certain government contracts that schedules could only be delivered in a P3-compatible format.

In the late 1990s, with the rise of networks and the Internet, it became clear that the future of project scheduling software lay beyond a single product installed on one person's desktop. Instead, project scheduling was moving towards systems that could be accessed simultaneously by multiple people in different locations.

In 1999, Primavera acquired Eagle Ray Software. This company had created a product in 1998 called Eagle Ray 1000 Project Management Suite. Primavera took ER1000 and released it as two products in 1999: P3 e/c, which was marketed for Engineering and Construction, and TeamPlay for IT and Financial services. Over the years, the products have appeared to merge and diverge, adding capabilities such as timesheet entry, integration, and portfolio analysis, eventually evolving into what is now called P6. In 2004, Primavera 5.0 was released, and in 2007, P6.0 was released, followed by P6.2 in 2008.

In 2008, another major change occurred. Primavera, a privately held company, was bought by Oracle, a publicly held corporation.

Enter Oracle

In 2008, soon after P6.2 came out, it was announced that Oracle Corporation was buying Primavera. Starting as a database provider in 1979, Oracle had grown over the years into a large and influential company, focused not only on databases, but on providing an array of software products that are fundamental to managing modern businesses. This array included **enterprise resource planning** (ERP) systems, content management systems, analytical and reporting systems, and application servers and technology, to describe just a few. In order to ensure that they also owned the best-of-breed in project scheduling software, Oracle acquired Primavera Systems in 2008.

Since the acquisition, P6 has undergone a number of changes. First, the various names were consolidated into one: P6. Oracle also spent considerable resources improving and adding to the product. For example, P6 now supports a standards-compliant Web Services API; it can run from a cluster of WebLogic or WebSphere application servers; and the full capabilities of the system are now available through a web browser.

P3 and SureTrak

Some users may confuse P3 and SureTrak with P6. P3 is the heir to the original Primavera Project Planner product. It is a standalone desktop application. SureTrak was a lighter version of P3 designed for users with simpler requirements, and so had a limit on the number of activities it would support. Both products have reached the end of their life cycles, and sales of P3 and SureTrak officially ended on December 31st, 2010.

Yet this is not the end of the standalone desktop client. With P6 version 8.1, a true standalone version of P6 was created, finally closing the gap that sprang open in 1999 when Primavera bought Eagle Ray, and set separate tracks for its desktop and enterprise solutions. Now users can have the power of P6 on their laptop with P6 Professional, or deploy P6 Enterprise and gain the additional benefits of enterprise-wide capabilities. P6 release 8.2 allows these two products to work even better together.

What's in the name?

The product that we all know as P6 is officially named Oracle Primavera P6 Enterprise Project Portfolio Management, which is quite a mouthful. But the name accurately reflects the scope and purpose of the software:

- **Enterprise**: Unlike P3, which was a standalone application designed to be used by a single user on a dedicated machine, P6 is designed to facilitate multiple users across a large organization. It is a true multi-tier system, with a database on the back end, an application server in the middle, and a web server to which users can connect through an internet browser client such as Microsoft Internet Explorer or Mozilla Firefox. This means that the system is very scalable, and can support hundreds of users working on thousands of projects with millions of activities. This also means that it can support companies with geographically diverse projects and a workforce spread across the globe.

- **Project**: At its heart, P6 supports projects. But what is a project? In the Project Management Body of Knowledge, a project is defined as a temporary endeavor undertaken to create a unique product or service. (*A Guide to the Project Management Body of Knowledge, 4th Edition*, The Project Management Institute, 2008). A project can mean different things in different industries, but projects comprise an amazingly large part of the commercial world. Traditionally we think of construction with respect to projects. But making entertainment is also a project. Think of all the people and equipment and coordination required to make a movie, television show, or album. Developing a new drug is a project as well, starting with basic research and moving to clinical trials, government approval, marketing, manufacturing, and distribution. Each of these is a project by itself.

  But what matters is this: A project has a scope of work to be done, a timeline for completing the work, and a set amount of resources to do the work. All of these can be measured within the boundaries of the project. P6 allows you to make these measurements, and it gives you the ability to react to these measurements (scope, schedule, and budget) to ensure that your project accomplishes its goals.

- **Portfolio**: With very few exceptions, a project does not stand alone. A studio creates many movies over the course of a year. A pharmaceutical company develops many different drugs. An energy company has facilities ranging from the frigid tar sands of northern Alberta to the tropical coastline of Brazil. When making strategic decisions about what projects to pursue, which ones to pour more resources into, and which ones to halt, you need to see the larger picture. This is the grouping of projects into a portfolio. P6 can handle thousands of projects and has analytical capabilities to roll up information across projects and perform analysis across the enterprise. This allows decision makers to understand their business from a broad perspective, and to take action on that information.

- **Management**: There is an old adage that says: *only what can be measured can be controlled*. P6 is about planning projects and measuring progress as the project moves forward. Although P6 is very flexible in how it can be used, it is also designed to help you manage projects well. And when used properly, you can maintain a reliable budget, anticipate cash flow and resource usage, and record and react to changes as they arise. What's more, you can bring the various members of the project team together, set standards, and define the right way to run projects at your specific company.

In a nutshell, P6 is designed to help organizations manage their projects in a coherent manner, giving them the power to make better decisions and allowing them to focus on the best strategies.

P6 core concepts

What is P6? At its heart, P6 is an application for scheduling projects. Yet as we mentioned earlier, what a project means can vary greatly. And though the end product is varied, every project shares some common characteristics:

- There are deliverables (what the customer is paying for)
- There is scope of work to meet the requirements of the deliverables
- There is the management of:
  - Time
  - Cost
  - Resources (people, materials, and equipment)
  - Communication among the project team
  - Project Documentation
  - Risks
  - Purchases

Project Management Life Cycle

A project has many phases, and these phases can be grouped in many ways using different terminologies and methodologies. One widely used and generally accepted categorization is as follows:

- Initiation – deciding whether to proceed finding funding and resources
- Planning – enumerating scope, creating the schedule, and planning resources
- Execution – performing the work to create the project deliverables
- Controlling – measuring progress and making corrective actions as the project progresses
- Closing – delivering the project and reviewing lessons learned

While many people associate P6 with the Planning stage, it can be used throughout the life cycle:

- **Initiation**: An initial project can be created to estimate the schedule, cash flow, and resource usage for projects that are still in the initial "what if" stages. *Chapter 14, Capacity Planning and ROI* and *Chapter 16, Resource Management* can help you decide on what projects make best sense to pursue and how pursuing those projects will affect your overall portfolio.

- **Planning**: Obviously, P6 can be used to create the project plan. This ability should never be underestimated, as the intelligent implementation of the CPM scheduling algorithms is the heart of what makes P6 the highly-valued tool that it is today.

- **Execution**: As the project progresses, the schedule is updated and adjusted as actual work is performed. Updated statuses can be entered directly into P6 and/or can be driven by timesheets.

- **Controlling**: As the situation on the ground changes and activities are completed, the scheduling algorithms will update the schedule to reflect new realities. P6 will show changes in anticipated resource usage and cash flow, so that you can alter the planned work as needed to stay on target.

- **Closing**: As the scope is completed, resources can be released to other projects. The completed project can then be converted to a project template (*Chapter 10, Project Template*), using the actual durations and resources expended to complete the project. Basing new projects on completed ones gives a well-grounded basis for estimating new projects.

At its core, P6 helps you manage these entities by breaking a project down into two main components: Activities and Resources.

Activities

An activity is a logical element of work to be done. Activities can occur independently, or can depend on one another. Managing the dependencies of activities is a core strength of P6.

When I was first learning software development, there was a certification test from Microsoft called *Analyzing Requirements and Designing Solution Architecture*, or the ARDSA. A common question on the test was to put a set of tasks into the best order to complete the work. For example, the job would be to turn on a flashlight. You are given a battery tester, a dozen batteries, only six of which work, and a flashlight that is broken down into three components: the case, the front casing, and a light bulb. What is the best way to order the following tasks?

- Turn on flashlight
- Test batteries
- Screw front casing onto case
- Insert batteries
- Identify two working batteries
- Insert light bulb into front casing

Solving such a problem may seem trivial at first. We make such decisions every day in our personal lives. But when the end product is not simply assembling a flashlight, but designing, building, and commissioning a power plant, the steps involved become quite complex. There are tasks within tasks, multiple teams to coordinate, and equipment to be delivered and assembled. A simple checklist will no longer suffice, and a single person cannot keep it all in his or her head. Activities track the disparate tasks required, and the relationships between activities form a network of dependencies that can be managed and modified with P6.

Resources

An activity can also have resources. Resources can be the people assigned to work on the task, the equipment that is needed to perform the work, or the materials to install. Each of these resources has an associated cost, and potentially limited availability. Knowing what resources you will need when and where is crucial in being able to make long-term plans on complex projects. For example, if you are sending a team to the South Pole station to assemble a new telescope, the logistics can be daunting, with a limited number of trips available in a given season. Heaven forbid that you send that team down and neglect to provide them with an essential piece of equipment. They can hardly drive down to the nearest Home Depot!

Resources also have calendars – when a given resource is available. For people, this is their work schedule. For equipment, there may be limitations on when it can be used based on weather, or a maintenance schedule. For the previous example, there is a calendar of when supplies and people can arrive at the station. If your team is working in arctic regions, there are seasons when the ground is too muddy to move equipment, and getting to the site can only be done during months when the ground is frozen.

There are also more mundane calendars. You may want to minimize the amount of overtime paid on a job, which can cut into profits. Certain employees may have religious holidays that affect the work schedule.

P6 posits resources as first-class citizens of the scheduling world. And it gives you the ability to manage resources across all of your projects, giving you the ability to make decisions from a high level.

What's new in P6 Release 8

Many changes were made between P6 Version 7 and release 8. Here we highlight the ones we view as most pertinent:

- Reporting through Oracle Business Intelligence Publisher.

  The reporting engine of P6 Enterprise is now Oracle BI Publisher. This is the same reporting application used across a range of Oracle products. This means that there are many people already skilled in its use and many references available, including *Oracle BI Publisher 11g: A Practical Guide to Enterprise Reporting, Packt Publishing*. See also *Appendix B, Integrations*.

- JBoss Application Server no longer supported.

  P6 version 7 was supported on Oracle Weblogic, IBM WebSphere, and JBoss, an open source application server. With Version 8, JBoss is no longer supported. Across many products, Oracle is standardizing on WebLogic. An excellent introduction to WebLogic is *Oracle Weblogic Server 11gR1 PS2: Administration Essentials, Packt Publishing*.

- Project Templates replace Methodology Manager.

  In prior versions there were two separate programs and two separate databases: Project Management and Methodology Management. Templates are now part of the main P6 database, and can be managed and secured from the web interface (Note that P6 Professional does not support templates).

- Integration with Oracle Business Process Management (BPM).

  Oracle's BPM Suite is a set of tools for allowing products to communicate with each other. Part of this functionality allows for the development of customized workflows which can interact with different products. Business Process Management and workflows are part of this set of products. Like BI Publisher, BPM is a well-documented technology which is explained on many websites as well as in books such as *Getting Started with Oracle BPM Suite 11gR1 – A Hands-On Tutorial, Packt Publishing*.

- Enhanced risk management.

  A risk register and risk scoring matrix provide a system for monitoring and tracking risks. This is shown in *Chapter 8, Issues and Risks*.

- EPPM is one hundred percent web-based.

  With prior versions, certain scheduling abilities were only available in the Windows Client. With the EPPM release of Version 8, users can completely create and manage their project schedules through the web, using Microsoft Internet Explorer or Mozilla Firefox.

- Tabbed views and configurable toolbars.

  Tabs and customizable toolbars make for overall easier navigation.

- Timescaled Logic Diagrams.

  Timescaled Logic Diagrams is a tool for viewing schedules in a time-driven chart which emphasizes the logical connections between activities in the project network.

New in Release 8.2

There are several new features which have been added to release 8.2:

- The installer has been made easier. The installer will walk you through setting up not only P6 but also many other applications that had to be installed separately before. This includes P6 Help, UPK, OCM, Progress Reporter, Integration API, Web Services, and Team Member.

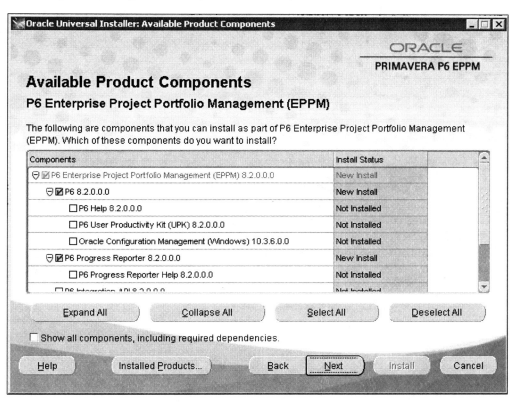

- **User Management**: When copying users, all of their current toolbars and preferences are copied over. You can take advantage of this by configuring one account with standard settings, and then create new users based on this account. It is now also easy to create a new resource directly from a user account.

- **Location**: Oracle Locator is a new technology that is being implemented in many of Oracle's products. This gives you the ability to associate data with physical locations. Project, activities, and resources can be given locations. These locations can then be used in other applications such as P6 Analytics.

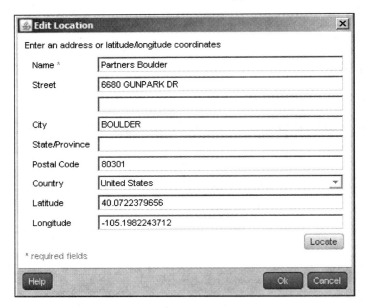

- **Searching columns**: P6 is notorious for containing dozens of fields: dates, properties, codes, variances, percentages, and so on. It can be a challenge sometimes to find the exact column you need when customizing your layouts. In 8.2 each of the **Customize Column** screens includes a search text box. If you want to see all the fields called "Actual", simply search for it.

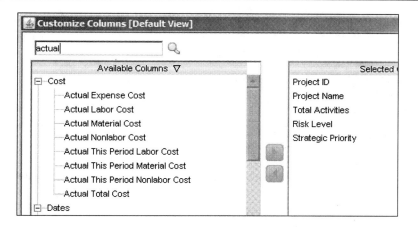

- **Exclusive mode**: Before 8.2 you could not check out a project in P6 Web. In 8.2, users can now check out a project. This is called **exclusive mode**. While a project is in exclusive mode, it will be tagged with a lock icon, and only the user who locked it may use it.

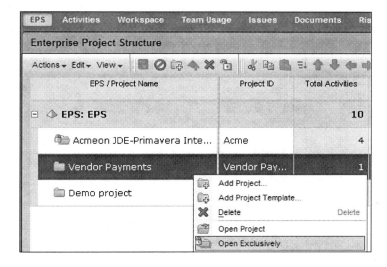

- **Is Under filter**: This is a new property used in filtering data which lets you filter by location of an item within a hierarchy. For example, you can filter for activities only under a certain WBS node.

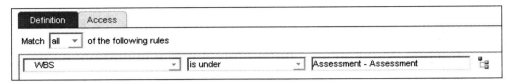

- **Microsoft Project 2010** is now supported. You can use MSP projects to update P6, which allows you to retain support for MSP users, yet still be able to take advantage of managing all of your enterprise data in P6.

- **P6 Professional unified**: There are no longer two separate Windows desktop clients. With 8.1, there was P6 Professional, which is purely a Windows Client, and P6 Optional Client, which was like Professional but with certain administrative features stripped away. Now there is one and only one P6 Professional client and it will support running stand-alone as well as running connected to your Enterprise system.

- **Line numbering**: You can now choose to display line numbers on the screen in P6 Professional. These numbers can be very helpful when you create screenshots of your projects and want to talk about items on specific lines without ambiguity.

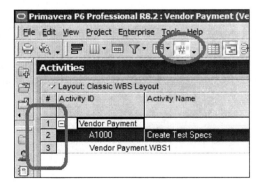

- **Mobile support** has been advanced. The Progress Reporter has been optimized to function on tablets as well. The iPhone application has gotten new features, and e-mail-based status is supported.

There are many more features in 8.2, such as the ability to group data by UDF. With this and so much more, it is an easy decision to use 8.2 to take advantage of these features.

Summary

Now the reader should have an idea of where P6 came from, what are its core components, and how it is used to accomplish a number of tasks across many industries. The reader should also be able to determine whether to continue reading in a linear manner, or to skip ahead to a chapter of interest.

In the next chapter, we will dive right into P6 and quickly go through logging in, customizing the screens, and finding your way around the system.

2

Getting Around: Understanding and Customizing the P6 Interface

In this chapter, we introduce readers to both the P6 Web Client and the P6 Professional Client. We first give a brief overview of P6 EPPM Web Client and point to the relevant chapters where the reader can learn more. Then we take a detailed walk through P6 Professional. After that, users will learn how to customize and save screen layouts. In general, we'll cover the following topics in this chapter:

- EPPM Web Client overview
- Logging into P6 Professional
- Screen overview
- Main menus
- Customizing screens and saving layouts

By the end of the chapter, readers should be comfortable navigating in Oracle Primavera P6 R8 EPPM and customizing the interface to suit their needs.

EPPM Web Client overview

When you log into P6 Web Client, you will see a screen similar to that shown in the following screenshot:

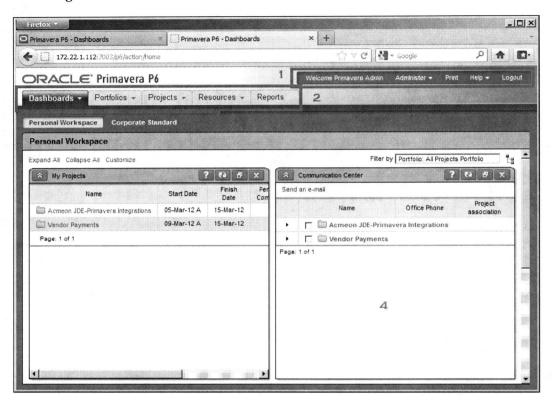

The screen can be divided into four main areas:

1. Application menus
2. Tabs
3. Modules
4. Main screen

Application menus

The Application menus are always present. **Administer** lets you manage your own application settings. If you have the right privileges, then you may also use this menu to access application-level settings and data.

Print will print the current screen. In *Appendix B, Reporting*, we will discuss screen printing and reporting in more detail.

The **Help** menu offers three options:

- **P6 Help** is a set of web documents describing how to use P6. The content of that help is much like the content of this book.

- **P6 Library** is a set of web documents that describe how to set up and administer P6.

- **Support** takes you to the main website for Oracle Support.

Logout logs you out of the system and returns you to the main login screen.

Tabs

The tabs across the upper left side of the page are always present, and represent five areas of work:

- **Dashboards** show a set of portlets which give high-level information about projects. This is the default tab selected when a user logs in, and the specific portlets displayed can be configured per user. **Dashboards** are discussed in further detail in *Chapter 15, Dashboards*.

- **Portfolios** let you organize sets of projects and perform analysis on them. Portfolios are discussed in *Chapter 11, Portfolios, Chapter 12, Portfolio Analysis, Chapter 13, Measuring and Scoring Projects*, and *Chapter 14, Capacity Planning and ORI*.

- **Projects** let you manage projects from the EPS level, down to the activity level. A scheduler would spend most of his or her time in this tab. This is also where you go to manage **Issues**, **Documents**, and **Risks**. The tasks under Projects are discussed further in *Chapter 3, Organizing your Projects with EPS, OBS, and WBS, Chapter 4, Creating a New Project and Work Breakdown Structure, Chapter 5, Adding Activities and Relationships, Chapter 7, Scheduling and Constraints, Chapter 8, Issues and Risks, Chapter 9, Baselines and Statusing*, and *Chapter 10, Project Templates*.

- **Resources** tab is where you manage the people, equipment, and materials that perform the tasks which compose your projects. Here you can plan resource usage in projects, assign resources to specific activities, and analyze the use of resources in your projects. Resources are covered in *Chapters 6, Resources* and *Chapter 16, Resource Management*.

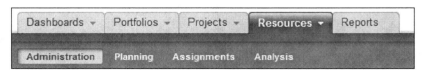

- **Reports** tab brings up the BI Publisher reports that are available for P6. Reports are covered in *Appendix B, Reporting.*

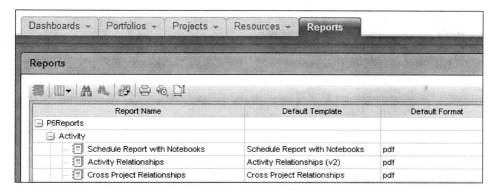

Modules

As shown in the earlier screenshots, each tab contains a set of modules in a strip directly beneath the tab. For Dashboards, this consists of one or more dashboards that you may choose. For Portfolios, this consists of the different actions you can take to manage and use your portfolios. For Projects, this consists of the many project-related activities you may wish to perform. For Resources, this list contains links for managing, planning, assigning, and analyzing resources. For Reports, there is no set of modules.

Main screen

The items displayed in the main area of the screen vary greatly, depending on which tab and module you have chosen. However, each item does consist of one or more Java applets, which must be downloaded and run. The first time you log into P6 from a new machine, you may experience a message stating that "this application is being run for the first time…". It may take a few seconds for the applet to download. But after the applet is downloaded, you should not get this message again for that specific applet.

Now that we have given an overview of the P6 EPPM Web Client, and have shown where each item is covered in the rest of the book, we will give a detailed walkthrough of P6 Professional.

Logging into the P6 Client

Let's start with logging into the system. If you have installed the windows client, you may already have a shortcut icon to it on your machine. If not, go to **Start | Oracle | Primavera Professional**.

You should see a screen as shown in the following screenshot. If you have an account, enter your login name and password in the displayed boxes:

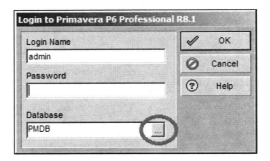

If you do not already have a connection set up, click on the **Database** ellipse button near the bottom of the screen to add and edit database connections. This will show the database connections that P6 knows about. If you are running the client for the first time, it is likely that there will be no items on this list.

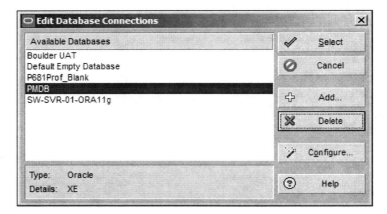

Click **Add** and you will get a dialog asking for two pieces of information.

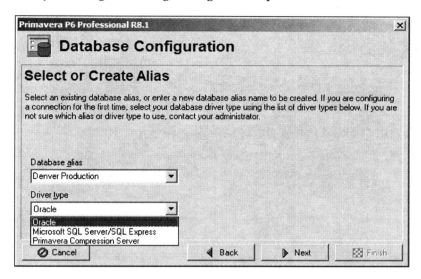

Database alias: This is a name for your own use to identify the connection. It can be anything. It is helpful to make the alias descriptive enough to remind you to which system it connects. A good practice is to identify the name of the server and the database that the alias represents.

Driver type: There are three options:

- **Oracle**
- **Microsoft SQL Server/SQL Express**
- **Primavera Compression Server**

The next screen asks you to specify the connection information.

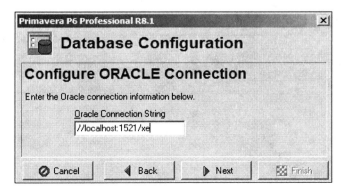

Configure ORACLE Connection: Specify the **Oracle Connection String**, which is given to you by the administrator. You may also notify your system administrator that the following syntax is also valid:

```
//<server>:<port>/<SID>
```

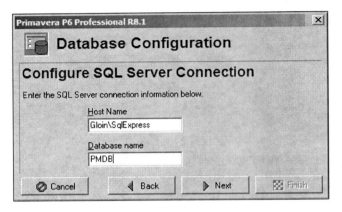

Configure SQL Server Connection: Specify the name of the server in **Host Name**, and the database in **Database name**. If your database runs on a non-default instance, then also specify the name of the instance, as in:

```
<server>\<instance>
```

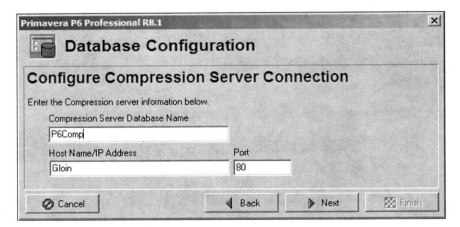

Configure Primavera Compression Server: The compression server is a technology that sits between the P6 database and the client, managing the data that is sent between database and client to ensure that the number of packets is minimized. The compression server requires an additional server which sits between the database and the client. Note that this technology is only relevant to the windows client.

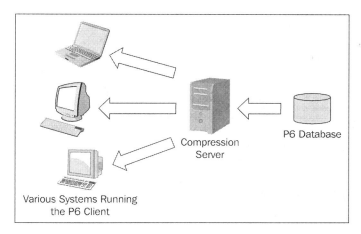

No matter which kind of system you are connecting to, the next screen asks you to enter public login information. These are the credentials of a database account set up specifically for the P6 client application. By default this is named **pubuser** and its password is **pubuser**, but the specific name may be different, so check with your system administrator. The **Public group ID** should be set to **1**.

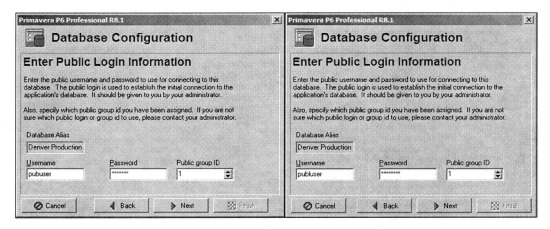

Click **Next** to validate the connection. If the validation succeeds, then click **Finish**. You will now see the new database alias in the **Edit Database Connections** screen.

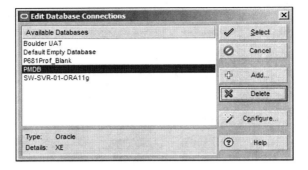

Choose the alias, press **OK**, and you will be logged into the P6 client.

Screen overview

When you log into P6 the first time, you should be presented with a screen similar to the following screenshot:

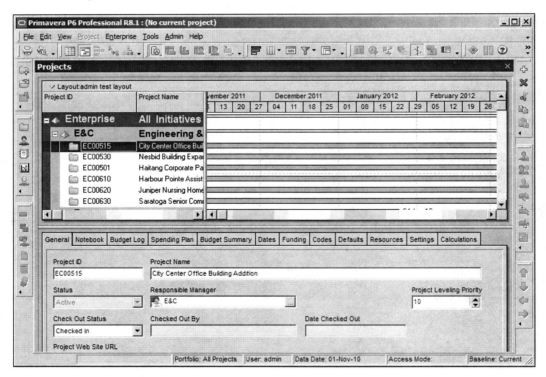

At the very top is the set of application menus that are standard to most Windows applications, such as **File**, **Edit**, **View**, and **Help**, plus a few that are specific to P6: **Project**, **Enterprise**, and **Tools**.

In the Professional Client, there is also an **Admin** menu:

The main screen also contains toolbars across the top, left, and right-hand sides. These toolbars contain icons which provide quick ways to access parts of the program. They are highly customizable. You can move any set of tools to any other toolbar, create a toolbar across the bottom of the page, or even detach a toolbar from the side and make it float!

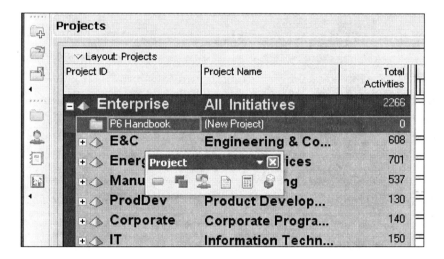

Floating toolbar: This toolbar will remain on top of the screen while you work on the main screen, and can be moved around as desired.

The central portion of the screen is filled with a set of screens which appear as tabs as you open up different modules. These are the main screens for working on projects.

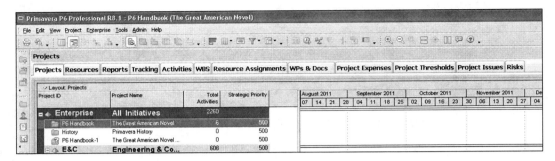

- **Projects** generally shows all projects available to the user. If a particular Portfolio is selected, then only those projects within the portfolio will be shown.

- **Resources** shows global and project resources available (*Chapter 6*).

- **Reports** shows the reports that are available within the Windows client (*Appendix B*).

- **Tracking** lets you compare project properties in a 3-pane window.

- **Activities** is the main screen for managing project activities (*Chapter 5*).

- **WBS** is the main screen for managing project Work Breakdown Structure (*Chapters 3 and 4*).

- **Resource Assignments** is the main screen for managing resources (*Chapters 6 and 16*).

- **WP & Docs** is for managing Work Products and Documents (*Chapter 8*)

- **Project Expenses** is for creating and managing project expenses (*Chapter 5*)

- **Project Thresholds** sets the threshold for triggering issues (*Chapter 8*).

- **Project Issues** lets you manage and track project issues (*Chapter 8*).

- **Risks** (not available in the Optional Client) is used to manage project risks (*Chapter 8*).

Main menus

Before we begin our overview of the menu items, let's address the issue of what shows up in the menu. By default the menu items only include recently chosen items with a set of arrows at the bottom which you can click on to see the menu items that have been hidden. This can be convenient if you have a small screen or if you don't use certain items. Personally, I prefer that the menu always shows all of the items every time.

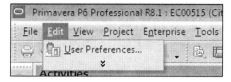

If you desire this behavior, you can set it easily. Right-click on any toolbar or on the menu bar, and choose **Customize...**. Then choose the **Options** tab as shown in the following screenshot:

Simply uncheck the item **Menus show recently used commands first**.

Then you will see the exact same menu every time, which is convenient if you want to use the application quickly.

Small Icon   Large Icon

This menu also allows you to use larger icons, which can be helpful when learning the application and the smaller icons may all look the same to you. The menu animations are cute, but not worth bothering with once you're doing serious work.

File menu

Each menu is grouped into sections, separated by a horizontal menu separator bar. The first group concerns projects: create a new project, open an existing project, or close all projects.

Each of these actions can be accomplished by a shortcut key:

- *Ctrl+N*: Create a new project
- *Ctrl+O*: Open an existing project
- *Ctrl+W*: Close all projects

(Where "Ctrl" means press the right or left "Control" key).

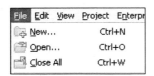

Many menu items have such shortcut keys. Knowing and becoming proficient at these can greatly enhance your experience of using P6.

The next group of items on the **File** menu concerns printing, beginning with **Page Setup**.

This screen is similar to **Print Setup** in other Windows applications. There are tabs for headers and footers. We highly recommend that the company name and current date be set in either the header or footer. This ensures that printouts are clearly marked as property of your company, and it is also clear when the data was printed out. Showing the project name and data date are also very helpful.

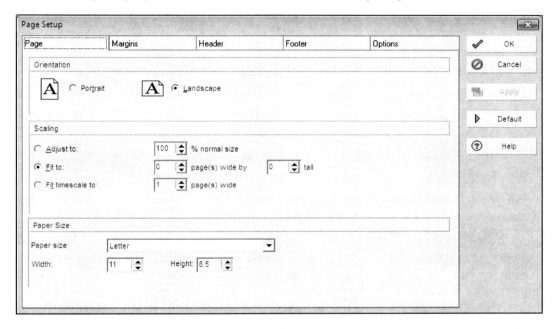

Print Setup concerns the settings for your specific printer, and so may vary greatly from person to person.

Print Preview shows what P6 will be sending to the selected printer. This is very helpful because you can adjust the **Page Setup**, view **Print Preview**, and continue to make adjustments until the preview shows the printout how you want to see it.

Print sends the printouts to the chosen printer.

The next section of menu items concerns working with projects:

Import lets you bring a project and data into P6 from specially formatted data sources. These may come from a variety of sources, including earlier versions of P6, P3, Microsoft Project, and Excel. Care should be taken while importing data into P6 because external data sources may introduce *trash* codes and values into the database.

Export lets you send projects and data out of P6 into a data file. This file may be exported to a variety of formats, including earlier versions of P6, P3, Microsoft Project, and Excel.

Send Project exports the project to XER format and opens your e-mail client so that you can e-mail the project to someone. It is simply a convenient shortcut for exporting the project and emailing the file separately.

Check Out creates an XER for the project and then changes the project's status to "checked out". The expectation is that the user will then take this XER file, import it into another instance of P6 or perhaps even another application, and make changes to it. While the project is checked out, no one else can make permanent changes to it until the person who checked it out checks it back into the system, effectively re-importing the modified XER file.

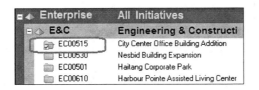

Check In is very similar to importing an XER file, and the menu items asking for what actions to take are the same. Once a project is checked back in, other users can make modifications to it.

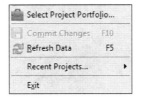

Select project portfolio lets the user choose from the available portfolios. These are sub-sets of projects. For example, a portfolio could contain all capital projects above a certain budget, or could be the set of projects that are the responsibility of a specific project manager. Portfolios will be covered in more detail in *Chapter 11, Portfolios*.

Commit Changes writes any changes you have made back to the database. This item can be confusing because certain actions (for example, renaming a project) will always be written immediately back to the database regardless of whether you click on **Commit Changes** or not.

Refresh Data is very helpful when multiple people and/or processes are making changes to the system. Pressing **F5** will update the data to reflect changes from others.

Recent Projects lets you choose from a list of projects that were opened recently.

Exit is the standard Windows command to close the application. Choosing **Exit** will always prompt you to answer the question **Are you sure you want to exit P6?** Responding to this query may grow quite tiring, but the prompt is a safety measure for people who repeatedly tell the program to exit by accident.

Edit menu

The **Edit** menu is a standard Windows menu that lets you do common actions such as cut, copy, and paste.

Undo removes the latest change you made. Though **Undo** is not implemented for all actions, it is implemented for certain very crucial actions, such as renumbering activities.

For example, suppose you need to renumber 50 activities. You can select them, choose **Edit | Renumber Activity IDs**, and then have all of them renumbered according to a new scheme. But suppose you chose the wrong prefix, or wrong increment value. If you make such a mistake, you can undo the change with **Edit | Undo**, or via the common Windows shortcut, *Ctrl+Z*.

Cut will remove an item, and place it into a buffer so that you can paste it later. You can cut simple text, or complex items such as activities. The shortcut for this is the same as in most Windows programs, *Ctrl+X*.

Copy, like **Cut**, makes a copy of an item. However, **Copy** will not delete the original after the paste. The shortcut is *Ctrl+C*.

Paste will insert the last item cut or copied. The shortcut for this is *Ctrl+V*.

The **Cut**, **Copy**, and **Paste** functions can save a good deal of time, especially when the shortcut keys are used. They are powerful functions, allowing you to copy objects as simple as some text characters or as complex as an entire project!

Add: The results of **Add** function depend on the screen on which you are located in the main application. If you are viewing Activities, **Add** will add a new activity. If you are viewing WBS structure, **Add** will add a new WBS element. Though no shortcut is shown, you can usually achieve the same result by pressing the *Insert* key.

Delete: As with **Add**, the results of the **Delete** function depend on which screen you are on. If viewing activities, **Delete** will delete activities; if viewing projects, **Delete** will delete projects. Fortunately, whenever you press *Delete* you will be prompted before the delete is committed, which is a great safety valve. This can also be done via the **Delete** button.

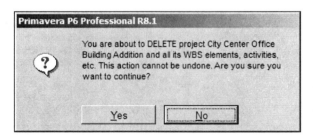

Dissolve is only available when you select an activity that has both predecessors and successors. It allows you to delete the activity. The predecessor activities are then assigned to its successor activities.

Renumber Activity IDs lets you change the ID numbers on a group of activities. Since Activity ID is a key piece of data, this is an incredibly helpful function. Suppose that at the beginning of a project, all activity IDs under a certain WBS element are to be prefixed with "PD" and incremented by 10. But later on, it is decided that these same activities are to be prefixed with "PR" and incremented by 5. Rather than having to update all of the activities manually, **Renumber Activity IDs** can be used.

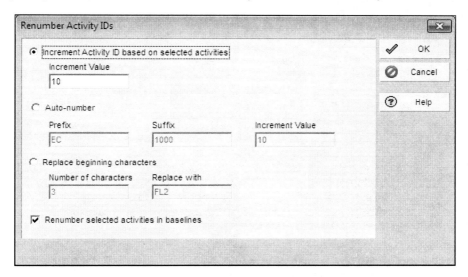

Assign lets you assign additional entities to activities. Such entities include **Resources**, **Roles**, **Activity Codes**, **Predecessors**, and **Successors**.

Link Activities: If you choose two activities, this menu item will be enabled. If you choose **Link Activities**, then the two activities will be linked via a Finish-Start relationship. The default behavior is that the upper item in the activity view will become the predecessor of the item below it. So if you sort by Activity ID ascending, such that A100 appears before A200, and link the two, then A100 will be a predecessor of A200. Yet if you sort by Activity ID descending, such that A200 appears before A100, and link the two, then A200 will become the predecessor to A100. Linking in this manner can be convenient, but use it with caution.

 Dissolve, **Renumber Activity Ids**, **Assign**, and **Link Activities** are out of place on the menu. These actions are specific to activities, yet they always appear on the menu even when editing projects or resources. Though this seems nonsensical, it also indicates the importance of Activities in P6.

Fill Down lets you copy the same value into different rows. For example, you can quickly rename activities using this function. The shortcut is *Ctrl+E*.

Select All will highlight and select all items on the screen. The shortcut is *Ctrl+A*.

Find will search the *currently selected column* for the entered text. To find on another column, select that column. The shortcut is *Ctrl+F*.

Find Next, with the common Windows shortcut *F3*, will repeat the last **Find** and take you to the next matching item in the grid.

Replace will let you search for text in the currently selected column and replace it with a new value. The shortcut is *Ctrl+R*.

Spell Check performs a check of the spelling of all values in the currently selected column, but only if that column contains text data, such as Activity Name. As in many other Windows programs, the shortcut is *F7*.

User Preferences: This menu item is quite unrelated to every other item found under the **Edit** menu. It brings up a dialog box that shows a plethora of user settings:

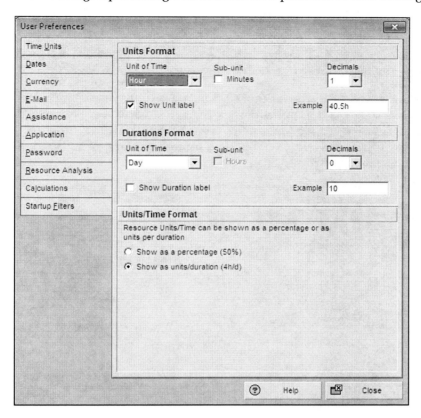

User Preferences | Time Units lets the user choose a number of settings.

Unit of Time is used with Resources. The options are **Hour, Day, Week, Month**, or **Year**. The subunits are relative to the units chosen. If **Show Unit Label** is checked, units and (if checked) subunits will be displayed. The user can choose 0, 1, or 2 decimal places, and the **Example** fields will then show an example for previewing.

Durations are used when displaying **Activities**, and the choices are similar to **Unit of Time**. For example, if the **Unit of Time** is set to **Hours** and **Duration** is set to **Day**, then an Activity's value "Budgeted Units/Time" will be displayed as "h/d" (hours per day).

User Preferences | Dates lets the user choose how dates will be displayed throughout the application. Users can choose 2-digit or 4-digit year, whether to show month name or number, and whether to show leading zeros so that, for example, July will show up as 7 rather than 07.

Time can be displayed as 12 hours with the AM and PM suffixes, or as a 24-hour clock. Users can also choose not to show time at all.

Shown in the screenshot is the author's preferred setting: year-month-day with four-digit year, dash as the separator, leading zeros displayed. Showing the clock and minutes is highly dependent on the event being scheduled. It may be a great hindrance on a five-year schedule. But on a three-day plant turnaround, displaying hours (and minutes) is critical.

User Preferences | Currency sets the currency to display in P6, as well as the type of currency symbol and whether to show decimal places. Note that the exchange rate for currencies is set through **Currencies** under the **Admin** menu.

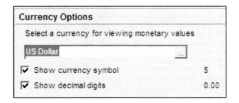

User Preferences | E-Mail sets e-mail information for the user.

E-mail Protocol can be either:

- Internet (i.e. SMTP or POP)
- MAPI

If choosing **MAPI**, the **Mail Server Login** will be enabled. Contact your system mail administrator for the appropriate profile to use.

If using **Internet**, choose the outgoing mail server and your e-mail address.

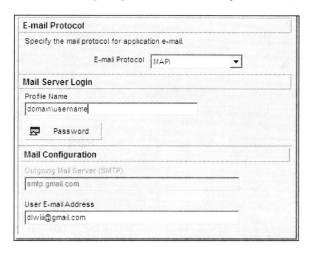

User Preferences | Assistance turns on and off flags telling whether P6 should use its built-in **Wizards** when creating new activities or resources.

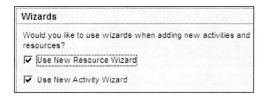

User Preferences | Application establishes a number of user settings. You may choose which window opens at startup:

• Activities	• None
• Project Issues	• Resources
• Project Thresholds	• Risks
• Projects	• Tracking
• Reports	• WBS
• Resource Assignments	• WPs and Docs

Startup Window

Application Startup Window

`Activities` ▼

☐ Show the Issue Navigator dialog at startup

☐ Show the Welcome dialog at startup

Application Log File

☐ Write trace of internal functions to log file

Group and Sorting

Labels on grouping bands

☐ Show ID / Code

☑ Show Name / Description

Columns

Select financial periods to view in columns

`[          ]` ... to `[          ]` ...

Job Alert Polling Interval

Poll for job alerts every `10` ▲▼

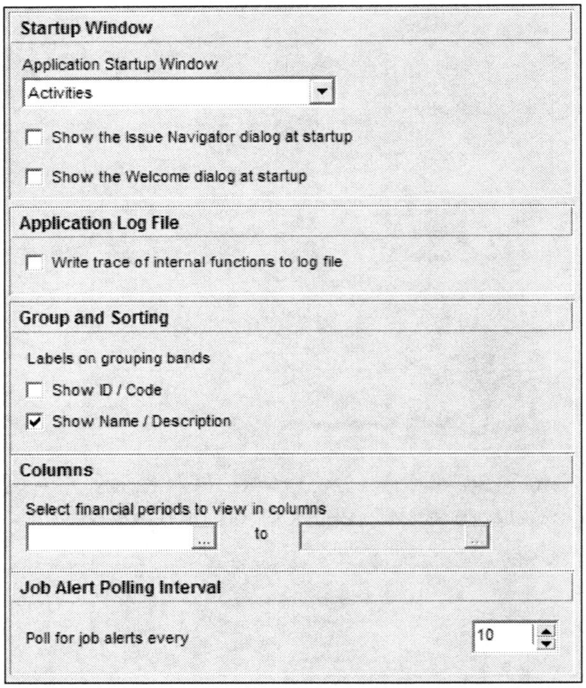

For example, if you primarily work with project risks, you may want to set this as the window that is opened on startup of P6.

This screen also lets you turn on logging, which can be helpful when diagnosing application issues.

You may also choose how grouping and sorting is done and which financial periods to view. If you have jobs, such as summarization, which run on a schedule, the polling interval will determine how often the application will look to notify you when a job runs.

User Preferences | Password lets the current user change their own P6 password.

Note that an Administrator can always change anyone's password.

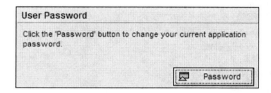

User Preferences | Resource Analysis allows the user to choose which projects are displayed on the **Resource Usage Profile** screen. The user can view:

- All closed projects except what-if projects
- All closed projects with a leveling priority
- Opened projects only

Remaining Early data can be shown using **Remaining Early Dates** or **Forecast Dates**.

The user may also choose the interval to use when making time-distributed resource calculations:

- Hour
- Day
- Week
- Month

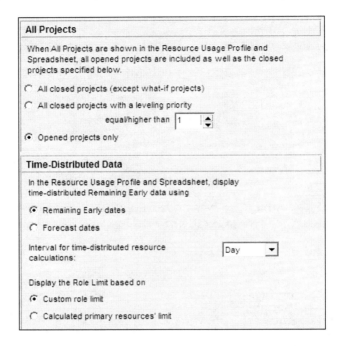

The **Role Limit** may be selected from either the resource limit of the **Primary Resource** or the custom limit assigned to the **Role**.

User Preferences | Calculations: This screen lets the user choose whether existing Units, Duration, and Units/Time are affected when adding and removing resource assignments.

This screen also lets the user choose whether to use the resources Units per Time and Overtime when assigning to an existing activity, or to use the current assignments values, or whether to prompt the user each time.

It also allows the user to choose what to do with Price per Unit when a resource and a role share the same activity.

While it is convenient to choose one of the "always" options, it is important to be aware of how you make these assignments and how that affects your project.

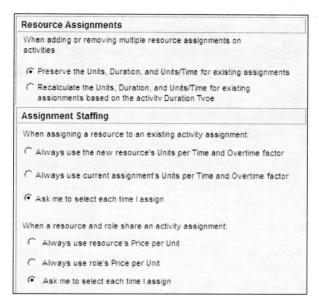

User Preferences | Startup Filters lets the user choose whether to see certain data, such as resources, filtered by project by default.

If you mainly work in one project, then it can be helpful to filter by project by default. However, if you find yourself frequently using resources, activity codes, and other items from different projects, you may prefer to have no filter by default.

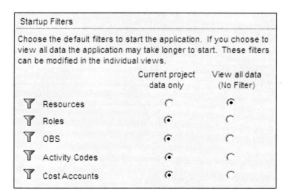

View menu

The **View** menu is quite extensive, and the items available vary as you view different modules. The items on this menu will be discussed as they occur in relation to other screens, and also in the section *Customizing screens and saving layouts*. Note that near the bottom of this menu there are two very helpful items:

- **Reset All Toolbars** — for when you have customized too much and want to start over again
- **Lock All Toolbars** — for when you have found the perfect setup and do not want to lose it by accident

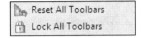

Project menu

The **Project** menu lets you perform a number of project-related actions, such as working with Activities, Resources, and WBS elements. These and other project-related activities will be covered in-depth in future chapters such as *Chapter 4*, which walks through setting up a new project.

However, one element of this menu is immediately useful: **Set Default Project...** When you work with multiple projects opened at once, this becomes the project selected when you choose to open a group of projects. It is also where new activities and issues are placed, unless you actively choose another project.

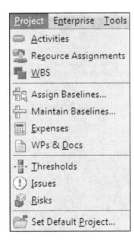

Enterprise

The **Enterprise** menu will show different items, depending on whether you are running P6 Professional or the P6 Enterprise Optional Client. The following screenshot shows **Enterprise** menu from the P6 Professional Client on the left-hand side, and the same menu from the P6 Enterprise Optional Client on the right-hand side.

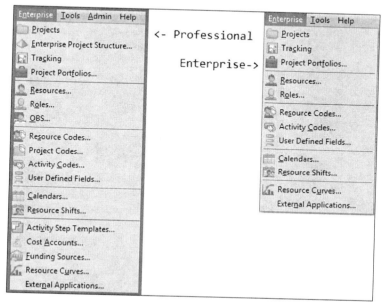

The differences in these two menu items reflect that P6 Enterprise assumes that the system will be installed in an environment where the administrative responsibilities have been separated from the daily scheduling of jobs, while P6 Professional will be installed at places where schedulers have more responsibility and ownership of the entire P6 installation.

The following menu items are found only in P6 Professional. For the Enterprise Optional client, these items are set through the web interface:

- Enterprise Project Structure
- OBS
- Resource Codes
- Project Codes
- Activity Step Templates
- Cost Accounts
- Funding Sources

Tools

The **Tools** menu contains a range of items. The first section deals with progressing project status. These topics will be covered in further chapters, particularly in chapters 7 through 9. In this section we will focus on the items below that first section in the **Tool** menu.

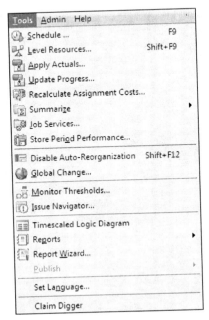

Auto-Reorganization determines whether a screen of data will be automatically re-sorted when you change data. Take, for example, the list of activities in the following screenshot:

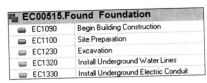

In this screen, activities are sorted by Activity ID. Let us take Activity EC1230 and change it to EC01230. If Auto-Reorganization is enabled, the activity will be moved to the top. If Auto-Reorganization is disabled, then the activity will remain where it is on the screen.

Global Change is a powerful utility that allows you to alter all of the data within a project. Note that this tool does enforce security, so if your global change attempts to affect any data to which you do not have access, it will not be allowed to proceed.

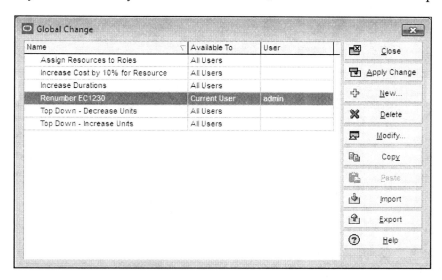

In the following example, task Renumber EC1230, we use global change to change Activity ID EC1230 to EC01230 and to change every other Activity ID by prefixing them with three asterisks.

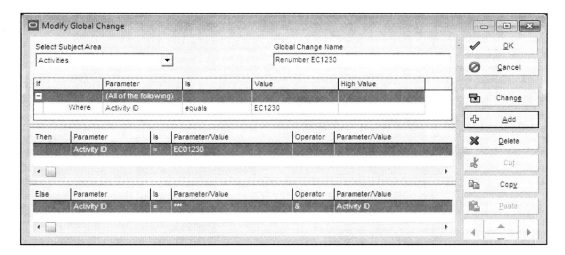

When you click **Change**, the change is not made immediately. Instead, a screen appears showing a preview of all the changes that will take place. You may then choose to save the results to a text file for review, cancel the changes, or commit the changes.

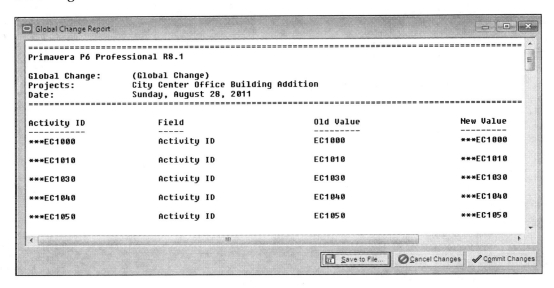

If you develop particularly helpful global changes, you can share them with other users within the same database instance and you can export them into a file that can then be imported into a different instance of P6.

Monitor Thresholds and **Issues Navigator** will be covered in *Chapter 8*.

Timescaled Logic Diagrams bring back a feature that had been missing in between P3 and P6 v8 (also implemented in P6 v7 service pack 3). It is a separate program which is invoked from the P6 tools menu, but which reads data in from P6 and then runs independently. A Timescaled logic diagram has been described as a cross between a Gantt chart and a Logic diagram, and is helpful when reviewing the logic and critical paths of the project as a whole.

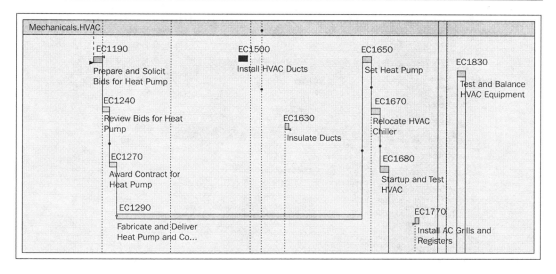

Admin

This menu is only visible for the P6 Professional client. For P6 Enterprise, all administrative functions are accessed via the web interface.

Users and **Security Profiles** lets you set up users and administer profiles and security.

Admin Preferences allows the user to alter a number of global settings.

Admin Categories manages a number of global categories used to describe and organize items.

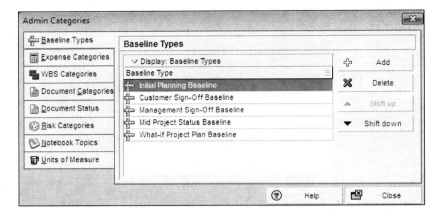

Currencies manages conversion rates between currencies and how currencies are displayed throughout P6. It is very important to update any currency conversion rates that you use in your projects.

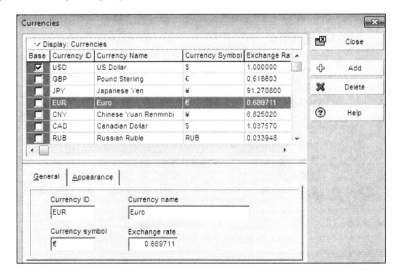

Financial Periods lets you set the reporting periods for financial reporting. The **Batch Create** function can be used to quickly generate financial periods. Note that this setting is enterprise-wide and not project-specific.

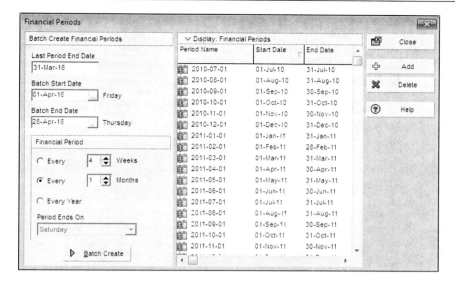

Help

This is the standard help menu.

Contents brings up a full help system that documents all features of P6. The second item brings up a screen telling you about the current system setup. The **System** tab on this screen can be very helpful when trying to diagnose issues. There is a convenient **Copy** button that will allow you to send this information to your local support staff or Oracle Support.

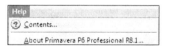

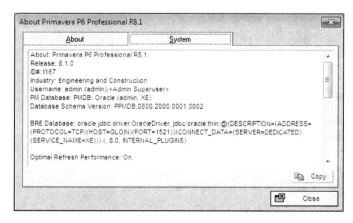

Customizing screens and saving layouts

There are a number of ways to view P6 data. In order to help make it easy to compare "apples to apples", P6 allows you to create and save customized views that can be shared by one or more people.

At the top left of almost every screen is an inverted triangle with the label **Layout**.

This feature lets you alter the appearance of the data screens. While the specific items in the list will change depending on the kind of data you are viewing, there are some common elements.

When you save a layout, a screen appears offering a number of options:

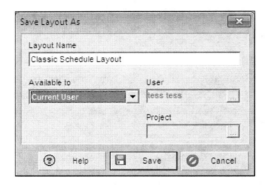

Layout Name is a name to assign to this layout.

Available to lets the user choose who may use this layout. Layouts can be saved at three levels:

- Global: Everyone in the system has access to the layout. This is a good practice for establishing a common set of layouts to be used across the company.

- Project: The layout is only available to a specific project. This can be helpful if a project must be viewed consistently by all users.

- **User**: The view is only accessible to the user, which is helpful when each person needs to view project data in a different way. Users can also share their layouts with other users.

When a user goes to **Open Layout**, they can see all Global ones, all the ones that they may have created or have been assigned, and all that are set for the current project. Thus, users have a great deal of flexibility in choosing how to view their data.

Summary

In this chapter, we have given a grand overview of P6, from how to log into the system, to all of the main menu items, and to customizing screens. Although there is much more depth in following chapters, we hope that the reader will now have a feel for what capabilities are present in the product and where to find things.

At this point the experienced P6 user who is mainly interested in how things have changed in version 8 may wish to skip ahead to specific topics of interest. Novice users will wish to continue to the next chapter, where we begin to lay out the foundations for managing projects in P6.

In *Chapter 3, Organizing your Projects with EPS, OBS, and WBS*, we discuss three key structures for organizing information across and within projects: Enterprise Project Structure, Organizational Breakdown Structure, and Work Breakdown Structure.

3
Organizing your Projects with EPS, OBS, and WBS

In this chapter we start with the big picture – how will you organize your projects and your people, and how will you organize the work within the projects themselves? This organization may be quite simple for a small company that is only managing a handful of simple projects. However, for larger companies, organizing can become quite complex. Fortunately, P6 can handle a wide range of user needs. In this chapter we will go through the basic elements of project structure:

- Organizational Breakdown Structure (OBS)
- Enterprise Project Structure (EPS)
- Work Breakdown Structure (WBS)

By the end of this chapter readers should feel comfortable designing and setting up EPS, OBS, and WBS for their own systems.

 The industry standard term is Enterprise Breakdown Structure, or EBS. However, in P6, this is called Enterprise Project Structure or EPS.

Enterprise versus project data

If you come from a background where you work with projects individually, the concept "enterprise" may seem foreign. Simply put, "enterprise" means information that is shared across all projects. For example, people are resources in P6 and resources are defined at the enterprise level. While an individual may work on only one project, they may be assigned to other projects as well. So having them at the enterprise level allows you to allocate people across projects.

Another quite different example of enterprise data is screen layouts. These are customizations of the various screens in P6, such as the view of activities in a Gantt chart. Layouts can be stored and shared globally, so are enterprise data.

Project data, in contrast, is limited to a single project. An activity, for example, belongs to one and only one project. Likewise, project work and reference documents are specific to projects.

However, some data can be stored either at the enterprise level, or at the project level. One such example is activity codes. Some activity codes may be enterprise, perhaps CSI codes to identify the type of work. Others, such as the specific floor in a multi-story construction, are particular to one project and meaningless in others. As we go through the various features of P6 we may sometimes refer to enterprise data as **global**. Let us begin with the top level of enterprise data, the Organizational Breakdown Structure.

Organizational Breakdown Structure (OBS)

The Organizational Breakdown Structure (OBS) defines how people within a company are organized and what rights and access they have within projects. For example, a company that builds ships may have different facilities, with different staff at each facility. Yet certain functions such as the executive team or IT support may span the different facilities. The OBS reflects the *chain of command* within the company. It can often mirror the EPS, but the two may also diverge. The specific OBS elements may be a mix of specifically named people, business units, departments, and specialties. The OBS and EPS are interconnected such that the OBS can be used to apply security roles and access all projects below specific EPS elements.

The OBS should be considered as a security element, and the use of specific people and names in the OBS should be avoided. Simply look at each EPS element and choose which group should have access to each node. The list of access will guide your design of OBS.

The OBS assignment shows up on each EPS, project, and WBS in a field called **Responsible Manager** that indicates who has access to this project. Assigning OBS to the entities will be illustrated in the last section of this chapter.

To manage OBS in the web client, click on **Administer | User Access**. This will bring up a screen as shown in the following screenshot:

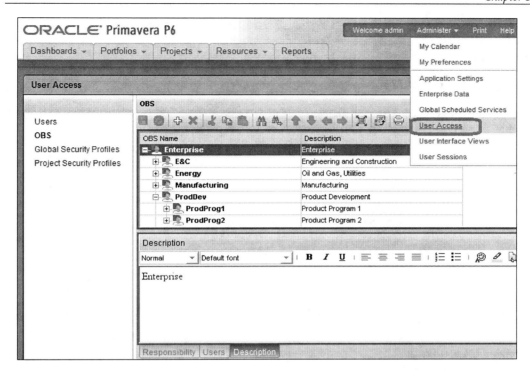

The management of OBS in the web client is very similar to management in the Professional Client.

In Professional, choose **Enterprise | OBS...** to bring up the OBS management screen.

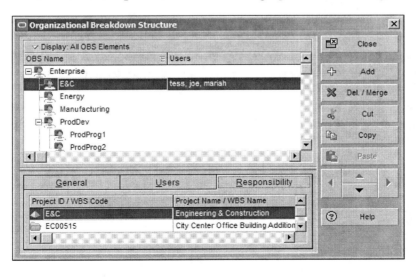

The main screen shows the OBS elements and the users who are assigned to each element. The OBS nodes can be moved by selecting a node, and pressing the arrow keys on the right-hand side of the main screen.

There are three tabs at the bottom of the OBS screen:

General displays the OBS Name and Description for the selected responsible manager (OBS element). The description is a rich-text description of the OBS element.

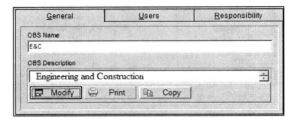

The **Users** tab shows which users are assigned to the OBS node. When users are assigned, they are also assigned a specific Project Security profile which determines their access within the EPS, Project, or WBS element associated with the OBS node. We will discuss project security roles in *Chapter 4, Creating a New Project and Work Breakdown Structure*.

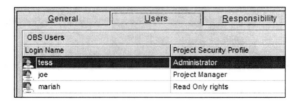

Responsibility is where users are assigned to specific elements in P6. An OBS element (and hence its users) may be associated with an EPS node. In that case the security level is passed down to all projects within that EPS node. An OBS can be associated with a specific project, or even with WBS elements within a project. The OBS assignments together with your security profile can create Read Only or Read and Write access privileges.

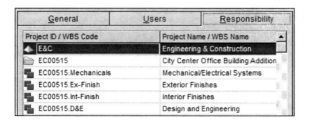

There are three icons of note on this screen, and each represents that the OBS element has responsibility at a different level of the EPS/Project/WBS:

- Enterprise Project Structure (EPS) responsibility

- Project responsibility

- Responsibility for specific WBS elements

Enterprise Project Structure (EPS)

The EPS is the *outsider's view* of your company, showing your lines of business. The EPS is laid out in a tree structure. A construction company may have an EPS tree with only two nodes: development, for work on existing sites and construction, for new sites. Or an oil company may split their work first between Natural Gas and Heavy Oil. The structure may be broken down further. For example, Heavy Oil may be broken down into Primary, Cold EOR, and Thermal. The idea is that all projects under an EPS node share common characteristics and may be managed by the same team. The following is an example from ExxonMobil:

- Refinery Division
    - US Domestic Operations
        California
        - Torrance
        Louisiana
        - Baton Rouge
        New Jersey
        - Bayway
        - Clinton
        - Edison
        - Paulsburo
        Texas
        - Houston
        Virginia
        - Fairfax

- Chemical Division
  - US Domestic Operations

    Lousiana

    - Baton Rouge
    - Chalmette
    - Plaquemine

    Texas

    - Baytown... and so on

In P6 web, the EPS is administered through the **Projects** tab in the EPS screen. The default view shows projects within the EPS, but you can choose a pre-defined view called **EPS Only View** to show only EPS.

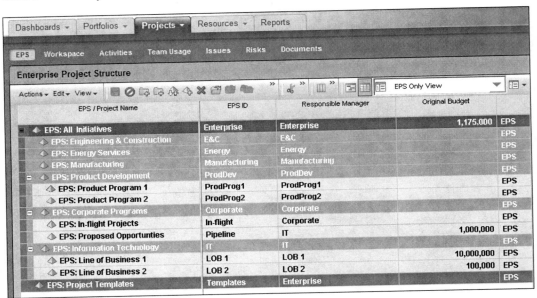

In Professional, choose **Enterprise | Enterprise Project Structure...** to bring up the EPS management screen.

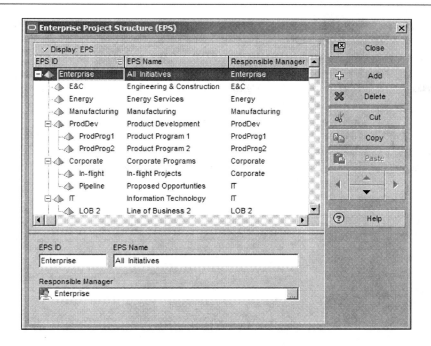

The EPS is basically a tree of information. When discussing this tree, the term node is used to describe each element of the tree. For example, **Enterprise** is the top node in the previous screenshot. The topmost node, also called the root node, has no parent. A node can have other nodes beneath it, and these are called child nodes. A child node, likewise, can have a parent node above it. In the previous screenshot, the children of the root **Enterprise** node are **E&C**, **Energy**, **Manufacturing**, and so on. The node **Corporate** has the children In-flight and Pipeline, and has the parent node Enterprise.

Each element of the EPS has three properties, shown at the bottom of the screen:

- **EPS ID**
- **EPS Name**
- **Responsible Manager**

The first two are straightforward. **EPS ID** is a unique identifier, a convenient and short way to describe the element, whereas the EPS name is a more verbose description. **Responsible Manager** shows what OBS element has rights over that particular EPS node. Note that the OBS elements shown have the same name as their EPS nodes. This indicates that the external organization of the company matches its internal responsibility quite well in this instance.

In the upper left-hand corner of the main EPS screen is a dropdown called **Display: EPS**. This can be used to alter how the EPS is displayed. By default the EPS screen is shown in table view, which lists the EPS elements in a tree. You can also choose **Chart View** to see a chart-centric display of the EPS.

The **Chart View** shows the EPS as you might display it on a wall chart.

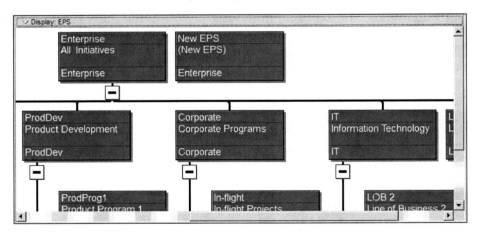

If you have a very large EPS, you can find elements by using the **Find** option or by pressing *F3* or *Ctrl + F*. Note that it is better to use the table view when attempting to find items because the chart view does not allow searching over all EPS properties.

Print preview shows the information on the screen in a printable report. This can be useful if you want to actually print and hang your EPS chart on the wall for analysis.

Columns lets you choose which columns to display. In table view the only options are EPS ID and Name. However, in chart view there are many other columns to choose from.

Table, Font and Row is another control that you will commonly see in many different layout menus. Use this screen to alter the font, color, and size of the displayed text.

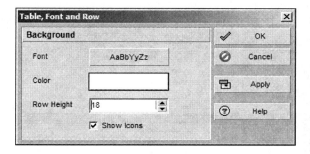

If you view the EPS in **Chart View**, there are more options on the display menu:

- **Arrange Children**
- **Align Children**
- **Chart Box Template**

These are all fairly straightforward and can be used to modify how the chart appears, which is helpful if printing out the EPS for display.

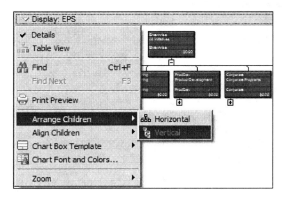

Now that we have seen how to manage the EPS, let us examine what EPS does. Every project in P6 must exist within a single EPS node. One of the standard project layouts in P6 shows all projects within the EPS structure. This is a common way of displaying projects.

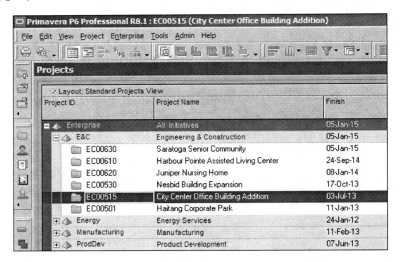

The EPS provides one of the many methods for organizing projects. Some projects may clearly fall under one EPS node, while others should span multiple ones. In later chapters, we will see how to organize projects into portfolios, which is a more flexible solution for organizing reports.

Work Breakdown Structure (WBS)

Within a project, activities can be grouped, filtered, planned, and organized by Work Breakdown Structure (WBS). The WBS classifies all of the deliverables of a project and is often formed into a hierarchy with an increasing level of detail. How WBS is defined varies by company and by project, but having a well-planned WBS is a key first step to implementing good project controls.

Consider any one of several standardized WBS structures:

- UNIFORMAT II Elemental Classification for Building Elements (Publication NISTIR-6389)

- UNIFORMAT II Classification for Bridge elements (NIST 1122)

- DOT Specs for use in almost every public entity road project. FHWA publication FP-03, also see specific state DOT website for more specific documentation.
- FAA Specs for use in every US airport/airfield construction project. FAA Publication AC 150/5370-10.

An example of WBS for a software development project could be:

1. Needs assessment
2. Design
3. Coding
4. Integration testing
5. Implementation and rollout
6. Maintenance

This would be the top level of the WBS. Each element could be further divided. Coding could be broken up as:

3. Coding

    3.1 Database Abstraction

    3.2 Business Layer

    3.3 User Interface

WBS elements are often added to track level-of-effort (overhead) work such as project administration. WBS elements representing milestones can be added as well to enable simplified reporting and tracking.

In P6, WBS elements are created within a project. First, open the project and then choose **Projects | WBS** or click on the double boxes toolbar icon

The WBS screen shows a tree-like structure representing the project. Each node can be moved up or down. An element can also be moved under another node or back up the hierarchy. You can move an element by selecting it and pressing the arrow buttons shown in the lower right side of the screen.

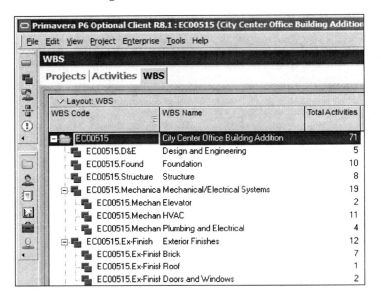

There are also a number of helpful shortcuts:

- *Insert*: adds a new WBS element
- *Ctrl* + Up Arrow: moves an element up
- *Ctrl* + Down Arrow: moves element down
- *Ctrl* + Right Arrow: moves under the adjacent element
- *Ctrl* + Left Arrow: moves an item from beneath the current parent element

Becoming proficient with keyboard shortcuts can help you work more efficiently.

Sometimes you may need to move more than one element at a time. If the elements are adjacent, then highlight them and move your mouse over the region just to the left of them. A "paper" icon will appear. This indicates that you may drag your elements to a new location.

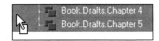

It is often the case that the same WBS structure is used across many projects. This greatly helps to standardize projects, which is critical to making meaningful measurements regarding planning, execution, monitoring and control, and close-out of the project management processes.

A simple example

We will now create a simple and fictitious example to illustrate how the EPS, OBS, and WBS can work together to implement proper project security. If you are able to create your own copy of a blank P6 database, you are invited to follow along so that you can get a feel for this firsthand.

In this example, our company ACME Inc. has two employees, Alice and Bob, and two projects, Project A and Project B. They work with two subcontractors, Charlie and Diane, who only work on Project B, and who also work on separate parts of the project. Here are the people involved:

- Alice: the owner of the company
- Bob: the Project Manager for Project B
- Charlie: Subcontractor working for Subcontractor 1
- Diane: Subcontractor working for Subcontractor 2

Your EPS is simple – there is your company, ACME, at the root level and then two EPS nodes: one for internal projects and one for external projects.

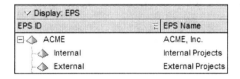

Project A is an internal project and only one employee will be working on it. Project B has the subcontractors working on it.

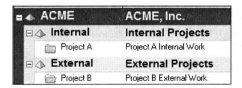

The EPS helps to separate these projects. In a more practical example you may have dozens of projects under several EPS nodes of varying depth.

Within Project B we will create two WBS elements. These elements will separate the work of Subcontractor 1 from the work of Subcontractor 2. This will allow both of them to work within the same schedule yet not interfere with each other's work.

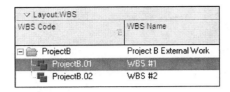

Now that we have our EPS, projects, and WBS set up, let's make assignments through the OBS. Note that we assign OBS elements to the EPS, Project, and WBS items, then assign users to the OBS.

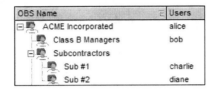

There will be a top-level node for the whole company. Under that is a node for ACME Class B Managers. Another node under the top level holds all of the subcontractors with one sub-node for each. Now let us use the OBS to assign users specific rights to different projects:

- Assign ACME to the top EPS, and let its default access propagate to its children.
- Assign Class B Managers specifically to Project B

Thus we have established the relationship between the EPS and Projects, and the OBS.

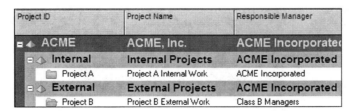

Next we assign rights at the WBS level:

- Assign WBS #1 to the OBS called Sub1
- Assign WBS #2 to the OBS element Sub 2

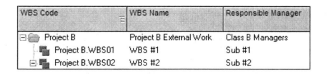

At last we may assign users to these OBS elements and then we can see what effect this has.

Open up the OBS view.

1. Assign Alice to ACME Incorporated
2. Assign Bob to Class B Managers
3. Assign Charlie to Sub 1
4. Assign Diane to Sub 2

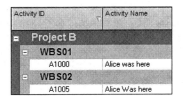

Now let us test the system. Alice should be able to log in and see both Projects under the Internal and External EPS elements. Alice is also able to edit activities in both projects.

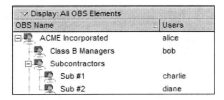

When Bob logs in, he can only see Project B under the External Node. He does not even see that there is a node named Internal in the EPS. Within Project B he has full access to edit activities in any WBS element.

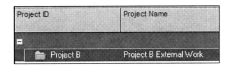

Within Project B, however, Bob has free reign to edit activities in both WBS elements.

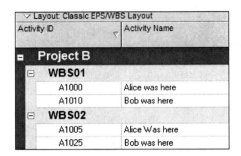

Next we log in as Charlie. What does he see? Like Bob, he sees only Project B. Within that project he can see activities under both WBS #1 and WBS #2. However, he can only edit items under WBS #1.

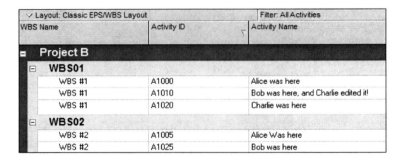

When Alice logs in, she only sees Project B. She is only able to add and edit activities under WBS #2. Thus, while Charlie and Diane are both able to view activities in Project B, they cannot alter each other's work.

With this setup, Alice has overall responsibility for all of the projects. Bob is responsible for Project B, and within Project B, Charlie is responsible for the work under his WBS element and Diane is responsible for the activities under hers. This combination of EPS, Project, WBS, and OBS allows companies to tightly assign roles and responsibilities so that teams can work together in the same P6 database.

Summary

You have seen how to organize projects under EPS, how to organize within projects using WBS, and how to assign user access to EPS, Projects, and WBS using OBS. The simple example showed you how to put these to work in practice.

In the next chapter we will walk through a more detailed exercise. We will create a new project, assign it a place in the EPS, parse out access in the OBS, and then break the work into meaningful sections with the WBS. We will then follow the project through a simple life cycle in order to illustrate how P6 is used from project inception to end.

4
Creating a New Project and Work Breakdown Structure

Now that we have discussed the organization of a project, we will walk through the process of setting up a new project in P6. By the end of this chapter, the reader should feel comfortable with:

- Creating a new project using the New Project Wizard
- Setting project properties
- Structuring the WBS of the project
- Importing projects into P6

You may also create a project using project templates. This is discussed in *Chapter 10, Project Templates*.

Creating a new project using the New Project Wizard

Let us suppose that you have gone through the exercises in the last chapter and created an EPS and OBS structure, which reflects how your company organizes and manages a project. Now that we have a place to put a project, and have created the parties responsible for managing our projects, we can create our first project!

Start a new project by choosing the **File | New** from the main menu. You may also press *Ctrl + N*, or press the following icon:

In P6 web, from the **Projects** tab, EPS module, choose **Actions | Add | Add Project**, or press the same icon as shown previously.

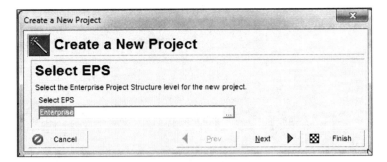

Once you do this a screen appears that will walk you through adding basic project information. The process is very similar in P6 Professional and the web.

The first choice to make is where to assign the project in the Enterprise Project Structure. Clicking on the ellipses button will bring up a screen that allows you to choose an EPS node under which to assign the project. See *Chapter 3, Organizing your Projects with EPS, OBS, and WBS*, for more about setting up EPS.

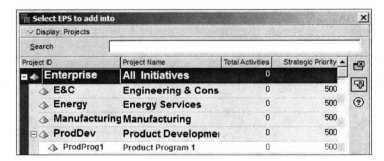

Next, provide a project ID and name. Choosing a good project ID is important, as this will simplify updates, reporting, and managing backup and restore files. The project ID is limited to 20 characters and is sometimes also referred to as the project's short name.

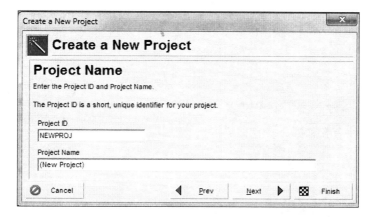

 It can be helpful to have a project ID that has meaning to your company. As an alternative to a standard accounting project number, for example, you could identify each project by state, year, and number, as in SSYYNNN.

In this case, project CA16020 would denote the twentieth project in California in the year 2016. Of course, if your projects are created within P6 through an integration from another system (see *Appendix A, Integrations*), the project ID may be assigned from that system.

The project name is what you would normally refer to as the project, as in "August 2011Turnaround" or "Heatherwood Elementary School Remodel". This is limited to 100 characters, the same length as a WBS element name.

The next screen lets you enter the **Project Planned Start** date and optionally, the date by which the project must finish. (Note that we highly discourage entering a project finish date. After all, a foundational strength of P6 is its ability to calculate the finish date!)

Next, choose the responsible manager for the project. This is the OBS element that will own the project. Additionally, see *Chapter 3* for more on organizational breakdown structure and how it relates to project security.

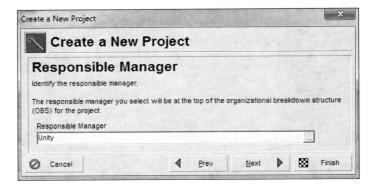

The next screen lets you choose the default billing rate to use for roles and resources assigned to activities. See *Chapter 6, Resources,* for more on Resources and Rates.

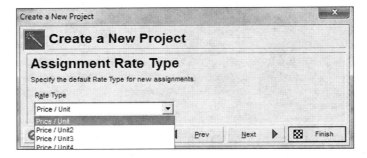

At last, the final wizard screen lets you press **Finish** to complete your project. But there is much more work to do. As the screen states, there are many project properties that need to be defined and modified after this process is complete.

Setting project properties

Project properties are set by going to the **Project** screen, choosing the project, and choosing **Project Details**. This will bring up a window as shown in the following screenshot in the lower half of the screen:

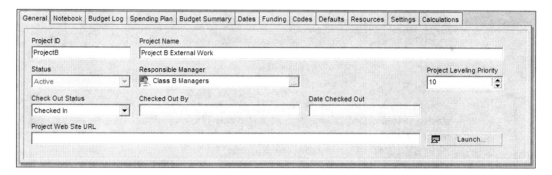

By default, not all of the tabs are shown in this screenshot. To add and remove tabs from the project details screen, right-click anywhere in the **Details** tab and choose **Customize Project Details...**.

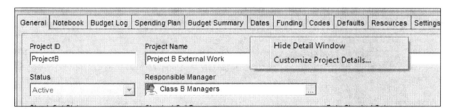

General

The **General** tab lets you set certain high-level information about the project. While the **Project ID**, **Project Name**, and **Responsible Manager** were entered in the wizard screens, they may be changed here as well.

Project Status can be set to one of four values:

- **Planned**: Progress Reporter users cannot access the activities
- **Active**: Progress Reporter users can access activities
- **Inactive**: Progress Reporter cannot access activities

- **What-if**: Progress Reporter users cannot access activities, and closed projects will not show in resource profiles

Your organization should have a policy in place as to when each of these status types is assigned to a project. The technical function of each one is as important as your reporting. Define in your lifecycle when a project moves from the **Planned** (where resources are shown as reserved but the project is not shown in the **Active** portfolios) or **Active** state when there are a few technical differences in how P6 handles the project—but big differences in how your company manages the project. Inactive is typically where a project has been in active state but is no longer being worked (cancelled or completed). In the inactive status, P6 does not show future reserved time for any resource assigned to an activity scheduled past the project data date. **What-if** projects do not report any of the data in assignments past or future—it is "off the radar" and therefore all copies or duplicate projects that exist to create different scenarios should be placed in the **What-if** status to avoid duplication of information and assignments.

The **Responsible Manager** was also set in the new project wizard and it is the OBS element responsible for the project.

Project Leveling Priority can range from **1** (highest) to **100** (lowest). When multiple projects are scheduled, this determines the order in which projects are considered when leveling resources across projects.

Check Out Status shows whether a project is checked in or out and **Checked Out By** shows who has checked out the project. The **Date Checked Out** shows when that user checked out the project. Check out is very helpful. It allows one user to lock the project for their exclusive use for a period of time. For example, a scheduler may want to ensure that no one is changing anything about the project while the schedule status update is being performed. It is important to always check a project back in after exclusive use is no longer needed.

If you have a project website, enter the URL in the **Project WebSite URL** screen. For example, if your project website is www.packtpub.com, simply enter this. Press **Launch** to view the site in your default web browser.

Notebook

Notebooks allow you to enter information about a project. The **Notebook** tab lets you enter a number of notebook topics, each with its own notebook entry. The notebook topics are set through the menu item **Admin | Admin Categories...**. Within each notebook, you can edit the text using HTML editing features, including formatting text, inserting pictures, copying, pasting, and adding hyperlinks. Notebooks can be used to enter project notes, such as the project's purpose, core requirements, or any other project-specific detail.

Notebooks exist not only for Projects, but also can be added to any EPS, WBS, or activity. So, for example, you could create a notebook that describes the purposes and objectives of each WBS element. These notebooks could then be gathered together in a report, which outlines the project by WBS, using the notebooks as summary paragraphs.

Budget Log

Use the **Budget Log** to enter project budget information. Note that budgets can also be entered at the WBS and EPS level. The budget information is not shared among the EPS, Project, and WBS. Instead, they are treated as independent values.

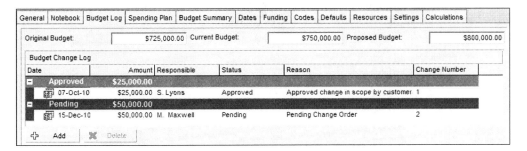

You may enter the original budget manually. Changes to the budget can be entered as change orders, and the status of a change can be **Approved** or **Pending**. Only approved change orders will modify the current budget.

The **Budget Log** is completely separated from costs in a cost-loaded schedule and will not progress as the activities progress. It is a disconnected area that is best used for the overall budget and change management to that budget. Spend plan and benefit tally are also not calculated or changed by the progress of the schedule in P6—it is a separate area.

Spending Plan

| General | Notebook | Budget Log | Spending Plan | Budget Summary | Dates | Funding | Codes | Defaults | Resources | Settings | Calculations |

Date	Spending Plan	Spending Plan Tally	Undistributed Current Variance	Benefit Plan	Benefit Plan Tally	Benefit Variance
Total	$300.00	$0.00	$300.00	$30.00	$0.00	($30.00)
11 - Jun	$100.00	$0.00	$100.00	$10.00	$0.00	($10.00)
11 - Jul	$100.00	$0.00	$100.00	$10.00	$0.00	($10.00)
11 - Aug	$100.00	$0.00	$100.00	$10.00	$0.00	($10.00)
11 - Sep	$0.00	$0.00	$0.00	$0.00	$0.00	$0.00
11 - Oct	$0.00	$0.00	$0.00	$0.00	$0.00	$0.00
11 - Nov	$0.00	$0.00	$0.00	$0.00	$0.00	$0.00
11 - Dec	$0.00	$0.00	$0.00	$0.00	$0.00	$0.00
12 - Jan	$0.00	$0.00	$0.00	$0.00	$0.00	$0.00

Enter monthly amounts into the **Spending Plan** tab. This allows you to set the expected cash outlay for the project. The months shown begin three months before the project start and extend to four years after the project start date. Unfortunately, there is no way to extend the spending plan beyond these four years for longer-term projects.

The **Spending Plan** tally and **Benefits Plan** tally columns are empty when viewing a project. However, for an EPS node, the tally shows the project totals for all projects beneath the node. Thus, you can plan your expected spending at the EPS level and compare it to the planned spending at the project level.

Budget Summary

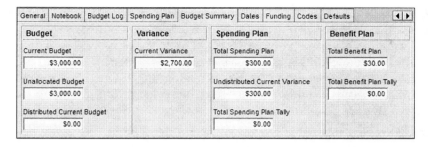

The budget summary table summarizes the information from the **Budget** tab and the **Spending Plan** tab. It is display only.

Dates

What is a schedule without dates? The **Dates** tab shows you high-level dates for your project.

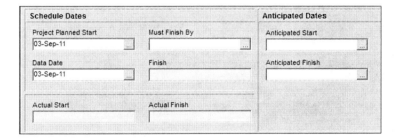

- **Project Planned Start** was entered when the project was created, and can be changed in this tab. If the project has activities, then this date is based on them. If the project as no activities but does have an **Anticipated Start**, then that value is used.

- **Must Finish By** is a constraint that can be added to a project if the project has a set end date. However, we strongly recommend that the project schedule be developed prior to setting the **Must Finish Date**. There are only a few examples where a mandatory **Finish Date** is appropriate at the project level.

- **Data Date**, also referred to as DD, simply equals the start date when a project is first created. Once a project is under way, the data date becomes critically important. The **Data Date** reflects the date as of which project progress is updated. For example, every week the scheduler could collect progress information about all work performed as of the prior Friday. The schedule is then updated to reflect the reported progress. After the scheduler enters that information, the schedule is updated using the *F9* key. The data date entered for the schedule update is then set to that prior Friday. Schedule updates and data dates are discussed more fully in *Chapter 9, Baselining and Statusing*.

- Finish is also a result of the last schedule calculation, and is the latest early finish date. If there are no activities scheduled, and there is an **Anticipated Finish**, then that value is used. Otherwise, this value is blank. If the project has started, the **Actual Start** date is shown here. Likewise, if the project has ended, the **Actual Finish** date is shown as well.

- **Anticipated Start** and **Anticipated Finish** are dates entered by the user as their best guess about the project schedule. These dates are completely free of constraints, and can serve as a helpful reality check on the dates that arise from the scheduling algorithm.

Funding

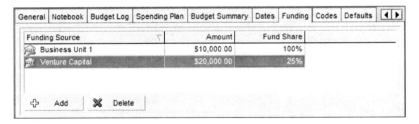

Your project may have funding sources that you wish to track. In the **Funding** tab you can choose funding sources and assign amounts and percentages. The list of funding sources is defined through the menu item **Enterprise | Funding Sources**.

Funding can also be assigned at the EPS level. Funding amounts do not roll up, and there is no logic connecting the percentages of each fund used. As such, this information is purely for reporting purposes.

Codes (project level)

Project Codes allow for grouping, sorting, and filtering projects. They are used extensively and allow you to organize your project in many ways, particularly for reporting and when performing portfolio analysis (See *Chapter 11, Portfolios*). Think of codes as categories or labels; they can be used individually or in combination to group or give totals for different categories in reports or portfolios.

In the previous screenshot you can see that for our project, there are many project codes assigned. The first code is **Business Process**, which describes the kind of work that is to be performed. Within **Businesses Process**, there are many different kinds of work, but for this project, we have assigned the **Business Process** to be **Construction**.

One key to manage a portfolio of projects is to have meaningful project codes. To edit project codes, go to **Enterprise | Project Codes**.

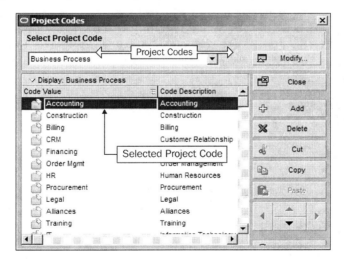

Here you see that besides **Construction**, there are other business processes, including **Accounting**, Legal, and **Training**. For a given project, you could assign any of these values to be the business process. These code values have two parts — the **Code Value** itself, which is limited to a maximum length defined for the code, and a **Code Description**, which is limited to 100 characters. This allows you to choose concise values for the codes, which can help in reporting, along with more descriptive text that can help an end-user understand the meaning of the code.

The project codes themselves can be modified by pressing the **Modify...** button that brings up the following screen:

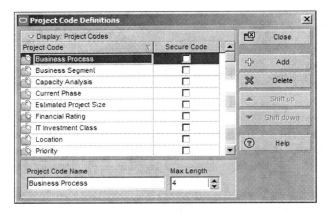

Here you can add new project codes, delete, or modify them. You can also set the maximum length allowed for a code value. Use this screen cautiously, as project codes are global across all projects. If you set **Max Length** shorter than existing code values, you can still use those values, but will not be able to add a code longer than the current **Max Length**.

Checking the **Secure Code** box will assign security to the code. Security can be assigned so that only certain users can view or assign these code values.

Once you have defined your project codes, you can enter the allowed values in the **Project Code** screen.

In practice, many codes are generally used. Codes can describe units within your company, physical locations, or geographical regions. How you define your project codes speaks volumes about how you view your business.

Think creatively about project codes. For example, if you find there is a grant for companies who use 10 percent green technology, then have a GREEN code. If executives want to know total hours of work in Texas this year, create a TEXAS location code for the projects, and so on.

Defaults

The **Defaults** tab lets you set a variety of activity-level defaults that help you to manage your projects efficiently. These defaults are project-specific, so apply to all users who are working on the project. Activities are covered in *Chapter 5, Adding Activities and Relationships*.

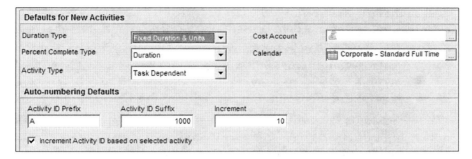

Resources

The **Resources** tab also lets you define default settings for resources. Resources are covered in more depth in *Chapter 6, Resources*.

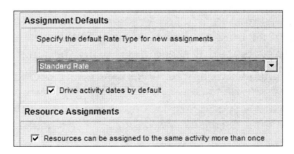

Settings

The **Settings** tab covers a variety of project settings.

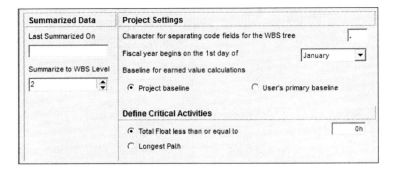

- **Last Summarized On** shows the last time that the project data was summarized. Summary data is used for reporting and project analysis.

- **Summarize to WBS Level** indicates the level at which the project is summarized. As summarization can be a slow process, and as summaries are not necessarily needed at every level, you can set the summarization value so that the level of summary is right for the specific project.

- WBS separator is the symbol to use when showing WBS names in the tree. For example, if you have WBS elements A, B, and C, each as successive children under the other, then by default, they will be displayed as **A.B.C.** But you can change this to use another symbol, such as a **>** so that it is shown as **A>B>C** instead.

- Fiscal year start month can be set as well to match your company's or your client's fiscal year.

- **The Baseline for earned value calculations** can be set to use the calculated project baseline or user's primary baseline. If you want all the users to see the same calculations, use the project baseline. At the very least, make sure that anybody who is comparing schedules is using the same baseline.

- How a project defines critical activities can be set as either those activities that are on the longest path to complete the project, or those activities whose total float is less than the specified amount. Critical activities and paths will be discussed further in *Chapter 7, Scheduling and Constraints*.

Calculations

The **Calculations** tab lets you set default behaviors for activities and resources in the project.

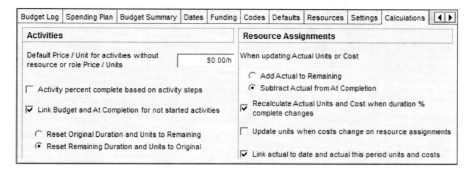

- If you create activities without assigning a role or resource that has rates assigned, then you can set the **Default Price/Unit...** that will be used to calculate the planned cost of the activity. This is very helpful if you have a rough average rate that you wish to use during the planning stages.

- The **Activity percent complete...** calculation can be tied to activity steps. If this is turned on, then as each activity step is completed, the percent complete is updated according to the weighted value of each completed step. (For P3 users, this is one part of the Auto Cost rules). See *Chapter 5* for more on activity steps.

- If an activity has not started, then you may wish to have the calculated amounts at completion remain equal to the planned budgeted amounts even as the schedule progresses. When you update activities you can tell the system to do one of two things:
    - The system can **Reset Original Duration and Units...** when you update the Remaining Duration and Units
    - Or, **Reset Remaining...** will tell the system to calculate the remaining duration and units based on the planned valued

If your activities have resources assigned, then the following settings may be chosen when updating actual units or costs:

- **Add Actual to Remaining** will calculate the new At Complete cost based on the actual values entered plus the remaining values. In this case it is important that when you enter actuals, that you also update the remaining values. For example, an activity is planned to take 40 hours to complete. You currently have 25 hours actual worked and 15 hours remaining for 40 hours At Complete. When you collect schedule progress you learn that 30 hours actual have been performed. If you simply enter 30 hours actual, then the new At Complete will be *30 + 15 = 45* hours remaining. This may not be correct. If the At Complete work is still expected to be 40, then you must update the remaining hours to 10. This is the option to choose for cost-plus contracts.

- **Subtract Actual from At Completion** is the opposite of the choice shown earlier. In this case, when you enter actual values, then the remaining work is set to equal At Completion minus actual. This is the appropriate choice for fixed-price contracts, as the budget is fixed and the At Completion budget should not change.

- Recalculate actual units and cost when duration % complete changes. This will cause the actual costs to be updated when the % complete duration of the activity is updated. The actual will be the duration percent complete times the planned units or costs.

- **Update units when costs change on resource assignments** will cause P6 to recalculate the units for an activity when the cost of the assigned resource changes.

- If you plan to store past period performance of actuals, **Link actual to date and actual this period units and costs** will cause the actual to date and the actual this period values to be linked to one another.

All of the settings mentioned are intimately related to how you manage your project activities. See *Creating a New Project using the New Project wizard recipe, Chapter 6, Resources, Chapter 7, Scheduling and Constraints*, and *Chapter 9, Baselines and Statusing*, for more information on setting up activities and resources, and planning and updating your projects.

Structuring the WBS of the project

As mentioned in *Chapter 3, Organizing your Projects with EPS, OBS, and WBS*, the WBS is used to organize and manage the work in your project. Also in that chapter we went over how to create and organize WBS. Now let's look closer at other properties of the WBS.

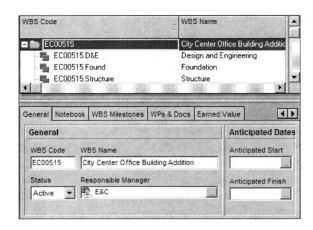

To see the WBS details, open up the WBS screen, right-click, and choose **WBS Details**. This will bring up a tabbed window as shown in this screenshot. If you do not see all of the tabs, right-click on the top of the **Tab** window and choose **Customize WBS Details...**.

General

The **General** tab shows high-level details about the selected WBS element. **WBS Code** and **WBS Name** can be edited here. See more about the WBS in *Chapter 3*. **Status** can be set to **Active, Inactive, Planned** and **What-if**. **Responsible Manager** is the OBS element responsible for this WBS item, and governs which users have which security access to the activities in this WBS item.

Anticipated Start is set during the planning stage, and does not figure into scheduling once activities are created.

Anticipated Finish is set during the planning stage, and does not figure into scheduling once activities are created.

Notebook

Notebooks for WBS behave the same as notebooks for Projects, as described previously.

WBS Milestones

Milestones at the WBS level allow you to set a list of items to be completed at the WBS level. These are merely milestones, and do not have dates or resources, or in any way affect the schedule. However, the **Earned Value** of the WBS element (as shown in the following screenshot) can be based on these milestones.

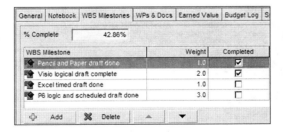

- **WBS Milestone** is a description of the milestone.
- **Weight** sets the relative value of the milestone with respect to all others and is used to calculate percentage completed as a weighted sum. To make the weights easier to understand, use percentage values that total to 100.0 percent.
- **Completed** is checked as each item is completed.

WPs & Docs

Work Products and Documents allows you to provide documentation for the project. Examples include material safety data sheets, punch lists, specifications, project manager notes and reports, product guides, and more. To add a document, choose **Assign**, and select the appropriate document. You may also specify whether the document is a work product, such as an engineering design.

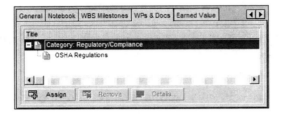

Before you can assign WPs and Docs, you must create them at the project level. Let's take a quick trip out of the WBS settings to see how that is done.

On the left-hand toolbar, click on the icon to open up the **WPs & Docs** window:

The **WPs & Docs** window is shown in the following screenshot:

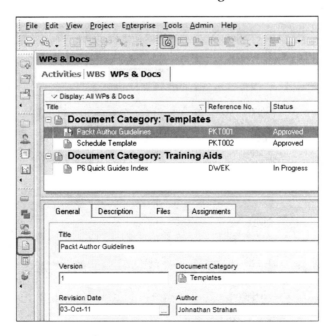

Here you can add new documents to your project and categorize them.

- **Title** is a description of the document.

- **Reference No** is a number to identify the document.

- **Status** helps to organize documents. Document statuses are set through the menu **Admin | Admin Categories...**.

- **Document Category** helps to organize the document. Categories are set from the menu **Admin | Admin Categories...**.

- The **Description** tab lets you create a rich-text description of the document.

- The **Files** tab lets you set the public and private locations of documents. **Private locations** are only available to P6 users from within P6. Public locations are available when work products and documents are included in published project web sites. Such files may reside on a publically available shared drive as well.

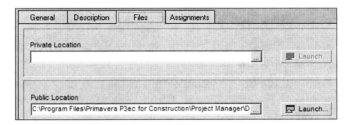

- The **Assignments** tab lets you see to which WBS elements or activities a document is assigned.

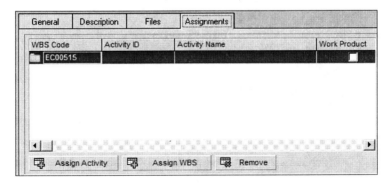

Earned value

Earned value is a large topic. In this section we will briefly review the EVM settings available for the Project WBS.

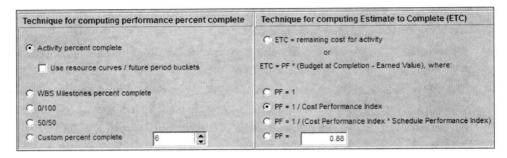

The way that earned value is calculated can be set at the WBS level, so that you can have each WBS node calculate EV differently. The methods available for calculating percentage complete are as follows:

- **Activity percent complete** calculates earned value based on the percentage complete specified at the activity level
- You may optionally choose whether to utilize **resource curves** and **future period buckets** in the calculation. That is, resource curves offer an earned value based on the expected resource expenditure
- One fairly simple way to calculate earned value is to use **WBS Milestones**, as discussed earlier in this chapter
- In **0/100** calculation, an activity is 0 percent complete until it is finished, at which time it becomes 100 percent complete
- **50/50** sets the value to 50 percent once the activity begins, and 100 percent once it finishes
- **Custom percent complete** is like **50/50**, but you can set the starting percentage to be other than 50 percent

The method used to calculate **Estimate to Complete** (ETC) can be chosen from the two main options:

- *ETC = remaining cost for the activity,* with no regard to earned value
- *ETC = (Budget at Completion - Earned value) * a factor, PF*

PF stands for Productivity Factor, which can be set to a number of values:

- *PF = 1*
- *PF = 1 / Cost performance Index*, where the CPI is the earned value cost divided by the actual cost
- *PF = 1 / (CPI * Scheduled Performance Index)*, where the SPI is the earned value cost divided by the planned value cost

PF can alternatively be set to any value. This is helpful when you have quality metrics of performance for this particular work

The Budget Log, Spending Plan, and Funding screens for the WBS are very similar to the corresponding screens for projects, described previously.

This is very important for all users, not just for those managing earned value. If you do not cost-load your schedules, these calculations can be deceiving because earned value calculations come from the actual costs in some of these choices. This means you must input actual costs on your schedule for accuracy. Educate your users which setting has been chosen for your system. Consistency across projects is also very important for enterprise reporting.

Importing projects in the web client

You can also create a new project by importing it from other systems, such as **Microsoft Project (MSP)**, earlier versions of P6, even Excel files. As each system manages and organizes schedule data differently, care must be taken when importing. However, when receiving schedules from subcontractors or when building your historical data from a previous tool, importing is a quick route to get your data in quickly.

The best way to work with subcontractors is to request that they submit their schedules in P6 format. This way the import is simplified and the hard job of ensuring the accuracy of the data (risk) lies with the subcontractor and not you.

When importing into P6 there are several ways to import, and several formats available. If you are using the P6 Professional Client, then there is a little bit more flexibility over the formats and options than those available in the web. Web imports are limited to two XML-based formats.

To import from P6 Web, go to the EPS screen, and choose **Actions | Import/Export | XML Project Import/Export**.

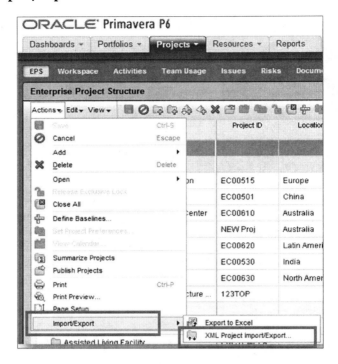

This will bring up a screen that looks similar to the following screenshot:

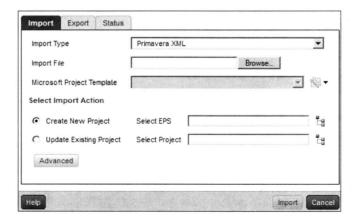

The **Import** window has three main tabs—**Import**, **Export**, and **Status**.

The **Import** tab has areas to choose—the import type, the particular file to import, the mapping template choices (if importing MSP XML), and an area to indicate the location of the project within the EPS after it is imported or if this import will merge with an existing P6 project already in the EPS.

There is also an **Advanced** button to make more selections for this import.

First, choose the **Import Type** drop-down field. There are two choices:

- **Primavera XML**
- **Microsoft Project XML**

Then choose the appropriate XML file to import by clicking on the **Browse** button.

Once your file is located, its path will be shown in the **Import File** field. Next, choose the EPS, where you want the newly imported project to appear. In this example, we have chosen **Energy Services**.

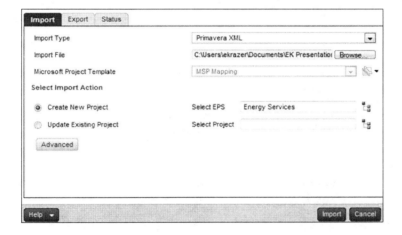

If you do not wish to indicate some advanced functions, click the **Import** button.

The **Advanced** button allows a user to indicate more details about how to handle specific items in the import process.

Modify the selected options by choosing the action to take when the same data exists in the import file and project being updated. Check Delete to delete those values in the database that are not contained in the file you are importing.				
Global Data		**Project Data**		
Name	Import Action	Name	Import Action	Delete
Project Codes and Values	Keep Existing ▾	Project Calendars	Keep Existi ▾	
Funding Sources	Keep Existing ▾	WBS	Update Exis ▾	
Resource Curves	Keep Existing ▾	Project Activity Codes and Values	Update Exis ▾	
Resource Codes and Values	Keep Existing ▾	Project Thresholds	Update Exis ▾	☐
Shift Names	Keep Existing ▾	Activities and Resource Assignments	Update Exis ▾	☐
User Defined Fields	Keep Existing ▾	Risks	Update Exis ▾	
Cost Accounts	Keep Existing ▾	High Level Planning Assignments	Update Exis ▾	
Roles	Keep Existing ▾	Activity Relationships	Update Exis ▾	☐
Admin Categories	Keep Existing ▾	Activity Expenses	Update Exis ▾	
Global/Resource Calendars	Keep Existing ▾	Issues	Update Exis ▾	
Resources	Keep Existing ▾		Keep Existing	
Global/EPS Activity Codes and Values	Keep Existing ▾		Update Existin / Do Not Import	
Risk Categories, Thresholds, and Matrices	Keep Existing ▾			

For each of the project components listed, choose to **Update Existing Data**, **Keep Existing Data**, or choose **Do Not Import the Data**.

For example, if you choose to **Keep Existing Data**, the Issues on the imported project will be created if they only exist in the imported version and will not touch or add to the existing issues for that project in P6. If you choose to **Update Existing Data**, all issue data will be overwritten and new incoming issues will be added. To prevent any issues being affected by the import, choose **Do Not Import Data** and no issues will be changed or added.

If you are importing an MSP XML file, the **Microsoft Project Template** option field is no longer grayed out. MSP formats data differently than P6, and this mapping template lets you choose how to translate certain MSP data into P6. Ever with these mappings, the import will not necessarily be perfect. When importing from MSP, always review your project data after the import to ensure that the data is still an accurate portrait of the project schedule.

To better manage some of the differences in the two software systems, there are choices at a more detailed level that you can manipulate for more desirable results. One note to remember is that MSP refers to work packages items as tasks but Primavera uses the term activity. Click on the **wrench** icon to see deeper detailed selections and options.

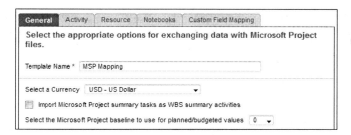

There are tabs with **General, Activity, Resource, Notebooks**, and **Custom Field Mapping** options. Once you have made all appropriate selections here, the group of settings can be saved as an import template to use on a future import.

General

- **Template name**: Enter the name for this group of settings you select to be used on a future import.

- **Select a Currency**: The database will take figures entered into cost fields in the original software and place a dollar sign in front of them in the P6 database.

- **Import Microsoft Project summary tasks as WBS summary activities**: These are not really a 1:1 match; but one option is to take the hierarchy created in the original file and assume it as your WBS in P6. There are values in the original file assigned to those levels, but the values shown in P6 on WBS summary bars are calculated. So the values will be different once imported and especially when the F9 calculation is performed on the newly imported P6 schedule.

- **Select the Microsoft project baseline to be used for planned/budgeted values**: MSP and P6 handle baselines very differently. This would take the selected MSP baseline and remove values from its planned fields and insert those same values into the field for planned or budgeted in P6. This does not mean that the baseline has imported nor does it mean there is a baseline in Primavera after the import. We recommend creating and assigning a baseline in P6 or importing a project to be used as a baseline in P6. See *Chapter 9*, for more information on baselines.

Activity

Milestones in MSP are also handled differently than in P6. They are simply milestones, with no distinction between start and finish milestones. Two options may be selected for how MSP milestones are imported. They may be imported as P6 **Start milestones with expenses**, where values in the cost fields are considered Expenses in P6 and not resource costs. Or, they may be imported as activities with resource assignments. After import, these can be designated as the appropriate milestone type in P6.

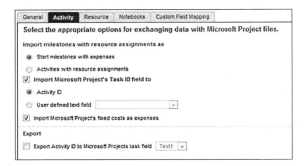

MSP calls work package items tasks, and P6 calls them activities. So choose to have the MSP task ID field become the P6 activity ID or create an activity-level-user-defined field that will be populated with the MSP activity ID after import to P6. This can later identify which activities to match up if you continue to import and update the same file periodically. However, the risk is that UDFs in P6 are a text box that can be typed into and the values may be overwritten before the next import, either by accident or some other reason. The UDF would have to be created in the P6 system before importing so it can appear as an option in the drop-down list.

You can also choose to take fixed costs in MSP and make them P6 expenses or uncheck this box to leave fixed costs only in MSP and not import them to P6.

It is a good idea to click on the **Save** button each time you change tabs or leave your screen unattended.

Resources

The **Resources** tab determines how resources will be imported. MSP has a field called **Resource Initials** and **Resource Name**, but P6 has fields for **Resource ID** and **Resource Name**.

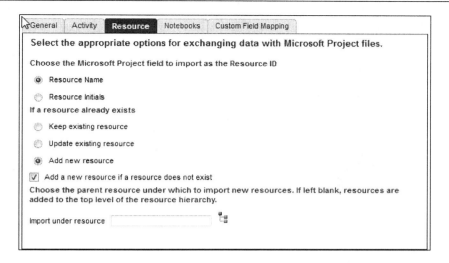

Here you can choose to make the MSP resource initials the P6 resource ID or to import the MSP resource name into the P6 Resource ID field.

If a resource already exists (spelled *exactly* the same in both systems), there are three choices:

- **Keep existing resources**: This does not overwrite P6 if the project is being re-imported.

- **Update existing resources**: This will completely overwrite whatever is in the current project.

- **Add new resources**: This will add every MSP resource as a brand-new resource in P6. The resource ID will be appended with sequential numbers in order to make it unique. For example, MSP resource 456 may become P6 resource 456-1 on the first import, then on a subsequent import be added as 456-2. Of course, this is not an ideal situation.

The **Add a new resource if a resource does not exist** checkbox will only add a new resource if it is not already in P6.

The next field allows you to identify the resource parent node of the hierarchy under which to put the incoming resources. (This makes the imported items children of what you select in this field.)

Notebooks

MSP stores descriptive notes at three levels: Project, WBS, and Task (Activity). The **Notebooks** tab determines how these will be brought into P6 and under which notebook topic:

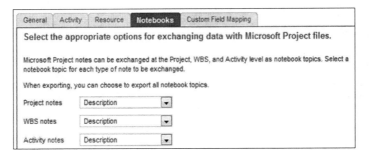

Custom Field Mapping

The last tab allows a user to select a P6 category and make additional choices within that category for the imported data.

As each category is selected, the listing below will have the MSP field names listed for that category in the right-hand column and the available custom fields in P6 in the left-hand column. The drop-down will show all UDF fields at the same level as of category that has been pre-defined in P6. So Project-level UDFs will be listed in the **Projects** category, and so on.

The categories are **Projects**, **WBS**, **Resources**, **Activities**, and **Activity Resource Assignments**. Basically you are to map items on the right with the P6 UDF on the left. To import the file, click on the **Import** button.

Importing in the Professional Client

To import using the client, choose the **Import/Export** function from the **File** menu on the **Projects** screen.

There are four formats to choose from.

- **XER Format**: The Primavera native format appends each exported file with a .XER. So any file ending in .XER was exported from Primavera. If you choose to import a .XER/Primavera file, select the first radio button then click on the **Next** button in the import wizard. No version needs to be referenced upon import as all current and previous versions are supported.

- **Primavera XML Format**: Choose the second radio button if your original file is in .XML format that was created by another Primavera user.

- **XLS Format**: Choose the third button for files coming from MS Excel or other spreadsheet program that created the .XLS file.

- **P3 Format**: The fourth radio button is for files generated by the P3 product. This selection will appear unavailable or grayed out if P3 is not installed on the same computer and appropriately licensed for use. If P3 is on the same computer as the client Primavera application, the item is available for use. P3 was actually a separate product, and not necessarily a version of Primavera P6, so there is a separate selection for importing P3 files. P3 is no longer sold or supported by Oracle.

- **MSP XML Format**: The final radio button is used to import from MS Project in XML or native MPX format.

Choose the appropriate radio button and click on **Next** to advance the wizard to the next step.

The MPX or the XER selections will take you to a screen where you can choose the data categories to import or to ignore upon import before asking which file to import. The other three formats will skip this step and ask where the file to import is located. Browse to the appropriate file location by clicking on the **Browse** button.

The next screen allows you to indicate how to handle the import:

- **Add imported project into an Existing P6 Project**
- **Create New Project**
- **Ignore this Project**
- **Replace Existing Project**
- **Update Existing Project**

The **Ignore this Project** option is only important when there is a list of several projects that you are importing at the same time.

The last column, **IMPORT TO**, is used to indicate the EPS location of your project file. Remember that this setting is a part of the EPS/OBS formula that allows a user access to read or write to the project after it is imported into P6.

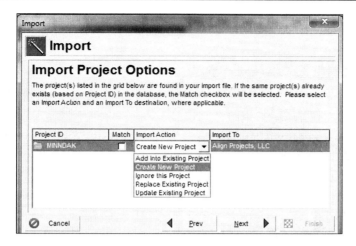

The next screen allows you to indicate further options for details, such as Resource Codes, Project Codes, and so on, and how to treat them during this import.

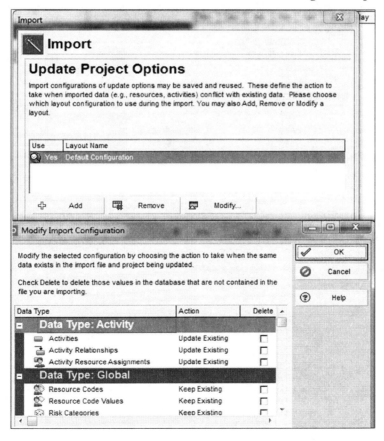

Choose the items to keep, update, or delete during import as appropriate.

Exporting projects

Primavera can export several formats including previous versions of P6 (R8x down to 4.2) as well as other products, such as MS Project, MS Excel, Contractor, and P3.

Exported files are good for several reasons. They can be used similar to a **Save As** function in other tools where you wish to keep a copy of the file under another name to ensure a backup or snapshot of its status remains intact, for later comparison or use.

Choose **Export** from the **File** menu of the **Projects** screen. Then choose the appropriate format to import. P3 will not be an available option unless it is installed on the same machine as this P6 client and is appropriately licensed.

Click on **Next** to progress the wizard to the next step.

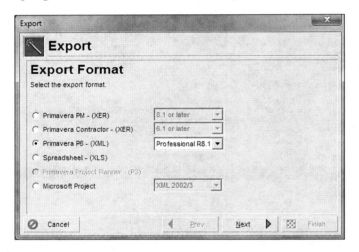

The wizard will walk you through the screens similar to the import functions, but in reverse of course. The list of projects will be those projects that you currently have open in P6.

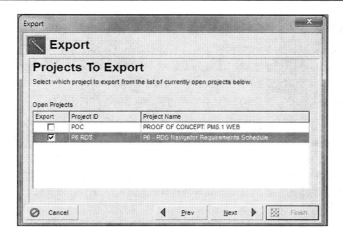

Finally, choose the location and name of your export file, and press **Finish**.

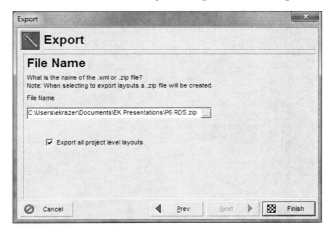

It is a good practice to export a .XER formatted file of a project, groups of projects, or even the entire EPS on a periodic basis to have a backup file of your data to revert to, should the system malfunction or should a user tamper with the information inadvertently. These files are easier to manage and revert to (less than five minute import) than a full backup of the database (a two to three hour process by which everyone's files are written over rather than just the one or two projects that are needed). I export my files right onto my current desktop as well as during specific timeframes, such as end of month, monthly report copy sent to client, as of last change order, end of fiscal year, or other pertinent time. These can be imported and used for comparison in claim digger or as a baseline to the project at some point.

Summary

In this chapter we have delved into all of the project's details that can be set to organize, prioritize, and describe project and WBS elements. We have also touched upon many settings that govern how activities and resources are used within a project. We defined several ways to create projects including import and using the wizard.

This short description of exporting should leave the reader wanting more. In the following chapters we will dive into activities, resources, and managing other project details. Up to now we have been working from the top-down. In the next chapter, we begin to look at a project from the bottom-up, starting with activities.

5

Adding Activities and Relationships

In this chapter we discuss the basic element of a schedule—the activity. An activity is a unit of work that must be done in order to complete part of a project. Though the specific definition depends on the nature of your work and your specific project, an activity generally lasts from a few hours to a few days. An activity can involve a crew of people, or could be a passive activity such as *waiting for the concrete to set*.

In P6, activities have many properties that can be combined so the activity will schedule, progress, and report in a way that proves that the project and schedule will meet the scope and requirements. This combination of settings represents a *chain* of features giving users a lot of flexibility. This is often is the main training and learning curve for new users, since the sheer number of activity options can be overwhelming. However, the reality is that there are certain settings which are more frequently used than others, and which meet the majority of your needs.

In this chapter we will cover:

- Activities
- Oracle Primavera compared to other tools
- Scheduling best practices
- Activity details
- Activity types
- Relationships
- Lag and Float

By the end of this chapter we hope that the reader will feel comfortable with the settings and options available for activities.

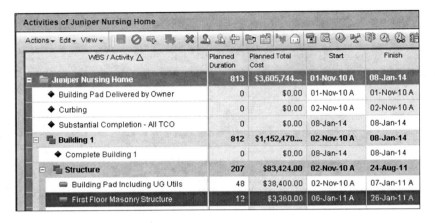

Activities

An **activity** is the basic unit of a schedule. It is defined as a specific thing which must be accomplished in order to complete a project deliverable. Within a project, activities are organized within WBS elements, as shown in the screenshot. An activity has a number of fundamental properties:

- **Duration**: The length of time the activity will last. In certain cases, this may be zero.

- **Start Date**: The time calculated for the activity to begin.

- **Finish Date**: The time calculated for the activity to be completed.

- **Relationships**: Activities must relate to one another in some logical way. If an activity does not relate to any others, then you must question whether it is an actual activity for the project. Only by logically connecting activities can you truly schedule a project. The logic is used to calculate dates, otherwise the default dates will be shown as they relate to the **Data** — more on this later.

Oracle Primavera P6 compared to other tools

In other software, an activity may be called a **task**, and even in P6 the two terms are often used interchangeably. Also in other systems, the activity is the lowest unit in the schedule, whereas Primavera has a feature called **steps**. These are basically a checklist for the activity and represent the lowest level of scope in a schedule.

Activity behaviour is a key differentiating factor among scheduling and project management tools on the market today. The limitations of some software is the biggest reason one tool is predominant in a specific industry more than another tool. While Oracle Primavera certainly has roots and a reputation in the Engineering and Construction industry, it is easily adopted in every major industry because of its scalability and flexibility.

Oracle Primavera is also the tool of choice among the most mature Project Management organizations because it fully supports project management standards and guidelines such as the world-recognized Project Management Institute (PMI ®) and others. Oracle Primavera performs best when using these standards.

A good scheduling tool should tell the user more than the input, it should forecast and give vision into the schedule rather than simply repeating or reporting what a scheduler already knows. Primavera P6 should be a data-driven decision support tool, not merely a reporting engine.

Oracle Primavera and scheduling best practices

To understand the most basic element of the schedule, we should first agree on the best practices. Under the conditions of these best practices, Oracle Primavera performs at its best:

- The schedule should follow the rules of a **Critical Path Method (CPM)** schedule. In such a schedule there is a list of all activities required to complete the project. Each activity has a duration to complete, and each activity has at least one predecessor and one successor relationship. The Start Project Milestone and Finish Project Milestone are the only exceptions to this rule. This creates a relationship-driven schedule in which one set of activities will be the longest path and the earliest the product can be delivered. The activities within that primary path are *critical*, meaning they must occur on the calculated dates in order to deliver the entire project *on time*.

- Lead times and Lag times are rarely used, though there are uses which are clear exceptions.

- Constraints are very rare within the schedule—and it is preferred they are not used at all. Dates are calculated by Oracle Primavera rather than input. See the baseline chapter for more on this topic.

- A logical sequence of activities is used which requires planning and agreement that one item begins before another, and so on. See the scheduling chapter for more on this topic.

- Progress is input and reported by the user with minimal auto-population of fields.

- A basic activity should be no longer than 80 hours of work or 14 days duration.

These practices, when used in combination, provide the best forecast and most accurate reporting of schedule performance, especially as the schedule should exactly mirror the work performance on the job site.

Activity details

When you are viewing activities, there are a series of tabs below the main screen. These display a wide variety of settings available for the activities:

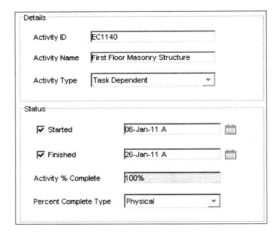

General

The most important tab is **General**, which lets you set fundamental properties of the activity. **Activity ID** should be a code which follows a set pattern that allows it to be grouped, sorted, and organized. For example, activities in the Engineering phase can begin with E. The **Activity Name** will be used on project reports such as the 3-week lookahead, and should therefore be meaningful to the people in the field performing the work on a daily basis. **Activity Type** is such a fundamental concept that it will be discussed in a following section solely dedicated to the topic.

The **Status** section shows the activitiy's start and finish dates. These dates may come from one of the following three different dates:

1. When the activity has not yet been scheduled, the dates are the **Planned Start** and **Planned Finish**.

2. After the activity is scheduled, but not started (finished) these are the **Remaining Early Start (Finish)**

3. Once the progress is input, the **Actual Start** is shown. Once progress is input as finished, the **Actual Finish** is shown.

An activity can have a **Percent Complete Type**, which can be duration, physical, or units. This property determines how you will measure progress on the activity. **Duration** means that if the activity is 10 days, and you set it to 60 percent complete, then there are four days remaining on the activity. **Units** means that the activity is governed by the number of labor and/or non-labor units assigned. For example, if the activity is assigned 100 man-hours, and it is 25 percent complete, it means that 25 hours of work have been performed. Similarly, if an activity has $2000 of non-labor units assigned, then 20 percent complete means that $400 of work has been performed. **Physical** percent complete means that the percentage is based on human judgment. For example, you may have a research activity that is 20 days into a 40-day planned duration, having spent $30,000 of the $40,000 budget. Yet the activity owner may declare that they are 60 percent complete on the task, even though 50% of the duration is complete, and 75% of the budget has been spent.

Durations

Planned Duration	12
Actual Duration	14
Remaining Duration	0
At Completion Duration	14
Duration Type	Fixed Units/Time

Constraints

Primary Constraint	
Secondary Constraint	

The other sections of the **General** tab concern durations. The **Planned Duration** is the amount of time that you expect the activity to take. Once an activity has started, you may enter the **Actual Duration** spent on the task, or this value may be updated through updating the percentage complete (if type is set to duration), or it may be indirectly updated through a number of ways to be discussed later. The **Remaining Duration** is the amount of time left on the activity. It too can be either entered directly or indirectly. The **At Completion Duration** is the amount of total time it is expected the activity will take. When the activity is new and unscheduled, this is equal to the Planned Duration. Once the activity is scheduled, it is the sum of the Actual and Remaining durations. The **Duration Type** is discussed in *Chapter 7, Scheduling and Constraints*.

Primary Constraint and **Secondary Constraint** can be applied to activities. The possible constraint types are:

- Start On
- Start On or Before
- Start On or After
- Finish On
- Finish On or Before
- Finish On or After
- As Late as Possible
- Mandatory Start
- Mandatory Finish

In general, constraints should be avoided, as P6 is designed to produce an optimized schedule. If possible, replace constraints with activity relationships by using calendars, by adding lag, or by other means.

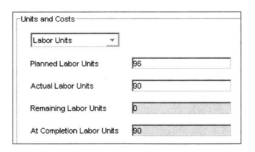

An activity can have two kinds of units: **Labor Units**, which are generally man hours, and **Non-Labor Units**, which can be miles of road, tons of backfill, feet of pipe, and so on. It can also have **Labor Cost**, **Non-Labor Cost**, and **Material Cost**. And each of these, in turn, has **Planned**, **Actual**, **Remaining**, and **At Completion** values. This is quite a lot of information, and how these values are filled depends on many things.

Material costs are generated by assigning material resources (See *Chapter 6, Resources*) to an activity. Likewise, labor and non-labor costs are added by assigning labor and non-labor resources, respectively, to the activity. These resources must have rates assigned to them.

Codes

Activity Codes can be defined through the **Administer | Enterprise Data** dialog, where they can be set at the **Global**, **EPS**, and **Project** level. Activity codes help to sort, filter, and group activities. In the following screenshot, the activity is associated with three different activity codes: **Department**, **Phase**, and **Responsibility**. **Department** describes which division within the company is responsible for the work. Possible values include Construction, Engineering, IT, and Purchasing. Of course, you may define your own activity codes with the values best suited to your projects.

Codes		
Activity Code	**Code Value**	**Code Description**
Department	CON	Construction Department
Phase	FOUND	Foundation Construction P...
Responsibility	FOLEY	Meg Foley

Expenses

Expenses are costs to a project that are not represented by resources, and it can be confusing at times to have activity costs originating in two different manners. In the following screenshot, the expense is crane rental for the activity involving erecting a structural frame. Expenses are any items that are not a material, labor, or non-labor (resources).

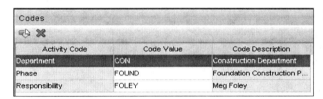

Expense Item	Expense Category	Planned Units	Price/Unit	Planned Cost
Crane	Equipment	1.000	$1,600.00	$1,600.00

Assignments

The **Assignments** tab shows what resources and/or roles have been assigned to the activity. From this screen the user may add and remove assignments as needed, and may add more than one assignment to an activity. It is important to understand that resource assignments are entities unto themselves, combining a resource and an activity. You can set specific properties on the resource assignment such as cost accounts and resource curves. These settings are independent of the underlying activity and resource involved in the assignment..

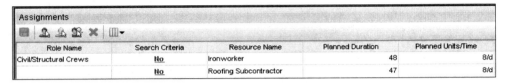

Documents

The **documents** assigned to the project (see *Chapter 8, Issues and Risks*) can be assigned to activities, just as they are assigned to WBS elements.

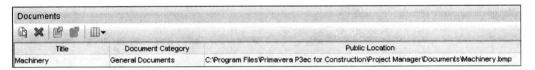

Feedback

Feedback allows a user, who is a resource on the activity, to enter information about the activity in a dialog with the activity owner. Each entry is a short note that is stamped with the date and time of the feedback entry, along with the name of the user entering the feedback.

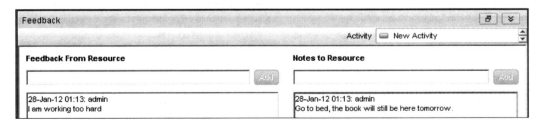

Issues

Issues, also covered in *Chapter 8*, shows all the issues that have been related to the activity.

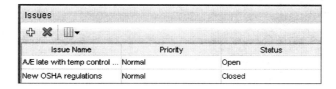

Notebooks

Notebooks are text entries on specific topics. Topics are created as part of the Enterprise Data setup. For each topic a large amount of text may be entered. For more on Notebooks and Notebook topics, see *Chapter 4, Creating a New Project and Work Breakdown Structure*.

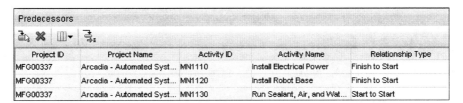

Predecessors/Successors

The **Predecessors** and **Successors** tabs show a list of activities that either precede or succeed the current activity. Note that the small icon, 🔧, will bring you to the selected activity, which is a handy way to navigate through the logical relationships of a project. Also note that the first column shown is the **Project ID**, indicating that activities can be related to activities in other projects.

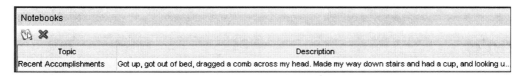

Trace Logic

This tab shows the activity in a trace logic diagram. By default the diagram shows successors and predecessors, three levels removed. However, you can change this in the **Options** setting (the wrench icon).

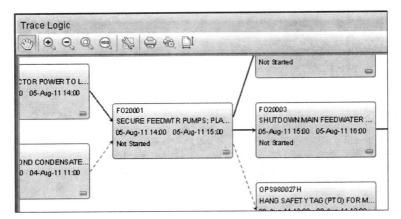

Risks

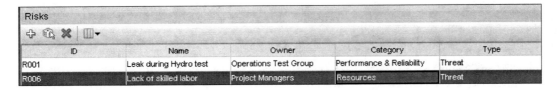

Risks show all of the risks associated with the current activity. Risks are covered in more detail in *Chapter 8, Issues and Risks*.

Activity types

As mentioned earlier, one of the key settings you will select for each activity is the **activity type**. There are six different ways that activities can behave:

- Start milestone
- Finish milestone
- Task dependent
- Resource dependent

- Level of Effort
- WBS summary

 Each of the following examples assume there are no constraints assigned to activities. It is a bad habit to rely on constraints as a substitute for schedule logic.

Start milestone

A **milestone** represents an activity which has no time associated with it, though it can have costs and a resource assigned as responsible for noting this activity as completed. Use these in the case where an activity needs to report when it starts, not its progress or finish date.

An example start milestone would be the beginning of the construction phase of a project once all of the design phase has been completed. In this example, the start milestone serves as a placeholder that marks the end of one set of tasks and the beginning of another.

Another example of a start milestone would be the delivery of a certain item to a job site. The item is scheduled to be delivered at a certain date, and that is the milestone. In this case there may be expenses associated with it, such as the payment for the delivery. There may also be a resource assigned; perhaps a specific person needs to be there to receive the delivery.

Progress payments can be milestones in the schedule, too.

These activities will have a start date, Early Start date and Late Start date. The start date will be calculated as the day after the predecessor finishes work, but can vary based upon calendar settings and settings within the scheduling options. About 5-10 percent of the schedule activities are designated as this type in a typical schedule.

Finish milestone

This is very similar to a start milestone, but represents the completion of a set of tasks. The main difference between start and finish milestones is that start milestones cannot have finish constraints and finish milestones cannot have start constraints. (Activity constraints are discussed later in this chapter and within best practices section of this chapter.) These activities will have a finish date, Early Finish and Late Finish date. The finish date will be calculated as the day after the predecessor finishes work, but can vary based upon calendar settings and settings within the scheduling options.

Use these in the case where an activity needs to report when it *finishes*, not its progress or Start date.

A good metric is that about 5-10 percent of the schedule activities are designated as this type in a typical schedule.

Task dependent

Task dependent activities are those that use the predecessors and successors to derive the sequence of activities. These *depend* upon predecessors to finish and their successors *depend* upon them to start. This is most like the *natural order* of the work and behaves in that way if all settings are correctly set. Choose this setting to have the schedule calculate all dates (Early and Late Start, and Early and Late Finish) based on the progress of its predecessor.

The activity calendar is used to calculate dates in addition to predecessor progress.

About 80 percent of the schedule activities are designated as this type in a typical schedule. Therefore, the most common Activity Type default should be *task dependent*.

Resource dependent

This activity *depends* on the resource for scheduling. Resource dependent activities are principally used in conjunction with resource loaded schedules where resources have their own resource calendars. Resource dependent activities rely on the assigned resource calendars to calculate all dates (early and late). For this scenario to be successful entirely, the activity should only have those resources with their own calendars assigned to it. This dictates that each resource's calendar be meticulously maintained either as a specific person's or craft's (shared) calendar. The activity can only be scheduled using timeframes in the assigned resources' calendar that was designated as working time. The resource, as a specific person, should have a valid P6 license in order to manipulate their respective calendar. This type of activity is only appropriate when the work simply cannot be scheduled or worked by another person or resource and work will stop and resume only during available timeframes in the resource calendar.

 In the case of a non-labor resource, to schedule accurately, the resource calendar needs to be up-to-date and indicate that resource's availability in terms of working time and non-working time. Material resources do not rely upon a resource calendar since units of measure are not *hours* as in the case of labor and non-labor resources.

In the following example, a resource dependent activity has several resources, even though the activity duration is 32 days—the **Start** is July 23, 2012 and the **Finish** is Sept 6, 2012, an elapsed duration of 45 days. Calendar days would have an earlier Finish. Another link in this *chain* is that some resources are assigned four hours per day. Non-working time in each resource's calendar is a part of the calculation.

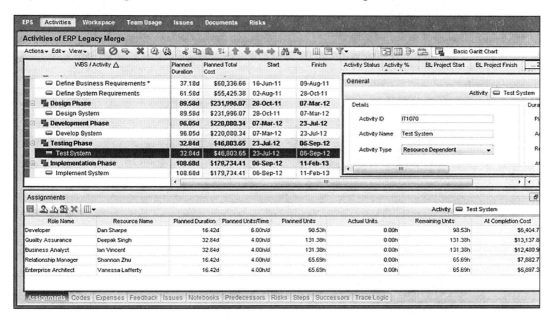

Level of Effort

A **Level of Effort** (LOE) activity is an activity that is not discrete in timeframe, and is supportive of other work in the project. This type of activity automatically expands or contracts with the activities it supports. Typically this activity is related to a Start Milestone as its predecessor and a Finish Milestone as its successor. When the milestones move, the LOE activity duration in between those milestones expands and contracts the duration of the LOE activity.

A good example is security. If you are capturing the time a security team is engaged on the job site, you would tie the **Start Mobilization at Job Site** Start Milestone activity as a predecessor to the **Monitor Security of Job Site** activity, and place a Finish Milestone (Complete Job Site Removal) as the successor.

Another good use is for Project Management time. If a Project Manager spends two hours per week in Project Meetings and 4 hours a week in travel, the activity could have a PM assigned for 6 h/w to accommodate meetings and travel. The costs for that travel can be added as resource costs on the Project Management activity with LOE activity type selected. Then, as the project duration lengthens, additional hours and travel are automatically budgeted. Should the project end early, that time is diminished accordingly.

This is shown in the following screenshot. Note the ties to both **Project Start** and **Project Complete** milestones and its anchors on either end in the **Trace Logic** window.

Also note the calculated start and finish dates for the Project Management activity.

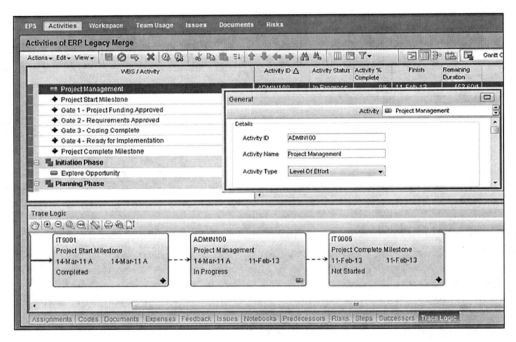

WBS summary

This activity is merely a summary of all activities that occur within a given WBS element. The activity Start date is the Early Start of the earliest activity within that WBS and its Finish date is the Late Finish of the latest activity to finish within that WBS element. This is a convenient way to show a higher-level of information for reporting or input without sacrificing the ability to manage or track a lower level of detail in the schedule.

For example, Actual hours are reported via Oracle Progress Reporter or another time sheet application at a higher level than the activities in the schedule. Using a WBS summary activity, the Budgeted or Planned hours will be a sum of all activities within that WBS; but the Actual Units can be input on the WBS Summary Activity. The WBS dates are also derived from the activities within it.

In the following screenshot, the Robot Controller WBS element has an activity called **Robot Controller Summary** with its **Activity Type** set to **WBS Summary**. Note the planned duration of 159 is a sum, the **Start** is the earliest start within that WBS and the **Finish** is the latest finish. Since the earliest start is an Actual (indicated by an A after the date) then the WBS Summary activity also shows an Actual Start date. The % complete is also a sum.

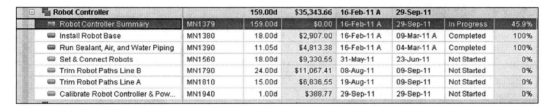

⊟ 🖿 Robot Controller		159.00d	$35,343.66	16-Feb-11 A	29-Sep-11		
Robot Controller Summary	MN1379	159.00d	$0.00	16-Feb-11 A	29-Sep-11	In Progress	45.9%
Install Robot Base	MN1380	18.00d	$2,907.00	16-Feb-11 A	09-Mar-11 A	Completed	100%
Run Sealant, Air, and Water Piping	MN1390	11.05d	$4,813.38	16-Feb-11 A	04-Mar-11 A	Completed	100%
Set & Connect Robots	MN1560	18.00d	$9,330.55	31-May-11	23-Jun-11	Not Started	0%
Trim Robot Paths Line B	MN1790	24.00d	$11,067.41	08-Aug-11	09-Sep-11	Not Started	0%
Trim Robot Paths Line A	MN1810	15.00d	$6,836.55	19-Aug-11	09-Sep-11	Not Started	0%
Calibrate Robot Controller & Pow...	MN1940	1.00d	$388.77	29-Sep-11	29-Sep-11	Not Started	0%

Relationships

The very definition of a project includes a set of inter-related activities done by a group of people (according to the PMI®). Activities are linked to each other using relationships in the sequence in which those activities must be performed. There may be one or more paths of related activities, but one subset of them will be critical, meaning that the rest of the schedule is driven by the activities on that path.

There are four ways to relate activities to one another (types of relationships):

- Finish to Start
- Start to Start
- Finish to Finish
- Start to Finish

Relationships will be described using three abstract activities, called A, B, and C.

Finish to Start

This is the most logical and most often used relationship type. In this case, A must finish before B starts. This is an expression of a relationship between these *two* activities only. For example, the frame of a building must be put up before any electrical work can begin; or the rig must be assembled before drilling can begin; or a specification must be written before writing code can begin.

Start to Start

This is the relationship when two tasks must begin at the same time. For example, as soon work begins on a job site, a nightly watch must be set. Another example is when procurement and resource acquisition may both begin at the same time. Another way of saying this is: as far as A is concerned, the start of A controls the start of B. Many times these are found following a milestone in a project schedule.

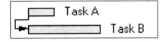

Finish to Finish

This is when two tasks must finish at the same time. One example is two lines of a railroad starting on each coast, with a planned meeting point at some predefined spot and time. In this case, your plan is that both of the lines be completed at the same time. By scheduling this way, you ensure that both crews arrive at the junction point simultaneously, and neither crew has to site idle waiting for the other. Another example is obtaining a permit and performing landwork, both of which must be complete prior to drilling. Another way of expressing this is: as far as A is concerned, the *finish* of A controls the *finish* of B. Many times these are found prior to a milestone in a project schedule.

Start to Finish

This is the least common of the relationships, and can be a bit confusing. It means that B may not finish until A starts. A good way to consider this relationship is *just in time*.

As an example, imagine that you are building a facility in an area that has no power transmission lines. Activity B can be: run a generator to power up site X. Activity A can be: turning on a power line to the site, which is being built while the rest of the project progresses. B must continue as long as A has not started. It is not necessary that B finish once A starts, but it is allowed to finish once A starts.

Another example is when *concrete the foundation* cannot finish until *plumb the foundation* starts—so pipes can come up through the foundation for water lines.

Lag and float

A good schedule will optimize the relationships among activities. Sometimes there must be a time between two activities when no project work is done. In this case, a **lag** is introduced into the relationship.

An example would be the time between pouring concrete and sanding it. The concrete must have time to dry before the sanding can begin, and this drying time can be represented as the lag between those two activities. There is no work nor resources involved, just time passing.

In another example, excavation can begin five days after a permit is submitted. There would be a 5 day lag on *Begin Excavation* as a successor to the *Submit Permit* activity.

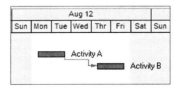

In the screen above, activities A and B both have two-day durations, and the start of activity B depends on the finish of activity A with a one-day lag.

Float is the amount of time that an activity can be moved without affecting the schedule. *Float is often also referred to as slack.* There are two main kinds of float in P6: free float and total float.

Free float is the amount of time a task could be delayed without affecting its nearest successor. This is illustrated in the following diagram:

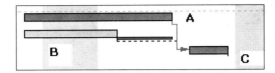

Tasks A and B are Finish-Start successors of task C. A has a longer duration than B, and so its finish date is what drives the start of C. B can remain where it is, or even be moved ahead a few days, with no effect on C.

Total Float is the amount of time a task could be delayed without impacting the project finish date.

 Watching float activity by activity is only one way to manage the slack you have within the schedule. With more modern tools and the calculating power of Oracle Primavera, it is better to manage variance. **Variance** is the difference between planned and actuals with planned data being contained on the baseline. Baselines are covered in *Chapter 9*.

Working with Activities

There are a number of ways to visualize a schedule.

Gantt chart

The **Gantt chart** is what most people think about when visualizing a schedule. It is sometimes referred to as a bar chart, though that term has less specific meaning than Gantt chart.

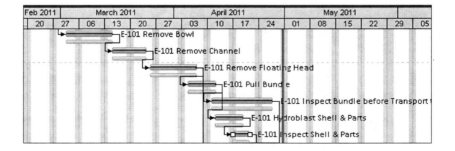

Table

The table view shows rows for each activity, and also optionally for each WBS. You may choose from among many different columns to display by pressing the icon, 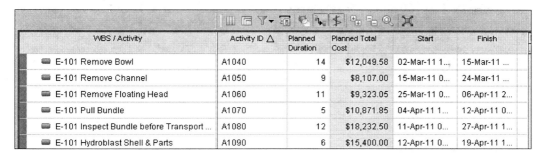.

WBS / Activity	Activity ID △	Planned Duration	Planned Total Cost	Start	Finish
E-101 Remove Bowl	A1040	14	$12,049.58	02-Mar-11 1...	15-Mar-11 ...
E-101 Remove Channel	A1050	9	$8,107.00	15-Mar-11 0...	24-Mar-11 ...
E-101 Remove Floating Head	A1060	11	$9,323.05	25-Mar-11 0...	06-Apr-11 2...
E-101 Pull Bundle	A1070	5	$10,871.85	04-Apr-11 1...	12-Apr-11 0...
E-101 Inspect Bundle before Transport ...	A1080	12	$18,232.50	11-Apr-11 0...	27-Apr-11 1...
E-101 Hydroblast Shell & Parts	A1090	6	$15,400.00	12-Apr-11 0...	19-Apr-11 1...

Activity network

The **activity network** shows the logical relationships among activities, with no time element involved. It is helpful for visualizing the pure logic of the system.

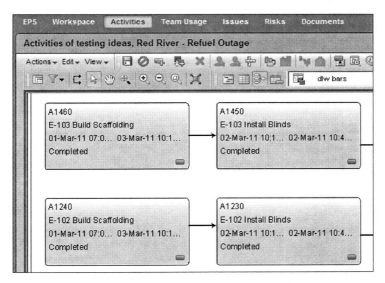

Summary

Activities are the foundation for a good schedule and are the focus of a scheduler's job. Learning the type to use, its contribution to the calculations, and the analysis of the critical path will make you successful as you use Oracle Primavera.

In the next chapter we will learn about Resources, the items which drive activities when they are Resource Dependent.

6

Resources

Resources are the entities that make the activities happen. They are the people doing the work, the equipment used, and the materials consumed. You *can* make a schedule without resources, using only activities and the logical dependencies of the activities. However, it is typically the resources in a project that are most limited, and lack of resources is a prime reason that projects are delayed.

In this chapter we will see how resources are used in P6. This will cover:

- Resources
- Roles
- Teams
- Resource assignments
- Resource curves
- Calendars

This chapter will focus on the fundamentals behind setting up and using resources and roles using the Professional client. *Chapter 16, Resource Management*, will discuss the many tools available for managing resource and roles across your project and across your enterprise.

Resources

The single pool of enterprise resources in P6 represents all people who will be working on projects. This is not the same as a Functional Organization Chart or payroll list, as the resources represent only the people assigned to work on projects.

Loading a schedule with resources and/or roles provides a number of benefits, such as:

- Potential head counts over time so that the project is properly staffed and funded
- Better coordination between the Human Resources department and the project group, based on valid forecasts that support the Project Staffing Plan
- Physical space or through-put overloads can be more easily forecast and proactively addressed
- Earned value can be more accurately measured according to industry standards
- Identification of many risks associated with limited resources/roles, such as vacations, hunting season, and weather impacts

You can view resources by clicking on the icon, or by choosing **Enterprise | Resources** from the main menu.

A screen appears as shown in the following screenshot appears:

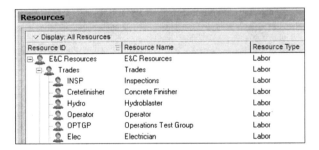

These resources represent people in an organization who do the work.

This screen is similar in design to the EBS or OBS screens, and the navigation and filters are similar. There are usually many more people listed as resources in P6 than there are items in the OBS. The OBS manages responsibilities, while the resources represent the people, organizations, and other components required to accomplish any given task.

Resources can be of three types: labor, non-labor, and materials.

- **Labor** is actual people performing the work. These are managers, operators, tradesmen subcontractors, and more. Labor type resources may have an overtime factor associated with them.

- **Non-labor** resources are things required to perform the work, such as a crane, scaffold, or other piece of equipment. Such items are not consumed by the work and can be reused later on for other tasks. Both labor and non-labor are measured in time units.

- **Material** resources are items that are consumed as the work is performed, for example, pipe and tubing that is being installed. As a pipeline is laid down, the quantity of pipe remaining decreases. A material also has a Unit of Measure, which can range from specific units such as cubic yards or meters, or can be the universally generic *each*. These units are defined through the menu **Admin | Categories** (see *Chapter 3, Organizing your Projects with EPS, OBS, and WBS*).

Let's look at the details available for resources. Like other P6 entities, these are shown on a series of tabs below the main screen.

Resources: General

The **General** tab lets you view and edit high-level information about the selected resource.

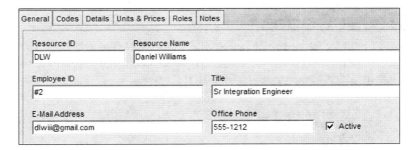

- **Resource ID** is a globally unique identifier for your resource. It is limited to 20 characters, so care must be taken for assigning these IDs in a meaningful manner. Employee ID is one reasonable standard to use for employees of your own company. For equipment, a serial number or tag number might be appropriate. For a specific subcontractor, each resource ID might have a common prefix, thus allowing multiple subcontractors to exist with the same type of resource.

[When resources are used in schedules but are not a part of the owning organization (such as subcontractors), it is a best practice to prefix the resource ID with an identifying character or set of characters so they may be grouped or not considered in total allocations. Example: Bob Smith working for NASA could be NASABSMITH.]

- **Resource Name** is a more descriptive title you will see when assigning resources in P6. This is commonly the user's full name, such a Bob Smith or Smith, Bob.

[Be sure to wisely choose your own **Resource Name** standards. In many searches and screens it can be easier to search depending upon the order of name and surname. If resources are listed as John Smith and Virginia Smith — the search would be done by entering J or V. But if the names are Smith, John and Smith, Virginia then both would show up when a user searches using S.]

- **Employee ID, Title, E-Mail Address,** and **Office Phone** are self-explanatory.
- **Active** determines whether a resource is available. This is a very helpful designation when, for example, an employee leaves the company. When you assign resources to activities, you can filter to show only active resources.

Resources: Codes

Resource codes behave like project codes and activity codes and are used to classify resources. They can also be used for grouping and sorting. You can edit them through the menu item **Enterprise | Resource Codes...**.

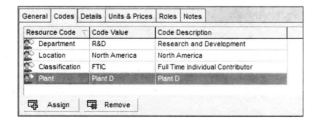

Like project codes and activity codes, resource codes are a powerful way to categorize your information so that it is fairly easy to make good reports.

Resources: Details

The **Details** tab sets a number of properties, such as the resource type, which we described earlier.

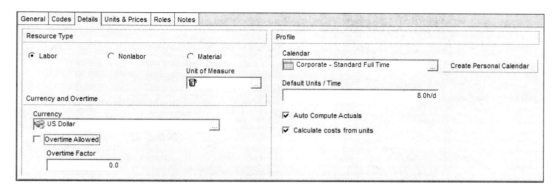

Currency determines the currency used when calculating the resource's cost and the symbol used when displaying costs. If the labor resource is allowed overtime, check the **Overtime Allowed** box. The overtime factor is used to calculate how much more the resource will cost when working above the normal time limits. The overtime factor can be from 0 (the same as regular costs) to 10 (ten times the regular cost for overtime worked!).

Under the **Profile** section of this tab you can choose the calendar for this specific resource to use. If this is a person, he or she may work five 8-hour days, four 10-hour days, or some other shift. A piece of equipment may use a calendar where the equipment is removed from service at predefined times. **Personal calendars** are specific to one resource. **Shared calendars** are often more useful when many resources are working the same schedule. These are resource-level calendars, but they can be used by any number of resources.

 The resource calendars only come into play when an activity is resource-dependent, as we will explain in the section on calendars.

A resource can also have a default number of **units per time (U/T)**. This is usually given in hours per day. For people this is usually 8h/d. A non-labor excavator could be shown as 24h/d.

Auto Compute Actuals, if set, will cause the actual amounts to be updated automatically according to project progress.

Calculate costs from units will cause the cost of an assigned activity to be automatically calculated and updated whenever the schedule is calculated using *F9*, or when actuals are calculated.

Resources: Units and Prices

The **Units & Prices** tab, shown in the following screenshot, is used to set workday shifts, limit the daily hours a resource is available, and set the resource's hourly cost.

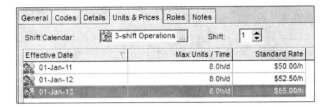

General	Codes	Details	Units & Prices	Roles	Notes		

Shift Calendar: 3-shift Operations   Shift: 1

Effective Date	Max Units / Time	Standard Rate
01-Jan-11	8.0h/d	$50.00/h
01-Jan-12	8.0h/d	$52.50/h
01-Jan-13	8.0h/d	$55.00/h

Additionally, **Units & Prices** information for a specific resource may be expected to change over time. The **Effective Date** determines the date on and after which a resource's maximum units/time and/or standard rate will apply. This is not required, and it is common to set rates without creating multiple effective dates.

There are five rate types available for each resource.

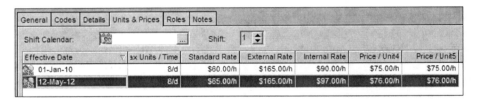

General	Codes	Details	Units & Prices	Roles	Notes				

Shift Calendar: Shift: 1

Effective Date	ax Units / Time	Standard Rate	External Rate	Internal Rate	Price / Unit4	Price / Unit5
01-Jan-10	8/d	$60.00/h	$165.00/h	$90.00/h	$75.00/h	$75.00/h
12-May-12	8/d	$65.00/h	$165.00/h	$97.00/h	$76.00/h	$76.00/h

To view these extra rate columns, right-click in the rate area, and choose **Customize Resource Rate Columns...**. For example, the **External Rate** can be what is charged to the client for hourly contracts, while the **Internal Rate** can be used for payroll purposes.

The fourth and fifth rate types can be renamed to descriptions that are meaningful to your company. This is done within the **Enterprise** menu in **Professional** or under the **Administration** screen in the web. Call your administrator to change these settings for your database.

Shifts can be created by choosing the menu item **Enterprise | Resource Shifts...**. This brings up a screen that lets you set the starting time and duration of each shift. A resource can then be assigned to work a particular shift. The maximum number of hours for all shifts cannot exceed 24 hours.

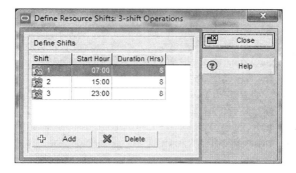

Shifts do not have to be used, but they are a helpful feature for certain industries such as manufacturing.

Resources: Roles

A number of **roles** can be set for the resource, with one role set to be the **primary** (default) role. We will cover roles in the next section.

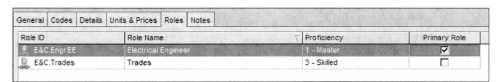

On this tab you can also assign a resource's **proficiency** in a given role. This skill level ranges from **1 - Master** to **5 - Inexperienced** and can be used to select the right person with the right level of skills for a given task.

Be careful using the proficiency feature. Make sure that the use of this feature is in line with Human Resource policy on reporting specific private information or identifying characteristics that would alienate some resources from their peers. It is a best practice to use a Resource-level User-Defined Field or Resource Code to identify when a resource is *Certified* or *Master* or *Journeyman Trained* rather than proficiency. These codes can be used as filter criteria when assigning activities in much the same way as proficiency so it's best to be on the safe side and avoid litigation.

Notes are notebook entries used to describe an employee, material, or piece of equipment. Throughout all of P6, Primavera is consistent in the display and use of notes. *Chapter 4, Creating a New Project and Work Breakdown Structure*, explains notes in detail.

Roles

When planning a project, you will most likely identify the specific types of resources that each activity will require prior to identifying specifically named resources to perform the work. For example, you have a number of project managers, but before a project is initiated, you may not know which project manager will be available for the new project. These resource types are represented by **roles**. Generally, roles should be defined for your enterprise, and not for a specific project.

To edit roles, choose **Menu** | **Enterprise** | **Roles**, or click on this icon . You will see a pop-up window such as shown in the following screenshot. There will likely be no roles shown at all. This is because by default the screen has a filter so that it displays only the current project's roles. You can change this by clicking on the triangle at the left-hand side of the layout bar and choosing to show **All Roles**, as illustrated in the following screenshot:

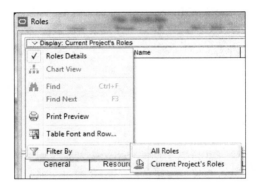

[🔆 The default filter can be changed in **User Preferences** both in the **Web** and in **Professional** to show **All** or **Current Project**.]

Roles are added in a hierarchy, similar to the EBS and OBS elements.

Roles: General

This tab shows the **Role ID** and **Name** of the role. A rich-text description of the role's responsibilities can be added by clicking the **Modify** button:

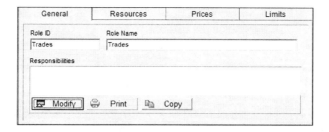

Roles: Resources

The **Resources** tab shows all resources that are currently associated with this role. Just as with resources, roles can also be assigned a proficiency level, from **1-Master** to **5-Inexperienced** (but see the note mentioned previously). In the following screenshot you can see whether each resource has this role as its primary role.

You can also assign resources to roles here, through the **Assign** button. This will bring up the **Resource Selection** screen, allowing you to choose resources to add to the role.

Roles: Prices

Just as with resources, you can assign a number of rates for a role. These can be used for cost calculations. For example, you can calculate the cost of the work using the internal rate, and the earned revenue using the external rate.

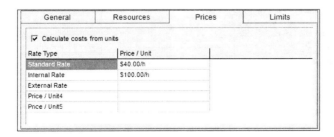

When you assign a resource to an activity, you can choose to use the rate based on the role or the specific resource. See the section on Resources for more on the **Rate Types**.

Roles: Limits

Limits set a cap on the number of units that a role can work for a given unit of time. Typically this is set in hours per day. These limits are tied to effective dates, so that different amounts can apply for different time periods.

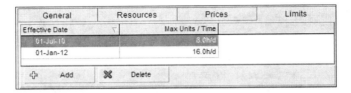

General		Resources		Prices		Limits
Effective Date			Max Units / Time			
01-Jul-10			8.0h/d			
01-Jan-12			16.0h/d			
⊹ Add		✖ Delete				

The **Limits** and **Prices** tabs for **Roles** serve a similar purpose to the **Units** and **Prices** tabs for **Resources**. But unlike resources, role prices do not have effective time periods. Keep in mind that this is the maximum hours per day for the role/resource to work on *projects*. This is not necessarily the same as the total hours of work per day.

Many organizations choose to limit all the project work to six hours per day (6h/d), so schedules are calculated using this "burn rate" rather than a typical workday that would include meetings, holidays, non-project work, administrative tasks, general communication, training, and so on. The six-hour workday more accurately represents the project work that can be accomplished. If an employee does spend the entire workday on project work, then the project could be delivered ahead of schedule.

Teams

With very few exceptions, no one works alone. This is quite true in project work. In fact, for a given activity, you do not in general assign one resource, but are more likely to assign a number of resources all together, working as a crew or **team**.

Teams is a concept that does not exist in the Professional client. They only exist in the Web client of EPPM, but are relevant to discuss here. If you wish, you can mimic teams using resource codes in P6 Professional. However, this does not grant you the ability to mimic role teams.

A **Resource Team**, as you may expect, consists of a number of resources. In the following screenshot we have a team called **Assessment Ninjas**, consisting of **Daniel Williamsen** and **Justin Quahog**. In *Chapter 16, Resource Management*, we will see how to make planning and assignments based on teams.

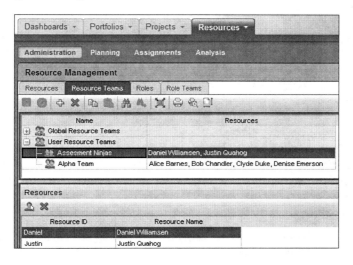

In a similar manner, you can create a Role Team, which consists of a number of roles. This is for when you do not have specific people to assign, but know the general skills that will be required. In the following screenshot we have an **Integration Team**, which will have a developer, an architect, and at least two subject matter experts.

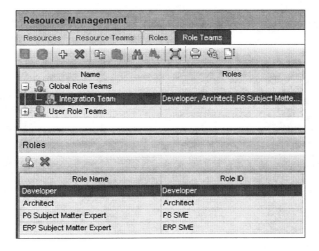

Both **Resource** and **Role Teams** are great ways to organize resources and roles in a way that is more intentional than resource codes. You can assign the same resources and roles to different teams, and these teams can be used as building-blocks of your projects. In *Chapter 16*, we will see how these can be used more efficiently.

Resource assignments

In order to appear when using the project-level filter, a resource or role must be assigned to an activity. A schedule in which all relevant activities have roles or resources assigned is called a *resource loaded* schedule. Resource loading is necessary when you want to utilize the resource availability analysis tools, as described in *Chapter 16*. It is also necessary if you want to use any of the status using tools such as **E-Mail** or the **Progress Reporter** module, or if you want to use the mobile solutions such as Team Member on the iPhone, iPad, or Android devices. Assigning resources to activities also allows personal data to show accurately in the Personal Workspace Dashboard.

 If you assign resources or roles in Resource Planning, as per *Chapter 16*, those resources or roles are still not considered *in the project*.

Let's start with a project that has no resources, in fact the project schedule for writing this book. We have an activity to write *Chapter 6*. Currently there is no one assigned to it.

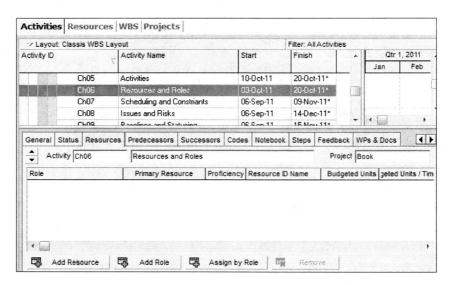

View the **Resources** tab for the activity. There are four action buttons.

Add Resource allows you to assign a resource to this activity. This brings up a resource selection screen, which is initially filtered to show only resources in the current project. You can change the filter to show all global resources, or only all active global resources. When you add a resource the role chosen is the resource's primary role, but this can be altered as needed.

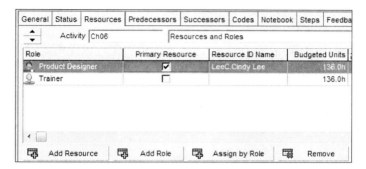

The first resource that you add to an activity becomes the primary resource for the activity (only resources, not roles, can be the primary resource). You can change this by selecting the **Primary Resource** checkbox. By default this checkbox does not appear, but you can display this column by right-clicking on the list of column headings and then choosing **Customize Resource Columns...**

Add Role brings up the role dictionary of available roles. When you assign a role to an activity, the default values of the prices/unit and units/time are populated.

Remove removes the chosen resource or role from your activity.

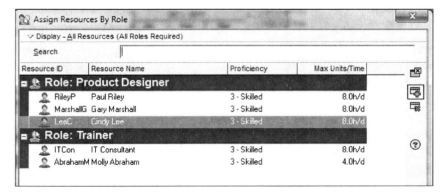

Assign Resources By Role is very helpful if roles have been assigned to an activity, such as in early planning when specific resources were not yet known. For example, when a project is estimated, it is very common that only roles, not resources, are known. Once the project is approved, then actual resource assignments can be made.

After choosing **Assign by Role** a screen appears that shows a list of only those resources that are associated with that role.

This screen has a number of options for filtering and displaying the Roles available. In this example, the screen is showing all resources in P6 which have the role of Product Designer or Trainer. The reason why these resources appear is that on the activity we have chosen one resource, Cindy Lee, who is has the role product designer, and one role of trainer. As the filter chosen is **All Resources (All Roles Required)**, these are shown. This happens when the resource is assigned prior to selecting the role.

To apply more filters, click on the display triangle in the left-hand side corner of the layout bar and select **Filter By**. This brings up a screen as shown in the following screenshot:

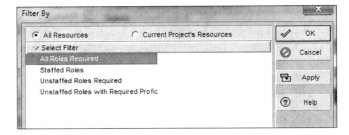

The first choice is in the two radio buttons that let you choose to see all of the resources available in P6, or only resources already assigned to the current project.

The filters are:

- **All Roles Required** is the default and it shows every available resource that has the roles specified in the activity. Note that certain resources may appear multiple times if they have more than one role.

- **Staffed Roles** lists only those roles to which a specific resource has been assigned. If you are filtering by project, you may want to view only the list of resources who are already currently assigned to a specific role within the project. For example, perhaps your project has a handful of crane operators already assigned. Rather than choose from a list of crane operators across all projects, you want to use only those who are already on the project.

- **Unstaffed Roles Required** is the opposite of the previous choice. This will show all resources capable of performing the needed roles who have not yet been assigned any work.

- **Unstaffed Roles with Required Proficiency** is where the proficiency setting comes into play. When assigning a role to an activity, you can choose the skill level required for that role. This filter will show you all resources which have that chosen skill level *or above*. For example, if you specify 1-Master, then only resources with mastery of that role will be shown. If you choose 5-Inexperienced, then anyone who has *any* proficiency in that role will appear.

Resource curves

When resources perform work on an activity, you can choose how the resource units or costs are spread through time. This is done using a resource curve. To see this column, right-click on the **Resources** tab on an activity, customize the columns, and choose **Curve**.

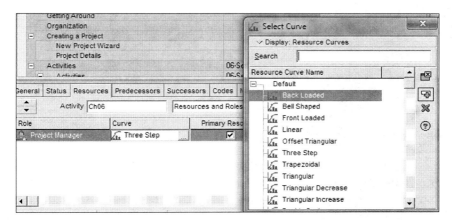

A wealth of curves from which to choose is presented. These curves will determine how the effort and cost of a resource is spread over time. This could reflect expected cost for labor or the expected consumption of a material resource.

To view and modify resource curves, choose the menu **Enterprise | Resource Curves**. A list of resource curves, much like the one shown in the previous screenshot, appears. This screen allows you to add, modify, and delete curves. In the EPPM web client, resource curves are defined in the Resource Curves section under the **Administer | Enterprise Data**. Because so many standard curves come standard with P6, there may be no need to define your own.

 Resource curves greatly affect earned value, duration calculations, capacity planning, and cash flow/cost forecasts.

If you delete a resource curve that is assigned to an existing assignment, you will be prompted and warned that the curve is previously assigned, and that deleting it will remove previous calculations affecting periods of performance reporting that occurred in the past. So only delete with good reason and with great caution.

When you add a resource curve, you are first prompted to select an initial, existing source curve to copy as a starting point, and are then taken to a screen much like the following screenshot:

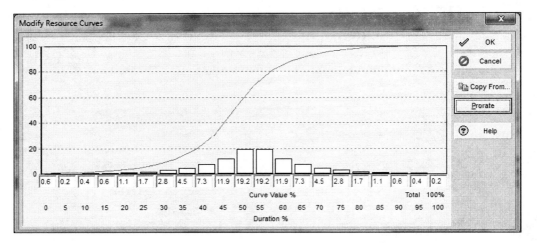

Here a curve is divided into 21 time slices, ranging from 0 to 100 percent in five percent intervals. You may enter any numbers from 0.1 to 100 in these boxes. These represent a time weighting of the resource usage. That is, based on an activity's state of progress, the specific resource will prorate the cost or resource usage accordingly. The cumulative total must be 100 percent, and you can *normalize* your curve at any time by pressing the **Prorate** button.

There are three components to the resource curve screen:

1. The *S* curve that provides a summary total for all the *to date* percent periods.
2. The histogram that provides an incremental portrait of the workload for the duration of the activity that will use this curve. The visual *weight* may be adjusted by clicking on the top of a histogram and moving it up or down.
3. The numerical value of the histogram. The specific value for a period may be modified directly in the respective field.

The sum total of the curve must equal 100 percent. To review the correct totals use the **Prorate** button to adjust the values to the appropriate periodic values.

Calendars

Resources by definition are constrained. A person works only so many hours per day. A person also has a defined set of non-work times such as weekends and holidays. Likewise, equipment may be available only at certain times. In the prior section on Resources, we mentioned that a resource can be associated with a calendar. Let us now discuss the definition and use of calendars.

Calendars describe the time available for project work. A calendar can be defined at three levels: global, project, and resource. A resource calendar is designed to work for a specific resource. Furthermore, calendars can be assigned to activities and to the resources assigned to that activity.

- **Global calendars** are available to all activities and resources.
- **Project calendars** can only be used within a specific project, and can be assigned to activities within the project. A project can also have a default calendar, which may be either a project calendar or a global calendar.
- **Resource calendars** can be assigned to resources. If a resource calendar is shared with more than one resource, it is called a **shared calendar**.

To edit calendars, choose from the main menu **Enterprise | Calendars...**.

A screen like the one shown in the previous screenshot appears. Use the buttons at the top to show global, resource, or project calendars.

- **Add** brings up a screen to add a new calendar. We will cover this further on.
- **Delete** will delete a calendar. If the calendar is being used anywhere, then you will be prompted either to select a replacement calendar or to replace it with the default global calendar.
- **Modify** lets you modify the calendar, as discussed further on.
- **Used by** will show which items are using the selected calendar. This is very helpful to view before attempting to delete a calendar.
- **To Global** allows you to copy a specific calendar to the global calendar list.
- **To Shared** allows you to copy a personal resource calendar to a shared calendar.
- **To Personal** allows you to copy a shared calendar to a specific resource calendar.

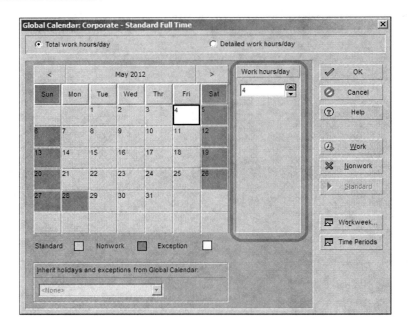

Modifying calendars

No matter what kind of calendar you are using, the screen for editing a calendar is always the same, as shown in the previous screenshot. You set up the normal hours of work for each day of the work week by choosing the button titled **Workweek...**

At the top of the screen are two main choices of how you want to assign hours on a daily basis: **Total work hours/day** and **Detailed work hours/day**.

If you choose **Total work hours/day**, then for each day you simply assign the number of hours available for work.

In the following screenshot, we choose Friday the 4th and set it to be a half-day with four hours. As it does not follow the standard or either an eight-hour workday or a nonwork day, it is colored differently as an exception:

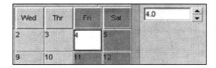

The following screenshot shows a standard work week with hours worked:

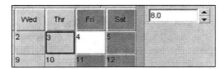

When you choose **Detailed work hours/day**, things become more fine-grained. The small section called **Work hours/day**, highlighted in the earlier screenshot, changes to show all hours available in a day, broken into 30-minute increments. You can set any 30-minute interval as available or unavailable for work by double-clicking on it. By doing this, you can, for example, set lunch hours or other break periods in your calendar.

On the main calendar screen you can also set a day to be a working day by selecting the date and double-clicking it, or by pressing the **Work** button. Likewise, you can make a workday a non-work day by double-clicking or pressing the **Nonwork** button.

Hours per time period can be set by pressing the **Time Periods** button. This tells P6 how to translate among the various time units. This setting affects the calculations for durations for all components using this calendar. Primavera stores time-based data in hours within the database and uses the values entered here as a multiplier to calculate the duration you entered into the hours stored in the database.

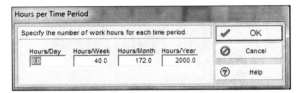

 Use caution when changing calendars and the hours per time period. For example: a user enters 10 days original duration onto an activity using this calendar shown in the previous screenshot. The database will store 80 into the original duration field of the database. If the calendar is changed to a 4.0 **Hours/Day calendar** for that same activity, the next time *F9* (schedule calculation) is used the database will deliver 80 to the **Original Duration** field and the new calendar will translate that into 20 days **Original Duration**.

A key functionality with calendars is the ability to inherit day and hours settings from other calendars. For example, a calendar for employees in a certain region can inherit from a global calendar which lists all company-level holidays. To that regional calendar, local holidays can be added.

Calendar priority

Calendars are used when a project is scheduled. The scheduling engine needs to know when activities can be performed and when certain resources are available. But with all this choice, how do you know when a given calendar will be used?

An activity that is *task-dependent* will use the activity calendar. An activity that is *resource-dependent* will use the calendar of the assigned resources to calculate the durations. For example, in the following screenshot we have two resource-dependent activities, each requiring 80 hours of work. Activity A1020 is performed by John Henry, who is using the standard five-day work week. It will take him two weeks to complete the task. Activity A1030 is performed by the Steam Drill, which uses a 24/7 calendar. It will complete the same 80-hour task in just over four days— not good news for John Henry!

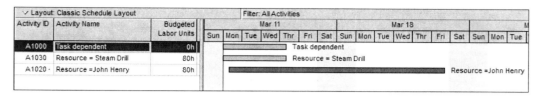

When new activities are added to a project, the calendar used is the default calendar for the project.

Calendars in P6 work like umbrellas: imagine overlapping umbrellas and the lowest level is resource calendars. Above that at the next layer is an activity calendar, then a project calendar, and finally a global calendar. They all combine to calculate dates in P6 for the scheduled project.

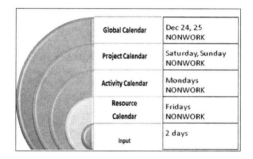

Example: Using the following sequence of activities, let's see calendars in action on Activity B. (Assume Finish to Start relationships for all shown and 8h/d workdays).

The Start Milestone is December 23. Shown here is the resource calendar with non-working days darkened. The activity calendar does not schedule work on weekends.

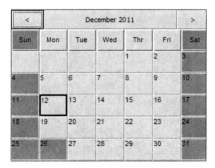

The user inputs 2 days (16 hours) for activity A planned duration, and A is set as task dependent activity type.

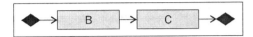

So, in this scenario activity A start date would be December 23 (beginning of day) and finish would be December 26 (end of day).

But if activity A was designated as resource dependent, the start date would be December 23 (beginning of day) and the finish date would be December 27 (end of day).

So you see, the individual layers of calendars are used in tandem to calculate dates.

For more information on dates and schedule calculations, see the next chapter.

 Primavera uses the default calendar in the Administrative settings for calculating summary durations on WBS or sort-by *categories* in activity views and layouts

Summary

In this chapter, we have covered resources and roles, which are key components of managing projects. You have seen the various properties of these items, and how to organize them into teams. You have seen how to add resources and roles, how to set their various properties, and how to assign them to activities. We also discussed calendars and how they are organized and applied.

In the next chapter, we will demonstrate how P6 can take all of this information, including the relationships between activities and the availability of resources, to generate a schedule.

Scheduling and Constraints

P6 is not just a way to enter sets of tasks into a pretty chart. Behind P6 is the scheduling engine and a set of algorithms which use a combination of project data and application settings to generate a schedule. The scheduling algorithms used are based on the **Critical Path Method** (CPM), a well-established technique for project scheduling that has a depth and history well beyond the scope of this book. CPM scheduling, simply put, is a method designed to answer two questions:

- When is the soonest I can deliver results based on my current estimates?
- On which items should I focus in order to deliver on a desired date?

In this chapter, we will cover:

- Scheduling activities
- Understanding scheduling algorithms
- Settings at the user level
- Settings at the project level
- Settings at the global level
- Settings at the activity level

Scheduling activities

Ideally, before using Oracle Primavera, a company or organization should have some scheduling or project management standards in place as approved and supported by upper management. This is particularly important for companies that will be using Oracle Primavera **Enterprise Project Portfolio Management** (EPPM), which enables and encourages a collaborative and multi-user environment. There are settings ranging from the user to the application level that can have powerful effects on reporting, progressing, and scheduling project data.

Oracle Primavera is designed to address projects within multiple industries, organizations with varying degrees of PM maturity, and scales from very small organizations to very large organizations. This means it is flexible, scalable, and robust. Add those factors together and you get a powerful, yet complicated, result. Let's clear up a few things.

Full clarity comes from understanding three principles:

- GIGO (Garbage In = Garbage Out)
- For data to be fit, we must commit!
- It is scheduling, not reporting

Garbage In = Garbage Out means that meaningful input is vital. To understand what input is appropriate, organizations and individuals must focus on the end-results first. For what purposes are you using Primavera? What activities will it govern? What output do you need? What reporting is required? When and to whom is the activity or project information required? How does the project activity reporting need to fit within the project communication plan?

Once these questions are answered, you can determine which settings are needed in Primavera. These settings should be established at each level—user, project, portfolio, and global. The end results should clearly dictate the settings and practices, and when the data input into the system follows these rules, then the output that Primavera creates will be consistent and will help to drive the business forward.

For data to be fit, we must commit! Once the system is configured properly, everyone who works with it must understand and agree upon following those rules. If people do not work within the rules, then the resulting data is neither good for comparison nor for decision making. Document the settings each user should follow. This governs how a project and its activities are structured and entered, how schedules are updated and progressed, and which scheduling options are to be used. These are in addition to the corporate/global settings for the common database. Without this level of consistency, the orange report your boss asks for may compare oranges, apples, eggs, and rocks.

It is scheduling, not fictional reporting; it is an all-too common occurrence for a scheduler to be asked, or forced, to adjust the schedule in such a way that it matches a contract, a promise, a deadline, or a report. This is a dangerous practice in that the P6 output will no longer provide an accurate, adaptive, and workable schedule.

If you are requested to make a change to a fundamental setting of P6 in order to satisfy a report, a good response is to suggest that instead accounting should simply edit their general ledger, or that payroll should re-issue their checks, or that accounts receivable should back out some paid invoices. Hopefully the people requesting these changes will then appreciate how fundamentally important it is to maintain schedule integrity.

Schedules should be transparent, in that they mirror exactly the work as it is being performed in the right sequence with the exact resources and with all the truth visible. If the project is behind and the reports present a different picture, then the organization is missing out on the opportunity that Primavera provides to become more efficient in project management. Organizations that ignore the truth behind Primavera often don't realize they are behind in schedule, cost, or profit until it is too late to make adjustments.

Understanding scheduling algorithms

The scheduling engine in Oracle Primavera is robust and powerfully complex. However, with a few simple rules and clear training, good schedulers will easily adopt Primavera as their tool of choice. Quite simply, the algorithm for determining start and finish for an activity is this:

Duration = Units / Units per Time

However, there are many other settings that can create a desired effect in that calculation.

 Keep in mind that each industry has a different database setting during installation. If you choose to install the engineering and construction database, then the word **Original** is used instead of **Planned** in column headings. In some industries, **Budgeted** is used instead of **Original** or **Planned**. If your organization uses the EPPM via web and is also using the optional client, install the **Information Technology (IT)** industry database to have the columns match in each tool.

Scheduling using CPM and P6

When you create a project, you will input activities with durations, units, units per time, and calendars. P6 uses the project management standard CPM for scheduling. The calculations begin by taking the string of activities created by relationships (predecessors and successors), and using the planned start of the project; P6 will calculate four dates per activity and populate those dates into four columns in the database. These dates are calculated using the standard practice for a forward pass and backward pass of the **Program Evaluation Review Technique (PERT)** chart created by the activities and their logical sequence of relationships.

Logic in the schedule should reflect actuality or reality at all times. This will clearly give a more accurate forecast on the project and allow better decision making based on the decision-support data from the project.

For example, it is logical that paint should dry within a room before painting a second coat or moving in the furnishings. So the network should look like this if it is using a retained logic (purest logic):

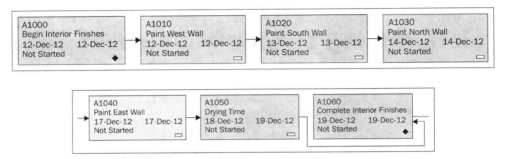

However, if you choose progress override when scheduling your project, the results can be different once the project is underway. For instance, if the team decided to move in furnishings after only two walls were painted, then you could choose progress override to schedule the remaining two walls and move up the decor activity. Typically, if you can no longer follow the logic of the schedule and must override earlier planning, then the planning was poorly done.

The scheduling algorithm

The only date you need to input is the start date of the project. This is the earliest date that any activity can start. All other dates (four dates per activity) are calculated and populate the database each time you use the scheduler (F9). This process has been done on projects since the 1950s and has been called forward and backward pass calculations of a PERT chart.

During a manual or automatic forward pass, the dates (days) are calculated by using a starting point (day one) and adding the duration of each activity in the chain. The calculation assumes that an activity ends at the end of a day, and begins the next activity on the next day. A forward pass calculates the earliest day that an activity can start, and the earliest day that it can finish (early start and early finish). A backward pass calculates the late start and late finish dates.

Additionally, the number of days that an activity can be delayed without affecting the overall project end date (called the total float) is calculated by subtracting either the early start from the late start, or the early finish from the late finish.

In this example, the earliest this project can finish is 31 days.

EXAMPLE:

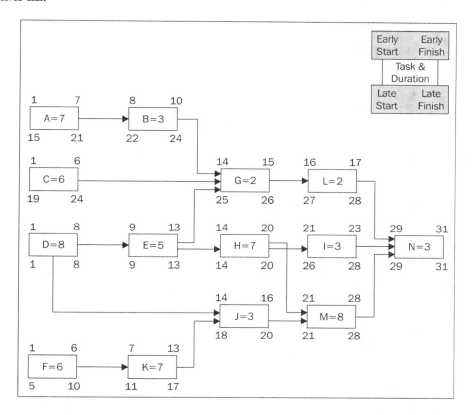

The formula for start and finish

Now that we know how the early and late dates are calculated, what about the other dates on each activity? The simplest answer is to use a formula, but there are other factors that can complicate the situation.

The simple formula is this (assuming retained logic):

Start =Data Date + Remaining Duration of Predecessor + Lead (if any) + Calendar + Lag (if any). If the project has not started and there are no predecessor activities, then Start is the planned start of the project. If the project has started and there are no predecessors, then the Start is the Data Date.

Finish = Data Date + Remaining Duration of Predecessor + Calendar + Lag (if any) + (Duration = Units / Units per Time)

Remember that milestones have only three dates, not six (Early Start, Actual Start, and Late Start for Start Milestones, and Early Finish, Actual Finish, and Late Finish for Finish Milestones).

The complications come from the settings and from the duration type and the activity type of the activity. Let's begin working with the settings. There are four levels of settings:

- User
- Project
- Global
- Activity

Settings at the user level

These are set in the menu **Administration | My Preferences** in the web client. Note that there is no corresponding setting in the professional client.

There are three tabs with multiple sections under each to review and ensure they will affect scheduling in the way your organization prefers.

Even though these are user settings, they affect a schedule enough that they should be agreed upon and consistently used by all users in that database. A corporate standard should be documented and followed.

On the **Global** tab in **My Preferences** (web) or the **User Settings** (Optional Client/ Pro), the following sections have an effect on scheduling:

- General
- Calculate performance and earned value information by cost or by labor units.

A fundamental decision must be made at your organization on how the project information will be reported in terms of progress in the schedule. One part of performance reporting is simply planned vs. actual, but overall it depends on the user preference **Calculate performance and earned value information by**, as shown in the following screenshot:.

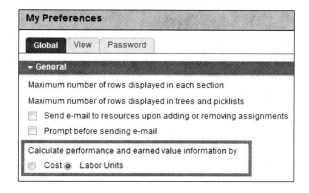

If you cost load schedules and use Progress Reporter (P6 Timesheets), then you are getting your actual costs straight from the source and may select the **Cost** setting. This is not a good option if neither your planned costs nor your actual costs are the best indicator or the best source of that data at your organization. For example, if you use another timesheet application and this information is imported into P6, then P6 is a secondary source and not the primary authoritative source for that data. Additionally, if you import your budget or do not place a true cost on your resources and resource-load assignments, then this is not the best option and you should choose **Labor Units**. The **Labor Units** setting means that performance and earned value data will be calculated using hours on labor and non-labor, and units of measure for each material assigned.

Labor units should be the default for any organization without a clear policy on costs or resource loading. P6 calculates units even if you only use durations in your planning or if you do not assign resources.

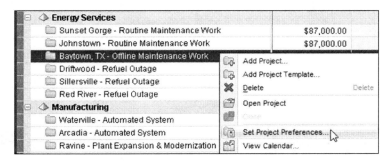

Settings at the project level

Project-level settings will affect the scheduling algorithms more than the user-level settings. For comparison with the project at different intervals or copies of the project, these settings must be comparable, too. On the EPS screen, highlight your project, then right-click on the project and select **Set Project Preferences** from the pop-up menu.

 These same settings are found in the professional client in the **Project Settings** and **Calculations** tabs.

Calculations

Under **Activities**, you can define how P6 will perform in the case that an activity that was designated as started is now changed to a not started status.

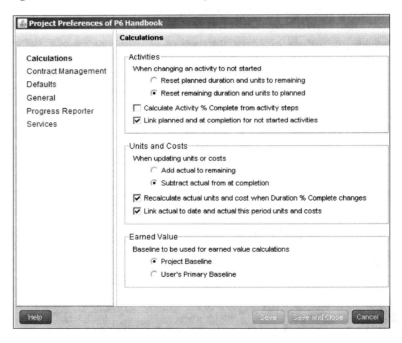

When choosing the top selection, P6 will place whatever number is in the **Remaining Duration** in the **Planned Duration** field. On a baselined project this can affect the scheduling algorithm. It will now be comparing the planned duration from the baseline to the currently (and newly) populated amount that was changed once the status of the activity was changed.

A general rule to follow is to never change original or planned dates or units on a baselined project.

Since actuals are not a part of the scheduling algorithm, the other settings here do not necessarily affect the scheduling calculations and are discussed in the *Creating a Project* section of this book.

Scheduling (F9) options

Other project-level settings are found when you actually run the scheduling algorithms on the project. View these options by pressing *F9* in the professional client. In the web client you may do this by going to the **Activities** view and pressing *F9* or pressing the icon that is shown in the following screenshot in the toolbar:

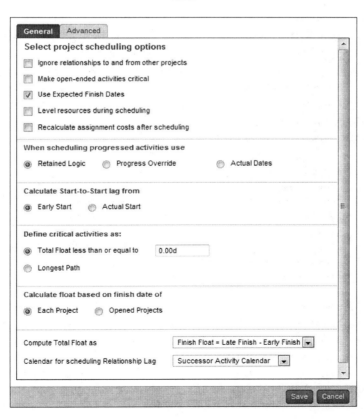

Keep in mind that these settings remain in effect for this project each time it is rescheduled and until the settings are changed. Please notify others on the project who have permission to run the scheduler, so they are aware of these settings.

- **Ignore relationships to and from other projects**: P6 is particularly good at allowing users to create cross-project relationships, such as when excavation activity on one construction site for project Y cannot begin until the excavation activity for project X is complete. Just as intra-project relationships affect scheduling, so too do these inter-project relationships. Whether these relationships should be considered by the scheduling algorithm is up to you. The top setting in the **General** tab allows you to calculate this project's schedule without regard for any relationships to other projects.

- **Make open-ended activities critical**: While it is a bad practice to have open-ended activities in the schedule, the **Make open-ended activities critical** setting would treat those activities as critical. It turns them red on the Gantt chart, calling attention to them so that you can determine if these activities should affect the project end date.

- **Level resources during scheduling**: If you choose to level resources during scheduling, then activities will be re-calculated based on the maximum hours per day of each assigned resource and will not allow more hours per day than that limit. This typically makes a longer project, but often makes for a much more accurate schedule.

 This setting is not often used because it requires tremendous discipline on the part of the organization and in particular on the scheduler. Prioritization of projects must be distinctive for this to be the rule and it must be a practice of the organization to not allow resources to work past working hours—it is a literal workday only. Most organizations would prefer that a resource arrange to work one extra hour that day than to delay the project by a day.

It is, however, a good practice to use this setting in the planning phases so the project is clearly communicating dates that are realistic to actual working hours instead of abusing the resources to cram in extra hours to meet an organizational deadline. While it is a common practice during execution to make resources sacrifice personal time, it is nice when you have built that assumption into the original plan. Then those extra sacrifices will only happen if and when corrective actions are needed to get back on schedule after the project falls behind.

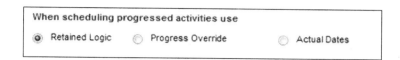

- **When scheduling progressed activities use**: The choice you make under this section can greatly affect the scheduling algorithm. P6 uses CPM scheduling, which is an industry standard. This setting allows a user to schedule the project using the logical ties in the schedule as originally input with appropriate predecessors and successors (**Retained Logic** is the preferred setting) or to simply schedule the remaining work based on actual work done (**Progress Override**). The **Progress Override**, therefore, may ignore logic if, for example, an activity has started earlier than constraints or logic would dictate. The third option, **Actual Dates**, uses the progress, but conducts a forward and backward pass to determine dates as described in the last section of this chapter.

- The last setting at the project level to affect calculations is perhaps the most pivotal—the **Data Date**. This date is input during initial planning on the **General** tab on the **Projects** or **EPS** screen. This date should be updated each time you recalculate the schedule and is also located on that screen (F9).

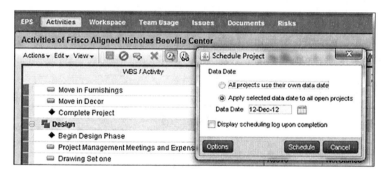

The **Data Date** serves as the point of calculation for all future work. It also answers the question *Progress witnesses as of what point?* and *Future from what point?* Think of it as your *as-of* date.

Consider this scenario where your company's timesheets are due on Fridays at 5.pm. and include all work done up to that point on the project. Therefore, the actuals or progress information you receive is up-to-date on Fridays and also includes Friday work. In this company, your data dates are therefore Saturdays. This indicates that *as-of* Saturday morning, this schedule represents all the work done up to that point.

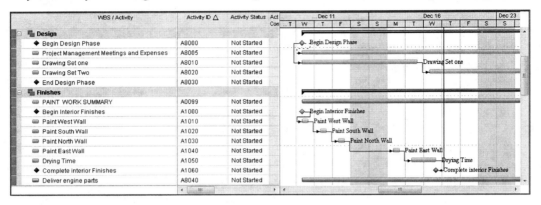

Here is how the **Data Date** is used in calculations. During initial planning, all activities are lined up along the planned start date, and the **Data Date** is the same as planned start. Once you calculate the schedule, the Start and Finish dates for each activity are calculated using calendars, predecessor, duration, and all other settings. Future work is all of work in front of the **Data Date**, and of course the entire project is in the future during initial planning.

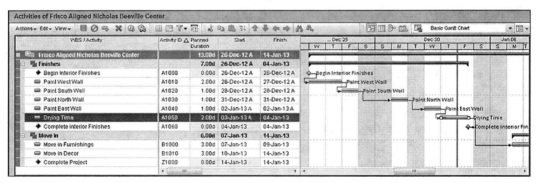

But once the project begins, the calculation changes. Now the **Data Date** is used as the point-of-calculation. All future work and associated dates use remaining units and remaining units per time in the calculation of new finish dates for in-progress activities and for new start and finish dates for all subsequent activities that are not started according to relationships. A forward and backward pass is conducted each time the schedule is re-calculated in order to populate Early and Late dates. For un-started activities, you can continue using **Budgeted** (Planned) columns.

Settings at the global level

Global settings can affect scheduling in two ways—the **Time Periods** setting in the **Application** section of the **Administer** menu, and the associated calendar setting **Use assigned calendar to specify the number of work hours for each time period**.

These values are a sort of default for the program to identify how many units (hours) are equivalent to a day when calculating duration from the standard equation (*Duration = Units / Units per Time*). Other equal values are defined here, such as hours in a week, hours in a month, and hours in a year. This becomes important at the activity level because P6 actually stores the duration as hours and displays the duration according to the calculations of a standard day. Likewise, if you enter an activity's duration as 2w, Primavera will use the same settings to convert to the appropriate number of days/hours.

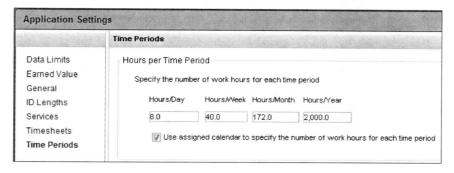

Using the sample settings shown (8.0 as **Hours/Day**); a user could enter 1d (one day) as the duration on an activity and the value of 8h (8 hours) is entered into the database.

Set this setting to the accepted amount of days or hours your organization typically works. The average human resource hours per year are 2,080 (if you include two weeks or 80 hours vacation) or 2,000 (without two weeks vacation). If your human resources department or financial bookkeeping does not have a specified amount, then use your best judgment for these values. Projects will schedule for longer time periods if these numbers are lower, and project schedules will be shorter if you place more units per time period. Be as close to accurate as possible to ensure realistic results.

The checkbox **Use assigned calendar...** can affect schedule calculations, too. If you would like to use the resource or activity calendars assigned to each activity as the definition of hours per time period and ignore the values set here for hours per time period, then check this box. Ensure that all the calendars have accurate working time and non-working time settings because these will be used to convert the input into hours for the database. For more information, see the section of this book regarding calendars.

If you would like to use these stated values per each time period for scheduling, then clear this checkbox. The values per time period will not be used for calculating duration of activities, but will be used in the planning resources functions, WBS views, and global change.

Settings at the activity level

Last but certainly not least, the activity level settings are paramount for schedule calculations. Most people know the activity settings and forget to look into all other settings when dates do not seem to calculate as expected.

Activities are the major component of a schedule, and there are several aspects to each activity that must be considered. Activity components can be categorized as **Mandatory** or **Optional**, and several of them together represent the chain that affects dates in P6.

Activity components that affect schedule calculation:

MANDATORY	Affects Dates	OPTIONAL	Affects Dates
WBS and OBS		Expenses	
Activity ID and Description		Steps	
Activity Type	Yes	Notebooks/Feedback	
Duration	Yes	WP & Documents	
Date (input)	Yes	Activity Codes	
Calendar Assignments	Yes	Relationships	Yes
Duration Type	Yes	Constraints	Yes
Percent Complete Type	Yes	Role and Resource Assignments	Yes

Activity types

Each type will react differently to scheduling and each type will have its own effect on dates. The available activity types are:

- Level of Effort
- Start Milestone
- Finish Milestone
- WBS Summary Activity
- Task Dependent
- Resource Dependent

Level of Effort (LOE) are activities that are supportive in nature and are often referred to by a legacy feature from P3—Hammock activities. This is an activity type where some work takes place regularly for the length of a phase or for the entire project. Therefore it is attached at both ends to targets that can change independently of each other. When the ends do move, then the work is automatically added to the schedule according to units per time. LOE can also be used to roll-up activity information from a separate project.

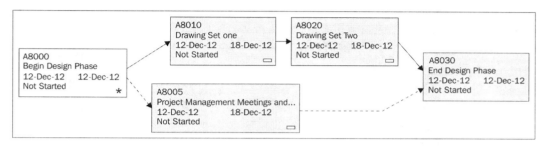

For example, two hours of travel time and a three-hour meeting takes place during the design phase of a project at a cost of $1,500 for room rental, gas, catering, and so on.

In P6 this work could be represented by a LOE type activity called **Project Management Meetings and Expenses**.

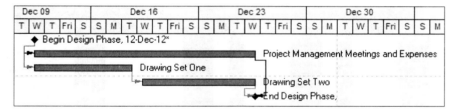

The planned duration was calculated by P6, based on the span of time created by **Drawing Set one** (five days) and successor **Drawing Set Two** (also five days) for a total of 10 days for the LOE activity. You can assign resources or materials to the activity as a burn rate or units per time totaling the $1,500 weekly cost. As drawing sets are added or delays occur (with appropriate relationships created) an additional $1,500 per extra week is added and the planned duration will expand on the LOE activity, too.

As the predecessor activities of the LOE are statuses with actual dates, the LOE itself will automatically inherit the earliest of these dates for its actual start date. As the data date is moved, and based on the balance of activities' cumulative remaining duration within the context of the LOE, P6 will adjust the progress accordingly. As the last successor to the LOE activity is "statused", P6 will automatically use the latest successor date for the LOE Actual Finish.

Start Milestone is an activity type that is used to define the start of a significant section of the project or of the entire project. Milestones have no duration and a Start Milestone completed typically indicates several other activities can now begin. Start Milestones only have start dates (early, late, and actual start).

Finish Milestone in the same way indicates the completion of a significant group of work or a project. Typically several predecessors lead up to the Finish Milestone, which has only finish dates (early, late, and actual finish).

In the following screenshot both a Start Milestone and a Finish Milestone are shown. Notice that the finish date is grayed out for the Start Milestone and the start date is grayed out for the Finish Milestone, indicating that these dates are not available for input:

WBS Summary activity is a type of activity that is rarely used but can be powerful when needed. The WBS Summary requires no relationships because it inherits its dates from all other activities within the same WBS component when the schedule is calculated (*F9*). This is useful when the project activities are more detailed than the level at which actuals or costs are reported and collected. For example, if the timesheets in use at your organization are not a part of the Primavera system and if time is input by cost account or by scope item rather than each activity in the schedule, then it makes sense to use WBS Summary activity when reporting against timesheets. Another frequent use of the WBS Summary is to cost load the schedule at the deliverable level rather than at the activity or commodity level, which is more granular in nature.

For WBS Summary Activities, the assignments, planned units, and other data are input to the activities, but the actual units and actual costs are input to the WBS Summary activity for that WBS component. The WBS summary activity uses the earliest early start among the activities and the latest late finish as its start and finish. Its duration is derived as the longest path among its fellow activities within the same WBS component.

In the following example, the WBS Summary activity is titled **PAINT WORK SUMMARY** and its start is the earliest from below (**12-Dec-12**) and its finish is the latest from below (**19-Dec-12**). Its duration is the total from all its sibling activities. If two activities were in parallel, its duration would be the longest path. Note that the summary activity itself is not a critical activity, but on the Gantt it does become a part of the critical path as it represents the longest path for that WBS component. Just as with LOE activity types, the WBS Summary will inherit the earliest actual start and the latest actual finish from the activities within its WBS group. If there is a remaining duration for activities within the WBS group, then the progress for the WBS Summary is based on the duration between the actual start, the data date, and the latest finish date.

When using this type of activity, clearly state that it is a summary activity in the description field. There are no other visual indicators that this is a WBS Summary type unless you look at the **General** tab of the activity details.

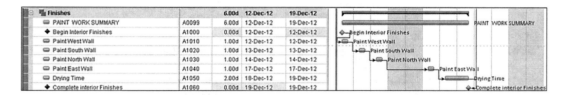

Task Dependent is the most common type of activity. Using this duration type, a Task Dependent activity will calculate its start as the next unit of time after the currently scheduled finish date of its predecessor in the logical sequence that is created by its relationships. If activity A has a calculated finish date of end of working time as Tuesday, then activity B will start at the beginning of working time Wednesday. But this will depend upon each item in this table (assigned resource or role, calendars, settings, constraints, and so on).

Resource Dependent is an activity type that will use the calendars of the resources assigned to calculate its start and finish dates. Use this type of activity when more than one resource is assigned and they can work independently from one another, not necessarily as a team.

The following chart shows the difference between a task-dependent activity and a resource-dependent activity during schedule calculations.

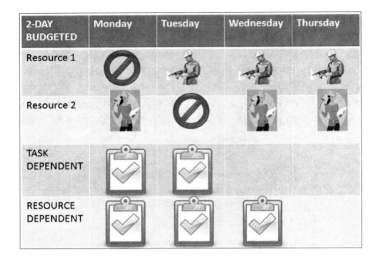

For example, assuming two days budgeted duration, two resources are assigned. Resource 1 is not available on Monday and Resource 2 is not available on Tuesday.

When the budgeted duration is two days, the start date is determined for a task-dependent activity type as the first day after the predecessor's finish date. However, for a resource-dependent activity type, the finish date is calculated as the earliest two days from which each resource assigned can be completed.

As a task-dependent activity, regardless of the resources' calendars, the activity is always a two-day planned duration.

As a resource-dependent activity, the activity depends on planned progress based on when each resource can complete two days of work each. If the activity starts on Monday, Resource 2 can begin work, but Resource 1 is not available. On Tuesday, Resource 1 can work, but Resource 2 is not available. On Wednesday, Resource 1 can complete his second day of work, and Resource 2 can complete her second day of work. Therefore, the activity will display three calendar days of execution for two days of work.

If the same activity were delayed by logic to begin on Wednesday, then the activity will display two calendar days of execution time for the two days of work.

The **Duration Type** of an activity is the next activity component that may affect dates. Duration Type is often misunderstood and often misused. Many tutors explain each one and examine how each affects the scheduling algorithm, but let's explain the algorithm and then test it using each type.

The duration type calculates using the standard algorithm already discussed:

Duration=Units / Units per Time

But the duration type lets the user decide what part is input and what part is calculated. Think of it as a triangle.

The Duration Triangle is shown as follows:

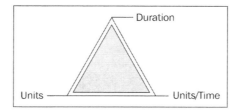

Here are the rules for using the triangle:

- Fix one side.
- Input or change second item.
- P6 calculates the third item.
- If your goal is to fix one item, that is to solidify that item so that it remains unchanged by the calculation, and you then input a second, then P6 will calculate the third item.
- To understand which item to solidify (fix) is to understand in general how your business (the project) runs, and specifically how activities will specifically differ. What input do you know during the planning stages of your project? Some know the durations, others may know the units, and many know that we have limited time per day or limited production (units/time).

Let's look at four scenarios:

Example A:

P.M.T. Company knows that the project has to deliver this activity within 20 days. Recent budget cuts leave no overtime dollars to expend and resources are spending six hours a day on project work, leaving two hours for training and meetings. A project manager at this company would be wise to select the **fixed duration and units/time** duration type. This P.M.T. project manager would budget 20 days duration (fixed) and then input the units/time as 6h/d. When the schedule is calculated (F9) the units would calculate 120 units (hours) for that activity.

Example B:

The planners at MISC Engineering know they have 12 drawings to deliver for an activity and they know that they typically can produce two drawings per day. The scheduler chooses **fixed units** duration type and inputs the 12 drawings as units, and inputs 2/d for Units/Time. The calculated duration is six days. After reviewing the schedule they need to make up three days time to meet contracted dates. So they add another resource (making production rate 4/d) and then recalculate (F9) to see that the duration is now three days.

Example C:

Zed Co Project Office knows it has 800 lines of code to deliver in four days. The IT PM chooses **fixed duration and units** activity type and inputs the 800 units and the 4 days duration. The F9 calculation results in 200 lines of code per day (200/d). If the PM adds another resource, the new calculation is more achievable at 100 lines of code per day for each resource. Of course this assumes that the coding can be accomplished independently, which does not often reflect reality.

Example D:

Davidoff Bentley Manufacturing has a production rate of 800 engine parts per day on its main production line. They are currently bidding on a competitive bid contract to deliver 80,000 engine parts. They will receive a premium bonus if they deliver in less than 90 days. The head of planning chooses **fixed units** duration type on the summary activity and inputs 80,000 units, then inputs 800/d units per time. The F9 calculation delivers a 100 day duration. The planner changes the type to **fixed duration and units** and inputs 90 days before recalculating. The result is 888.89/day. So he works with quality control to find a way to deliver 89 more parts per day or he adds shifts to the line.

Ideally, a project manager will be involved early in the planning, and some details and calculations will be a required input into the schedule. However, many times a project manager is confined to deadlines and promises made by sales teams or contract offices. In this case, the duration type can be used to optimize the schedule activity-by-activity to ensure that the schedule calculates for the desired results.

This helpful matrix details the duration types even further:

Duration Type	If Change Units	If Change Duration	If Change Units/Time	Add 1st Resource	Add Additional Resources
Fixed Duration & Units	Units/Time Changes	Units/Time Changes	Units Change	Units Change	Units/Time of each Resource Changes
Fixed Duration & Units/Time	Units/Time Changes	Units Change	Units Change	Units Change	Units Change
Fixed Units	Duration Changes	Units/Time Changes	Duration Changes	Units Change	Duration Changes
Fixed Units/Time	Duration Changes	Units Change	Duration Changes	Units Change	Duration Changes

Summary

No longer is the schedule simply used to report past behavior. Instead, the powerful calculations from P6 now provide a forward-facing windscreen view rather than a rear-view mirror. Put another way, P6 will let you drive the bus toward success rather than look behind the bus for collateral damage. P6 can tell a user much more than what is known. P6 delivers decision support data with calculated precision as long as the user understands the algorithms.

In the next chapter, we address what happens when things do not go according to schedule, as we discuss issues and risks.

8

Issues and Risks

What is life without risks and danger, the excitement of the unknown? Well, that may be fine for your leisure time, but when managing a project, risk is something you want to actively manage. If you cannot avoid it, at least you can measure and control it to some degree. The risks to projects are as diverse as projects themselves. In fact, some risks may be positive, such as when durations may have been over-estimated. Such risks are also called **opportunities**. Here are a few examples of project risks:

- There may be a shortage of skilled labor, possibly requiring higher salaries and/or delays to the project schedule
- A critical piece of equipment may have a known failure rate, and such failure could cost the project time and money
- A permit may have a delay, setting back several activities
- Material prices can fluctuate, affecting the cash flow of the job—even in a positive manner

P6 has a number of facilities for monitoring thresholds in your projects, tracking issues, and managing risks. The enterprise version of P6 has extended features and is a more robust solution for managing risk than the professional version.

Thresholds are triggers that fire when certain values exceed a defined limit. When a threshold is exceeded, it can generate an issue, which is then assigned to a specific manager who is responsible for addressing the issue.

Issues are automatically created by thresholds or can be created manually. They are used to document, track, and monitor problems that arise. An issue may have no impact on cost or schedule. The difference between an issue and a risk is that an issue has actually occurred and a risk is assumed possible but not yet occurred. Often an issue is a former risk that has now occurred.

Risks assign values to events that may or may not happen during a project. Project risk is defined as an uncertain event or condition that, if it occurs, has an impact on at least one of the project objectives. Objectives may include scope, schedule, cost, and quality. (*PMBOK Guide*, 4th Edition).

A risk has a probability and an impact. For example, there may be a three percent chance that a certain pressure vessel will leak, and the cost of such a leak could cost $100,000 and delay the project by seven working days.

Thresholds

To view thresholds, click on the icon or choose from the main menu **Project | Thresholds**. The icon looks similar to the following screenshot:

The **Select Threshold Parameter** window is shown as follows:

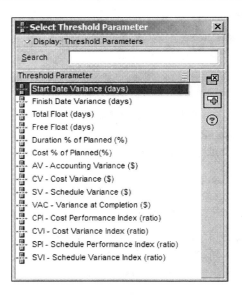

Thresholds monitor threshold parameters. These are pre-defined calculated quantities in P6 which can be related to costs and dates. A threshold looks for a variance in one specific parameter.

If the parameter exceeds the upper threshold, or is lower than the lower threshold, then an issue is generated. A user can then monitor issues to see when thresholds are violated. Within a WBS element, the threshold can be set to apply either to the WBS and its children, or to the activities contained within that WBS and its children. If the WBS level is chosen, then one issue will be generated for each threshold violation. If the activity level is chosen, then one issue will be generated for each activity which triggers the threshold.

Next, the Responsible Manager can be set for the threshold. This is the OBS element responsible for that threshold. You can also choose the graphical tracking layout, which is most useful for displaying the data involved in the specific threshold parameter.

A threshold can be disabled. This might be appropriate if it is known that a threshold will be violated for a short period, and you do not want to have issues generated for it.

Finally, for sorting and filtering purposes, thresholds can be assigned a priority, from **1** (most important) to **5** (least important).

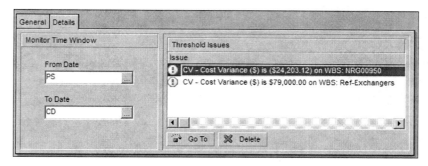

A time window can be set on the threshold. In the previous example, the threshold is monitored from the project start date (**PS**), through the current date (**CD**). Issues will only be generated for this threshold within this time period.

A number of dates are available, and the user can also enter specific calendar dates using **Custom Date...**.

If the threshold identifies issues, then the issues are displayed under **Threshold Issues**. The user can select an issue and go directly to it by selecting the issue and pressing the **Go To** button.

When a threshold is created, it does not automatically have issues identified to it. Instead, you must manually monitor the specific threshold. To do this, go to the menu item **Tools | Monitor Thresholds...**.

You may choose to use the monitoring window set in the threshold itself, or you may enter the start and finish dates manually. After you press **Monitor**, P6 will create issues for any thresholds, which have been exceeded.

Issues

There are two kinds of issues. The ones we have seen already are generated through thresholds. You may also create issues directly. To view issues, click on the exclamation icon, which looks like the following screenshot:

Or choose from the main menu **Project | Issues**. This screen shows all issues within any currently open projects. Note that the first one was generated from a threshold, easily identified by its unique issue name.

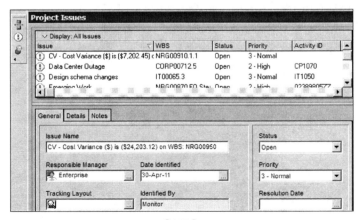

An issue can be assigned a **Responsible Manager**, a **Tracking Layout**, and **Priority**, just like a threshold. **Date Identified** gives the date that the issue was first recognized. The values for **Status** are: **Open**, **On Hold**, and **Closed**. If an issue is resolved, the **Resolution Date** can be set.

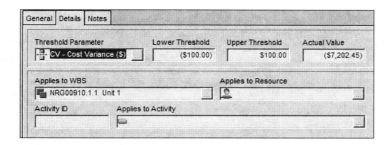

The **Details** screen shows more information about the issue. If it was created by a threshold, then the first row of information is filled in, based on the threshold. If it is not associated with a threshold, then all the data on this row will be blank.

An issue must be associated with a WBS element (group of several activities), and can optionally also be associated with a resource, or single activity.

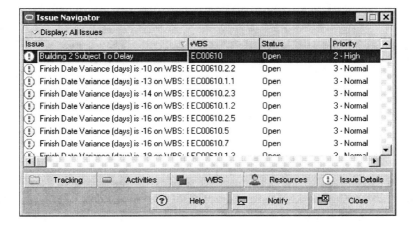

The **Issue Navigator** is opened from the menu item **Tools | Issue Navigator**. This brings a screen like the one shown previously. This screen will float above the main screen, and lets you quickly navigate between all items related to the selected issue, including the tracking view, activity, WBS elements, and any resource associated with the selected issue.

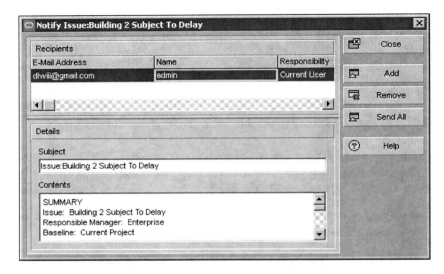

You may also choose **Notify** to send out an e-mail about the issue. The body of the e-mail brings in and formats information from the issue. However, you may edit the text to meet your needs. You may also add recipients to the e-mail by either entering the e-mail addresses manually, or by pulling e-mails from existing P6 resources which have e-mail addresses assigned.

Risks: P6 Professional

Only P6 Professional allows you to manage risks from the Windows client. For P6 enterprise, risks are not available in the optional client, but can be managed from the web. To open the risks window, click on the dice icon, which looks similar to the following screenshot:

Or choose from the main menu **Project | Risks**.

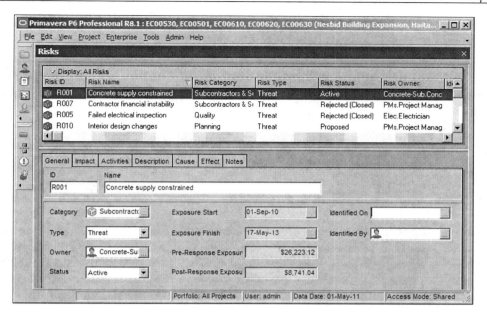

Whereas an issue or a threshold is associated with a WBS element, a risk is associated with a project. Within a project, a risk can then be associated with zero or more activities.

A risk has an ID and a name. It also has a category. Categories are defined through the menu **Admin | Admin Categories....** The risk type can be either a threat or an opportunity. A **threat** is a risk event, which if occurs, will have a native impact on the project. An **opportunity** is a risk event, which if it occurs, will have a positive impact on the project.

The owner of the risk is a resource assigned to it. The status of the risk indicates whether or not it is considered outstanding, or whether it has been resolved through impact or management.

Exposure start and exposure finish are the expected start and finish window of the risk exposure. If the risk is associated with multiple activities, the dates include the earliest start and the latest finish of all the associated activities. Similarly, the pre- and post-exposure costs come from the associated activity costs and the impact settings on the next tab.

Identified On is simply the date recording when the risk was first seen, and **Identified By** tells which resource identified the risk.

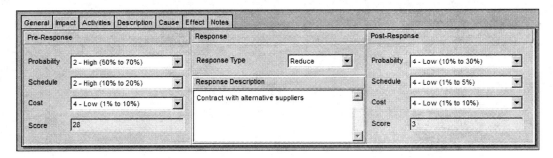

The **Impact** tab is used to quantitatively measure the effect of the risk on the project cost and schedule. The **Pre-Response** portion lets you set the probability that the event will occur. The schedule sets the magnitude of the effect on the schedule if the risk event happens. The cost lets you set the effect on the cost if the event happens. The schedule and cost are together called the impact. The highest value of the impact, taken with the probability, is used to generate a risk score. This measure ranges from **0** (negligible probability, negligible impact) to **72** (very high probability, very high impact). The score can then be used as a level yardstick to compare risks from a variety of sources.

The **Response Type**, when not set to **<None>**, shows the action chosen to address the risk. The **Response Type** values are: **Accept**, **Avoid**, **Reduce**, and **Transfer**. Given that a response is chosen, then the probability and impact due to that action can be assigned a risk score, just as in the **Pre-Response**.

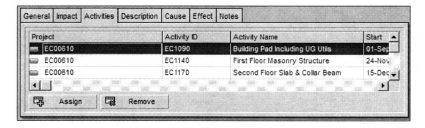

Activities are assigned to the risk in the **Activities** tab. Just as a risk can be associated with multiple activities, likewise, an activity can be assigned to multiple risks.

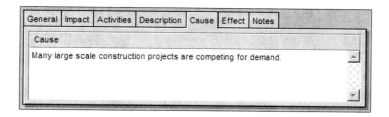

The remaining tabs are **Cause**, **Description**, **Effect**, and **Notes**. These are simply text areas to store notes about the risk.

Use **Description** to describe the risk condition. For example, there is a risk that labor costs will escalate by 20 to 30 percent above the estimated maximum ceiling labor price established in the project budget.

Use **Cause** to describe what conditions cause the risk to occur. For example, due to the many large scale construction projects in the region, there will be competing demand for these critical skilled trades.

Use **Effect** to describe the impact of the risk. For example, the effect is that the project may be impacted by an increased cost due to the regional demand for these critical skills. Given our cash allocations, we may be unable to procure critical supplies as our budget will be spent on labor.

Use **Notes** to describe any residual risks remaining after the primary response. For example, if we raise labor costs in this one region, we may receive pressure from our workers to increase rates in other regions that are not affected by this local risk.

Risks: P6 Enterprise

Risks in P6 Enterprise are quite different than in P6 Professional. For example, you can have multiple response plans, and there is a risk register and a scoring matrix.

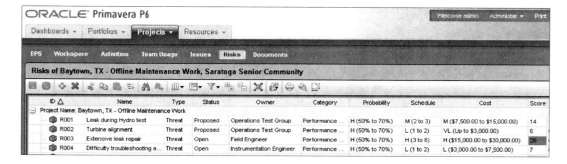

One item of note is the **Response Plan**, which is similar to the **Impact** tab in P6
Professional, but gives much greater flexibility in assigning responses.

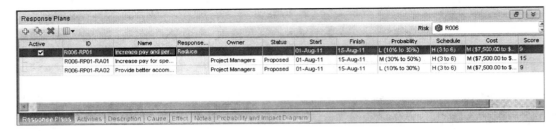

Rather than having a single response, you can create multiple responses to a risk,
and can provide much greater detail about how the risk will be handled.

Once you have established your risks, you can view the **Probability and Impact
Diagram**, which shows how the risks are coded. Several pre-defined PID matrices
have been provided from which we can choose.

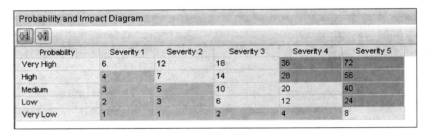

Different industries measure risk differently. You can customize your own risk
matrices by going to **Administer | Enterprise Data** and going to the section on
Risks | Risk Scoring Matrices.

> Risk management is an area in which P6 excels over most other
> tools. Proper use of P6 risks guides you to be more proactive
> about project risk. This allows you to gain insight into possible
> future outcomes and to be prepared for them ahead of time,
> which is much more effective than responding to past events.
> Think windscreen rather than rear-view mirror.

Summary

In this chapter we have examined a number of ways to anticipate and manage project issues:

- Thresholds to identify variances in certain quantities

- Issues, either keyed to thresholds or entered manually

- Risks, which can be measured as having quantifiable impacts on the project cost and schedule

The next chapter builds on the concept of threshold and risks. It addresses creating project baselines — snapshots of a project that are used to store historical information that can be used for comparison to the current project. These can be used to look backward when auditing a project's past performance, but can also be used to make projections on where the project is headed.

Baselines and Statusing

9

Schedules, just like our lives, rarely occur exactly as planned. In the world of Project Management, the better we are at planning, the better the results. However, there are still variances and unforeseen events which alter a schedule during execution. One way to look ahead is to see how our project has changed over time. A baseline is essentially a snapshot of a project at a given point in time which can be compared to the current project to highlight changes in the schedule. When you look at the trends between the baseline and the current project, you can identify and mitigate trends. A well-designed report can highlight which activities or areas are more prone to slippage, and point the way to prevent similar slippage in the future.

As a project progresses, what was once a planned activity becomes actual work reported on the schedule. This work performed can be tracked in a number of ways, all under the classification of "actuals". This can mean the actual number of hours worked, the actual duration of activities, actual resources and money spent, and so on. When the planned work is updated with actual reports of progress in the field, this process is called *applying actuals, progressing the schedule*, or *statusing*.

In this chapter we will cover:

- Creating and assigning baselines
- Assigning baselines to projects and users
- Managing baselines
- Statusing projects' date, costs, and resource hours

Maintaining baselines

A baseline at its core is a snapshot of your project at one point in time. You can use the baseline to compare your current project to that baseline, to see how the project is progressing compared to the original plan.

Two separate functions are present in the baseline feature of P6; **Maintaining Baselines** and **Assigning Baselines**. Simply, baselines are created in one place and assigned to the project for comparison in another place. This is separated because there are typically two different roles or users who would perform these functions as part of a balanced quality check. Since a baseline is used as a calculation for variances, the capability to create your own baseline is risky. For example, if original duration is six days and you realize there have been eight days on that activity; the variance between your original duration in the baseline and the current project actual duration is -two and you are late. If someone were to change the baseline to have eight days original duration, your project activity would not show as late, and you have lost the benefit of learning from that. First, let's create or maintain baselines.

You can get to the baselines by pressing the ⊞ icon, or by clicking **Project | Manage Baselines…**

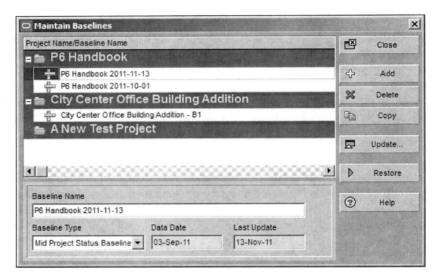

When you open this window, it shows you all the currently open projects, and under each project, a list of all its respective baselines. In the screen above we have three projects open: **P6 Handbook**, **City Center Office Building Addition**, and **A New Test Project**. (Note that the projects are sorted according to their Project ID).

The first project has two baselines, the second has one, and the third has no baselines assigned.

To create a baseline, choose the **Add** button.

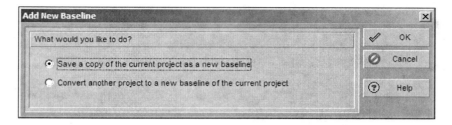

You are presented with two choices: **Save a copy...** will create a new baseline that is a copy of the project, whereas **Convert another project...** will take an existing project, convert it to a baseline, and allow you to attach it to the selected project. As a project is converted to a baseline of the current project, that project is *delisted* from the project selection list. This second functionality is needed, for example, when a project and its baseline are exported from another system and imported into yours. When a project is exported, its baselines are not attached. The only way, therefore, to import a project and its baseline is to promote the baseline to be a project, and then export it separately. This selection is also most helpful when you wish to compare this current project with any point in the past, or another similar project or template. Upcoming versions are expected to include a choice to determine copying baselines upon import.

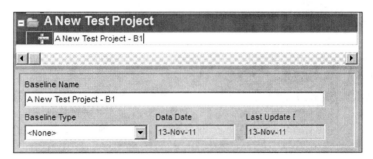

In the previous screenshot we have just added a baseline to the test project. By default, the **Baseline Name** will be the same as the project name, but with extra text at the end such as - B1. If we add another baseline, it will be called - B2 and so on. This is the default behavior of P6.

Note, however, that you can change this name at any time to something more helpful to users. For example, if the baseline has a **Data Date** of 13-Nov-2011, you can prefix the description with the date so that it is clearer; you can then append an additional clarification to the end. An example would be "2011-11-13 – A New Test Project – Daniel's Snapshot". This pattern will allow the baselines to be easily sorted in a date order. Or you could define the timeframe of the snapshot/baseline more clearly such as "A New Test Project Fiscal Year End 2011".

Remember that this name will appear on screen in a very short field on the bottom left of the project and activities screens—keep it simple, clear, and short for best viewing.

Baseline Type is a drop-down which allows you to set the type of baseline. This is used in grouping, sorting, and filtering. You can create new baseline types or edit the available baseline types through the menu **Admin | Admin Categories...**

The **Data Date** cannot be changed. It is the data date of that file at the time of creation of that baseline.

The **Last Update** date is the time that the baseline was last updated. This can change if you choose to update the baseline.

Copy baseline simply copies the entire baseline and names it with the next "B" number. All other properties of the new baseline match the copied one. However, the **Last Updated Date** is blank.

Restore baseline will take the baseline, remove it as a project baseline and restore it as a full-fledged project file. You may then modify that project as desired, and later on re-attach it as a baseline to the original project. Remember, as any "live" project is converted and attached or re-attached as a project baseline, it will be de-listed from the list of available projects.

Updating a baseline

While an original project baseline can be helpful, sometimes the information in a baseline needs to be updated to reflect changes in the project. It is a best practice to keep the baselines pristine and unchanged once the project is being executed—often this should be handled as a re-baseline effort. This is so that all original planning is captured for historical data and accurate variance reporting and trending. But, if during planning, the original baseline needs to be changed, then a baseline update is more appropriate than a re-baseline effort.

While the ability to update baselines does not exist in the P6 Enterprise web client, both the Professional and Optional clients give you the ability to update baselines with a fine level of detail.

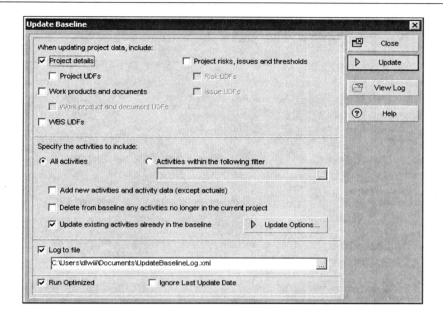

After clicking the **Update** button on the main Baseline screen, a new window will open up, as shown in the previous screenshot. This screen has many options.

The first section determines what entities to update, and whether UDFs (User Defined Fields) should also be updated. This includes Project details, Work products and documents, WBS, Project risks, issues, and thresholds. Updating these entities is fairly straightforward—the data and values in the original project are simply used to update information in the baseline.

However, the process of updating activities is more involved. First, you may choose to update all activities or to only update those that match a filter.

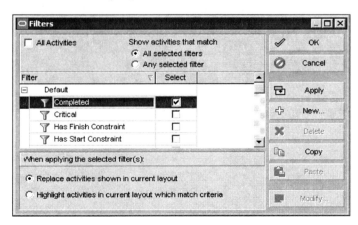

The **Filters** dialog box allows you to choose from a set of pre-defined filters, or make your own. These filters are the same ones you use to filter activities in the main P6 Activities screen.

You can choose to add new activities which are in the project, but are not in the baseline. They will be added to the baseline, but without any actuals from the current project file applied to them.

You can also choose to delete activities that are in the baseline but which are no longer in the current project. Presumably these would be activities which have been removed from the project scope and that you no longer want.

Adding and deleting activities as needed helps to ensure that your baselines are still comparing similar items.

When updating activities, there is a button called **Update Options...** which will yet again bring up many options, as shown below.

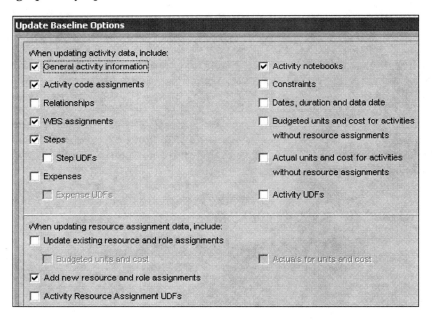

Here you can choose what activity properties to update at a fine level of detail. On this screen you can also choose how to handle resource assignments for the activities.

With such flexibility, of course, comes great responsibility. There should be a consistent policy of how baselines will be updated, and this knowledge should be understood and accepted by everyone who will be using baselines for project analysis. Often this is a required quality check and the security of creating or assigning baselines is a task done by the Project Management office or a Change Management/Controls board with strict procedures.

Baseline assignment

We have discussed a lot about how to create and manage baselines. This is all fine, but the purpose behind baselines is in project analysis. To do this, you must assign baselines to your project. There are two main kinds of baselines assignment:

Project Baseline is a baseline that is set as the official baseline for the project. This baseline is the one used to calculate all variance fields, to populate information on web dashboards and controls icons and indicators on charts and dashboards and in columns. This is the one used for the reporting engine. All users who view the project and look at baseline information will see the data from this and only this baseline.

User Baseline: Each user can have up to three personal baselines assigned in the Professional client. In the web client, however, there is only one user baseline allowed. This allows a user to compare the current project with up to three previous snapshots (baselines) at a given time. Some good examples for comparison include:

- Current versus end of last month
- Current versus end of year
- Current versus end of planning phase

Other items to compare include Original Planning, Original Early Dates, and Original Late Dates. Each of these would be interesting data for progress analysis.

The columns with BL will show variance from the baseline assigned as the Project Baseline. Columns for BL1 would show variances between the current project and the project baseline in the user's "Primary Baseline" assigned slot. BL2 is secondary, and BL3 is the tertiary User Baseline.

You can get to the baselines by pressing the 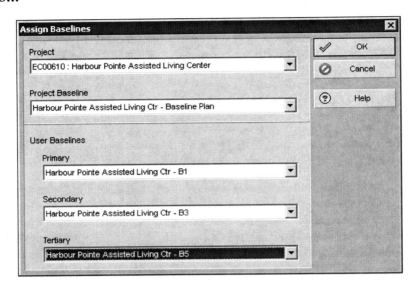 icon, or by pressing **Project | Assign Baselines...**

The earlier screenshot shows baselines that were automatically named by P6. Here we see that the **Project Baseline** is set to **Baseline Plan**, while the **User Baselines** are set to **B1**, **B3**, and **B5**, respectively.

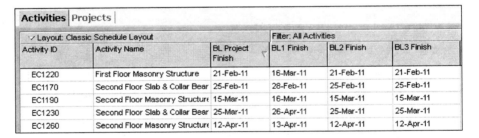

Activity ID	Activity Name	BL Project Finish	BL1 Finish	BL2 Finish	BL3 Finish
EC1220	First Floor Masonry Structure	21-Feb-11	16-Mar-11	21-Feb-11	21-Feb-11
EC1170	Second Floor Slab & Collar Bear	25-Feb-11	28-Feb-11	25-Feb-11	25-Feb-11
EC1190	Second Floor Masonry Structure	15-Mar-11	16-Mar-11	15-Mar-11	15-Mar-11
EC1230	Second Floor Slab & Collar Bear	25-Mar-11	26-Apr-11	25-Mar-11	25-Mar-11
EC1260	Second Floor Masonry Structure	12-Apr-11	13-Apr-11	12-Apr-11	12-Apr-11

When viewing the activities, or project, or WBS, there are many baseline-related columns to choose from. In the previous screenshot we simply choose to show the Activity name and ID, as well as the finish dates for the Project Baseline (BL Project), User Primary baseline (BL1), and secondary and tertiary. Note that if another user uses this layout, they will see the same dates for **BL Project Finish**, but may see other values for BL1 through BL3 if their user baselines are set differently.

Updating project status

Statusing refers to the practice of applying actual dates, costs, and hours to the project. This is when your planned schedule begins to reflect what actually happened on the project. This can mean simply updating actual start and/or finish dates and remaining durations for activities, or updating hours worked and remaining hours for resources, or updating completed activity percentage. But often the situation is more complicated than that and a number of questions must be considered:

- Who will perform the updates?
- How will the data be entered?
- How often will updates take place?
- What metrics will be used so that all team members view project status in the same way?

The answers to these questions will vary widely between companies, and will even vary among different types of projects at the same company. However, for any specific project, status updates should be performed consistently throughout the project's lifetime.

There are conceptually three ways you can apply actuals. They do have overlap but at a high level they are:

- **Auto Complete Actuals**: If an activity is set to auto complete actuals, then when you schedule the project, all work before the data date is set to actual and all work after that date remains planned. Duration remaining is then computed based on the remaining amounts of resource units and the finish date is set accordingly.

- **Percentage Complete**: You can set the percent complete or remaining duration for each activity. When you schedule (F9) or apply actuals, the percentage complete of work done as of the Data Date is considered actual, and the remaining percentage is used to forecast the activity finish date and cost.

- **Detailed Quantities**: You can enter the specific hours worked on each activity, on an aggregate or time-based basis. This is generally done through Progress Reporter or some other external application, though it could also be done directly in P6.

Typically, progress is reported on the project by entering remaining duration on the **Status** tab, entering actual and remaining hours for each resource on the **Resource** tab and updating percent complete (if it is a physical percent complete type activity). Then all other items are recalculated using the **Schedule** function (F9). If that information is reported through Progress Reporter or an integrated timesheet, then it populates those same fields automatically; but the F9 calculation still must be done to progress the schedule up to the Data Date. For more on Data Date and scheduling, see *Chapter 7, Scheduling and Constraints*.

Auto compute actuals

P6 can compute actuals automatically when you apply actuals. This can be helpful for certain tasks whose cost runs uniformly. One example would be a night watchman, whose hours and costs would never vary from the schedule, such that given a Data Date, all hours and costs prior to the date are actual, and all hours and costs in the future are remaining.

Actuals will be automatically updated when you click **Tools | Apply Actuals**. Please note this should only be done when all work on those activities is progressing exactly as planned.

Budgeted Expen			$16.88	$20.00	$20.00	$20.00		$20.00	$3.13
Actual Expense			$16.88	$20.00					
Remaining Exper					$20.00	$20.00		$20.00	$3.13
At Completion Ex			$16.88	$20.00	$20.00	$20.00		$20.00	$3.13

In the previous screenshot we have an activity which is budgeted to cost $20 per day in expenses. It is set to auto compute actuals. When we apply actuals, the actual expense amount simply becomes the budgeted expense amount. Note in the above example, the first period indicated less than the $20/day rate due to less than a whole day being charged for the resource usage. Likewise, the last period captures the remaining portion of the allocated work, which again is less than a whole day.

To turn on auto compute, view activities and customize the columns displayed to include this field, as shown in the following screenshot:

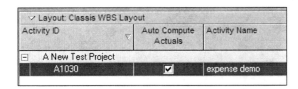

Turning this on for resources is done in the same way and can also be done from the **Resource Details** screen. However, this changes the *default* setting for the selected resource being added to activities, and it will not change the settings for current resource assignments.

 This is risky since all activities that person is assigned to throughout the tool will now auto generate actual amounts indicating all of that person's work is being done exactly as planned. This is rarely the case.

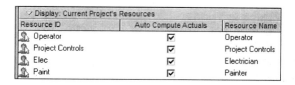

Note that if **Auto Compute** is set at the activity level, it will override the Auto Compute setting for the resources assigned to it.

Percent complete

You can also update activity status by entering the completed percentage against it. In the **Activity Details** screen, you can set the percentage complete for the activity to be one of these three types:

- **Duration**: It simply calculates the current date versus the start date and planned duration.

- **Physical**: It requires statusing both resource units (remaining duration or percent complete). This delivers a better representation of progress, but at the cost of requiring greater detail.

- **Units**: It requires statusing of remaining units. The percent of delivered units compared to planned units drives progress for the activity.

When you set this value, the activity status tab changes to reflect which of the three percent complete types you have chosen.

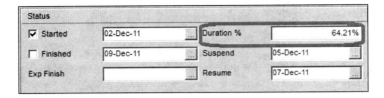

You can then update the activity by updating the percent complete. When you apply actuals, the remaining duration of the activity will be based on the percent remaining.

Be careful to choose the correct percent complete type on activities during planning. *Chapter 2, Getting Around: Understanding and Customizing the P6 Interface* and *Chapter 7, Scheduling and Constraints* for more information regarding percent complete types.

Entering hours

You can also enter the amount of work completed by the resources assigned to the activity. This can be done within P6, but is often done instead in a timesheet application such as Progress Reporter or, in Version 8.x, through the TeamMember iPhone application. This application is also pending availability in the Android market.

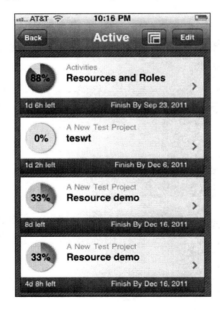

Note that hours entered through Progress Reporter are subject to approval before being applied, based on the P6 application settings, whereas hours entered through TeamMember are applied immediately

Actual dates

In its simplest form, this means finding an activity on the schedule, showing its **Details** tab, opening its **Status** tab, putting a checkmark next to its **Started** or **Finished** dates. This *solidifies* the date and removes it from calculations when the F9 Schedule feature is used to update the project.

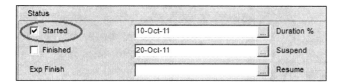

When you check the date on the **Activity Details** screen, the date is modified with the letter **A** after it on the screen, both in the column, and in the Gantt chart. In this example, we have updated the activity named **Activities** to have an actual start date of 10-Oct-2011.

 An asterix (*) will appear next to any date that has been constrained and not allowed to calculate with the progress information given.

What does this do? When you set an actual date, then you are telling P6 that the work has actually started or finished. If finished, then this activity is no longer affected by the scheduling process.

If we set the start date to actual, then all work before the data date is set to actual, and all time after the data date is now remaining. Next time you schedule the project, its start date can no longer change. The scheduling engine will instead calculate the finish date, based on how the activity is set up.

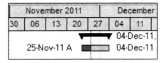

When the activity is completed, check the **Finished** box and enter the Actual Finish date. The hours worked then turn from remaining to actual for the entire activity, regardless of the data date.

Another way to status multiple activities is to include Actual Start/Actual Finish in the column display so that the user can enter the actual date directly in the column. If there are a number of activities with the same date, then the **Fill Cell** can be used to quickly populate all selected records based on the "First" selected cell.

Actual costs

Costs can arise from two sources: Expenses and Resources.

Expenses, as we saw in *Chapter 5, Adding Activities and Relationships,* are tied to Activities. You can view all project expenses by choosing from the main menu **Project | Expenses...**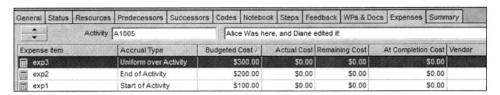

The costs of an expense can accrue in three ways:

- **Start of Activity**: It causes the actual cost to occur as soon as the activity begins.

- **End of Activity**: It causes the cost to be delayed until the activity ends.

- **Uniform over Activity**: It spreads the cost in time uniformly across the activity.

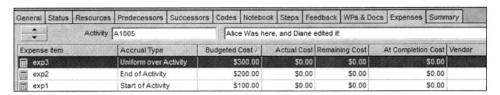

| General | Status | Resources | Predecessors | Successors | Codes | Notebook | Steps | Feedback | WPs & Docs | Expenses | Summary |

| Activity | A1005 | Alice Was here, and Diane edited it! |

Expense item	Accrual Type	Budgeted Cost /	Actual Cost	Remaining Cost	At Completion Cost	Vendor
exp3	Uniform over Activity	$300.00	$0.00	$0.00	$0.00	
exp2	End of Activity	$200.00	$0.00	$0.00	$0.00	
exp1	Start of Activity	$100.00	$0.00	$0.00	$0.00	

Expenses are simple to deal with, but the three ways of placing the costs in time are not always what you need. If you want to have finer control over actual costs, you should use resources and resource curves.

Resources

When you apply actual units to a resource, through whatever input method, the result is that the actual hours are updated and remaining units are calculated. If you wish you can update the remaining units, which will in turn update the **At Completion Units**, which is the sum of actual and remaining units.

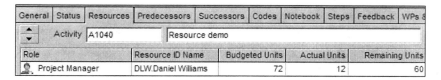

The resource's **Rate** from the resource's **Units and Prices** tab is used to translate these actual hours into actual costs. See *Chapter 6, Roles and Resources* for a detailed discussion of resource curves.

Summary

Now we have seen the use of baselines to measure how a project schedule changes over time. We have seen how to create and manage baselines, how to convert and restore them, how to update them, and how to assign them for reporting purposes. We have also seen how these schedules are updated with actual data.

If you are curious about the many ways to use baselines, look up the topic *Milestone Trend Analysis* on the Web. This powerful technique uses baselines and project milestones to view the *trajectories* of various project elements so that potentially dangerous trends can be observed and handled proactively.

At the end of all the work of creating baselines and updating your progress, one day your project comes to a close and the schedule is complete. But of course once you have successfully closed a project, it is time to create a new one! In the next chapter we look at creating new projects using templates, and we show how to create templates with the data you have collected in existing projects.

10
Project Templates

In *Chapter 4*, *Creating a New Project and Work Breakdown Structure*, we walked through the steps of manually setting up a brand new project. While creating a project, there are several important steps involved, and creating a full project from scratch can take a good deal of time. Project templates help you create new projects by providing a common set of project properties and items that can be used to create new projects quickly. This will allow you to get right to implementing your project plan.

For example, you may have a number of WBS elements that are commonly used in every project. You can create a template that contains these elements. When you generate a new project from this template, the WBS elements will be added automatically. Similarly, you can take an existing project and convert it into a template. This allows you to take successful projects from the past and use them as a blueprint for future work.

 Templates do not have to be entire projects, think of a template that can be only a single WBS element to add to projects, such as flooring finishes. Then add as many of these WBS templates to the project as needed to complete several floors of the building.

With templates, you do not have to start over at step one each and every time you have a new project. This is particularly helpful when you are working in an environment with many users, resources, and/or projects as it gives repeatability and consistency to projects in your organization.

Note that project templates are a new feature in P6 version 8.0. However, this functionality is only available in the enterprise version. Later in this chapter, we will show you how to mimic the templates feature using Primavera Professional.

By the end of this chapter you should understand how to:

- Create and customize a new project template
- Create a new project from an existing template
- Add a WBS from a project template

Creating a new project template

As mentioned, you can either create a template from an existing project, or create a template from scratch. Let's walk through the steps of creating a new template for the first time. From the main menu, choose the **Projects** tab and click on the **Add Project Template** icon:

The following screen appears, showing you the main properties to set on the new template:

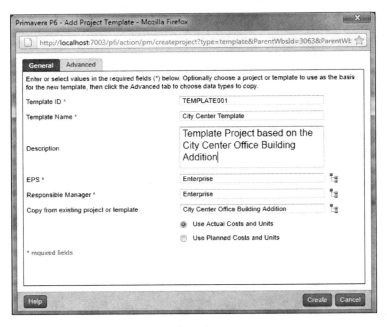

A template has a number of project properties which you must fill in. These are marked by red asterisks. The other fields are optional, and are explained as follows:

- **Template ID**: A short, unique name for the template.

- **Template Name**: A more descriptive name for the template.

- **Description**: This should describe how the template will be used, and/or where it came from.

- **EPS**: The default **Enterprise Project Structure (EPS)** node for the template. Some companies have one special node for holding all the templates, while others will place the templates under specific EPS nodes, which represent projects with common properties. For example, you may have one EPS node for capital projects, and one for turnarounds. These nodes would each have their own set of templates specific to each line of work.

- **Responsible Manager**: The default responsible manager or organizational breakdown structure node (defines who typically would be able to see this type of project).

- **Copy from existing project or template**: Allows you to create a template based on an existing project or template. Note that not all project items are copied into the template. The following items are not included:
  - Documents
  - Issues
  - Team usage
  - Workspaces

- **Use Actual Costs and Units/Use Planned Costs and Units**: These options are only available when creating a template from an existing project. When copying from an existing project, actual costs are often chosen, as this represents the true story of how past projects have performed.

If you are creating a brand-new template, this is all that is required at this point. However, if you wish to copy from a project or template, the **Advanced** tab will be enabled.

Creating a template from an existing project

If you choose an existing project or template, there are more decisions to make, as that project or template will have data in it already, and you must decide which data to use in the new template. The **Advanced** tab shows you a number of project data items to choose from:

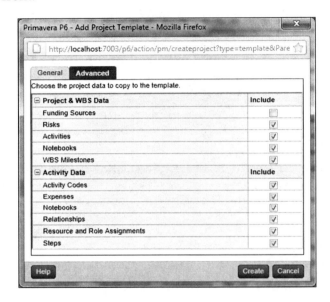

Why choose some items and not others? It may be that you only want the project skeleton in place, such as the WBS milestones, because you use the same ones on every project. However, you may not want to copy all of the resource roles and assignments, because different people will be working on new projects. Your circumstances and needs may vary greatly. As you can see, creating a new template is not that difficult once you have existing projects or templates to start from.

Once you press the **Create** button the new template will be created under the EPS node that you selected on the **General** screen. Next you will want to modify the template. Perhaps you copied it from an existing project, along with the project milestones, but now you want to use different milestones in your template. Simply open up the template, just as though it was a regular project, and modify the milestones.

Creating a new project from a template

Now that we have created a template, let's see how to use it. Imagine that you are starting five new projects, all of which share common features, such as WBS milestones and activity codes. Rather than typing the same information into each of the five projects, we will use a template to create all of them so that they are uniform to begin with.

From the main menu on the **Projects** screen, choose the **Add Project** icon shown as follows:

You can also use the button on the toolbar as shown in the following screenshot:

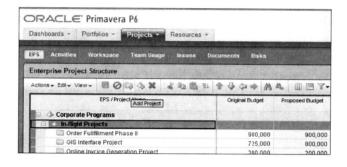

Then fill in the appropriate **Project ID**, **Project Name**, and **Description** in the pop-up window that appears. Using the **hierarchy** icon to the right of the EPS field, select the area of the EPS the project should reside within. In the **Responsible Manager** field, select from the OBS an appropriate assignment—remember this is a security setting allowing all those within that level of OBS to have access to this new project:

The **Project Planned Start** date should be the start date of the first activity within your critical path schedule (likely a project start milestone activity.)

It is a good practice to avoid using the **Must Finish By** date as it constrains your critical path. See *Chapter 7, Scheduling and Constraints* and *Chapter 8, Baselines and Statusing,* for more information.

Finally, using the **hierarchy** icon at the right of the **Copy from existing project or Template** field, select the appropriate template for this project. This is it—the one step that causes your project to obtain its properties from your template. Click on **OK**. Then select the **Create** button to finish creating your new project.

This works great if you are using the Enterprise version of P6. But what if you are only using the professional version? There is a poor man's template technique that we will discuss in the next section.

Inserting a WBS into an existing project

Historically successful projects should become templates for future use. Yet perhaps you do not want to use all of a template to start your new project, just part of it. A new feature in P6 allows you to do exactly this; to insert one or more WBS elements into an existing project from a template. This feature is used to add consistency, avoid duplication of effort, and to ensure compliance to organizational policies, even on projects that are not generated directly from templates.

To insert a WBS element into a project file follow the ensuing steps:

1. Locate your project file in the EPS screen and open it.
2. Then navigate to the **Activities** screen.
3. Highlight the parent WBS element into which you wish to add a template WBS element.

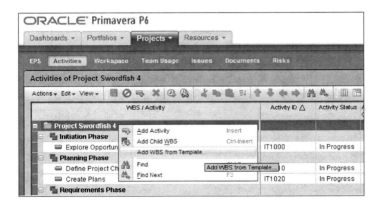

4. Right-click on the parent element, then select the **Add WBS from Template...** option from the pop-up features list.

5. Select the appropriate template and click on the plus (**+**) sign at the left-hand side to expand the WBS hierarchy within that template. Then highlight the appropriate WBS element and click on **OK**.

In the following screenshot, we are adding the **Key Milestones** WBS element from the IT template.

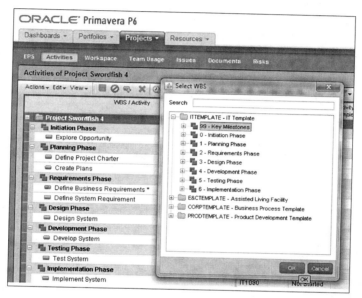

As you can see, the WBS elements are copied into the new project.

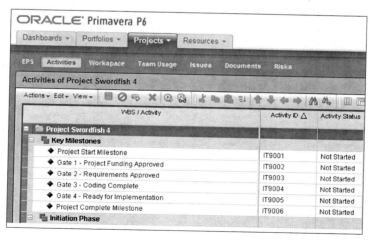

Now you have successfully copied those WBS elements from the template into your existing project. Remember that security settings will allow you to grant access to a specific WBS element across all projects so WBS elements from templates further allow this feature to be used as an analysis and comparison tool among all projects. For example, the engineering group could view the engineering WBS across all the projects and compare the **Key Milestones** within that element.

In the optional client or professional version of P6, WBS elements can be copied and pasted from one project to another, or one project may be used as a template for another project. The feature entitled templates does not exist in these tools, but a workaround is to open more than one project at a time, copy WBS from one project, and paste them into another. Alternatively, you can make a copy of one project and rename it, thus using the elements of the first project as a template. Be sure to keep these templated WBS elements or project files in the **What if** status to avoid reporting them as active activities and assignments.

 Create historical data by keeping an archive of completed projects. These can be analyzed for use in creating new project templates.

Summary

The reader should now understand the benefits of using project templates, how to create them, and how to use them. Templates allow a user to begin with a framework of WBS, activities, and other project data to ensure that new projects are consistent, have repeatable quality results, and that they comply with internal and external standard procedures.

Speaking of project quality, in the next chapter we discuss Portfolio Analysis, a powerful technique that allows you to compare sets of projects to identify their strengths and weaknesses. Hopefully, by using the standard practices in creating your projects through templates, all of your projects will be successful.

11
Portfolios

A project is rarely performed in a vacuum. More likely, it is one among many other projects that your company manages. It is very helpful to take all projects with similar characteristics and analyze them together as one portfolio (or grouping) of projects. This is a great way to see the *big picture*. P6 has a number of features to help you manage your project portfolios. The desktop client application is capable of grouping projects and summarizing the data, but the best features for portfolio management reside in the web application.

In this chapter we will cover:

- Managing portfolios
- Creating a portfolio
- Managing portfolio views
- Scenarios

Managing portfolios

The main P6 web page has four main tabs available: **Dashboards**, **Portfolios**, **Projects**, and **Resources**. Click on the arrow in the **Portfolios** tab to navigate to the **Portfolios** section.

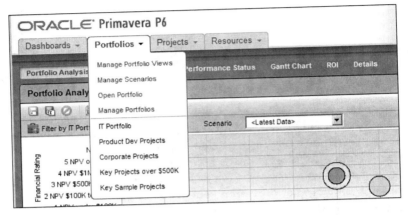

Choose **Portfolios | Manage Portfolios** to see a list of all current portfolios. This will show the portfolio descriptions, the number of projects in each, and the accessibility of the portfolio. Click on the down arrow in the **Projects** column to show the list of specific projects within a given project portfolio.

Projects are assigned to portfolios either through a set of criteria or manually (see next section). Portfolios may be grouped by project codes or other features which we will explore later.

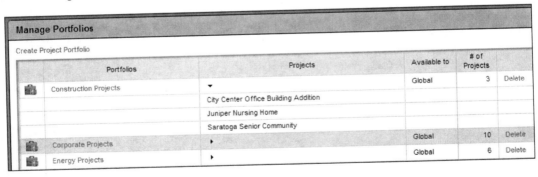

The composition of a portfolio varies widely. Different portfolios may cover projects in a specific geographic area. They may cover projects within different business units. They may be organized by project size. One of the great advantages of portfolios is their flexibility. In a single instance of P6, you may have portfolios that slice and dice your projects according to all those criteria so that each analyst can view projects in the way that makes best sense to him or her.

Creating a portfolio

Let's walk through setting up a new portfolio by choosing **Portfolios | Manage Portfolios | Create Project Portfolio**.

A screen as shown in the following screenshot appears:

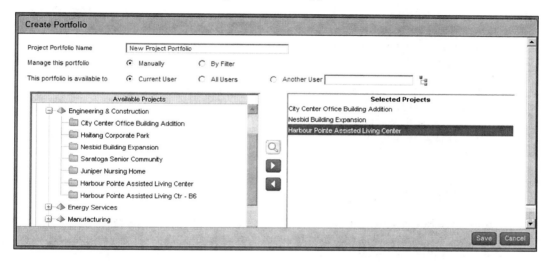

Project Portfolio Name should describe the nature of the portfolio. You may always rename the portfolio later on.

The projects in the portfolio may be added **Manually** or **By Filter**. In the previous screenshot, you can see that we have manually added three projects to our new portfolio. Projects are added and removed from the portfolio using the arrows.

If you choose **By Filter**, the screen changes to show a list of filters for the portfolio. You can filter on a number of properties and the filter can require either all criteria to match, or any criteria to match.

In the next screenshot we are filtering for projects that are integrated to **Fusion** and which have an **Estimated Project Size** within a certain range.

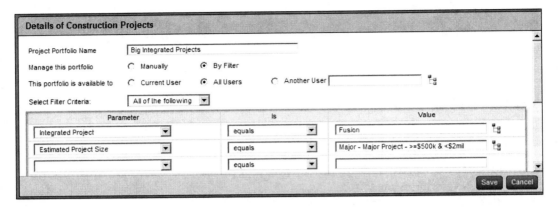

You can filter on many project properties, including Project Codes and user-defined fields.

Portfolios can also have different security. They can be global to all users, available to a list of users, or only visible to the user who created them.

Once the portfolio is created, you can view it and its list of projects in the **Manage Portfolios** screen.

Portfolio Views

Portfolio Views helps you to analyze the projects in your portfolios by providing a number of helpful graphics and tools. P6 comes with a number of pre-defined reports that allow you to quickly take advantage of a handful of industry-standard reports.

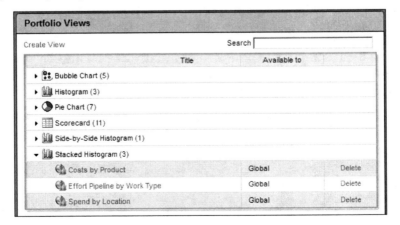

You can create your own view by clicking on **Create View**. A screen as shown in the following screenshot appears:

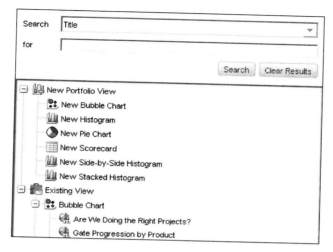

A number of view types are available:

- Bubble Chart lets you choose X and Y axes, and then a metric for the bubble size. This gives a visual for relative size and comparative analysis:

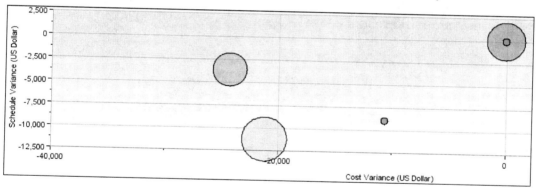

- Histogram lets you choose X as the base, where X is generally a discrete quantity such as phase or project name, and Y is a non-discrete quantity such as budget amount.

 This is not a true mathematical histogram, as in here there is no concept of bins or bin size.

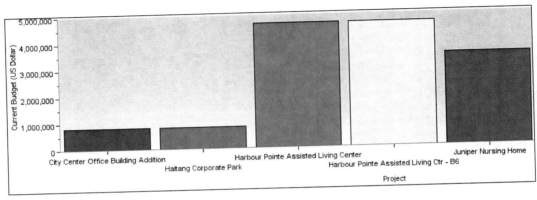

- Pie Chart: In this mode, you choose a quantity to measure, such as budget, and an item to group by, such as geographic area. In the example shown next, the chart groups projects by geographic area with the size of the pie slice proportional to the total budget:

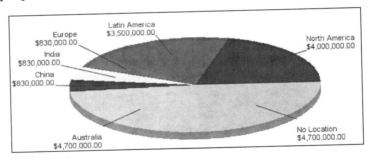

- Scorecard: This representation is an Excel-like document with rows and columns, subtotals, and headers.

☑	Name △	Original Budget	Proposed Budget	Current Budget
⊟ **Total**		**$19,390,000.00**	**$19,390,000.00**	**$19,390,000.00**
⊟ **Engineering & Cons...**		**$19,390,000.00**	**$19,390,000.00**	**$19,390,000.00**
☑	⊞ 📁 City Center Offic...	$830,000.00	$830,000.00	$830,000.00
☑	⊞ 📁 Haitang Corporat...	$830,000.00	$830,000.00	$830,000.00
☑	⊞ 📁 Harbour Pointe A...	$4,700,000.00	$4,700,000.00	$4,700,000.00
☑	⊞ 📁 Harbour Pointe A...	$4,700,000.00	$4,700,000.00	$4,700,000.00
☑	⊞ 📁 Juniper Nursing ...	$3,500,000.00	$3,500,000.00	$3,500,000.00
☑	⊞ 📁 Nesbid Building E...	$830,000.00	$830,000.00	$830,000.00
☑	⊞ 📁 Saratoga Senior ...	$4,000,000.00	$4,000,000.00	$4,000,000.00

Note the checkboxes to the left-hand side of each project. If you uncheck a box, then that project will be removed from the totals displayed. This will also remove that project from the accompanying portfolio view.

- Side-by-Side Histogram: This format is similar to the histogram above, but allows you to group by the items on the X axis. For example, you can show a histogram of total budget, per project sponsor, broken down by region for each sponsor, as shown in the following screenshot:

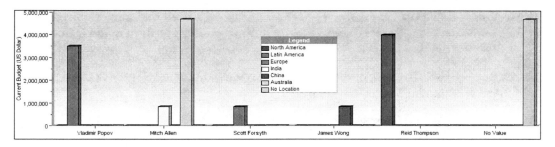

- Stacked Histogram is also similar to the standard histogram. But in this case, the vertical bars can be grouped to display their composition. In the following example, we show project size versus current budget and then split out how much each region contributes to each budget bar.

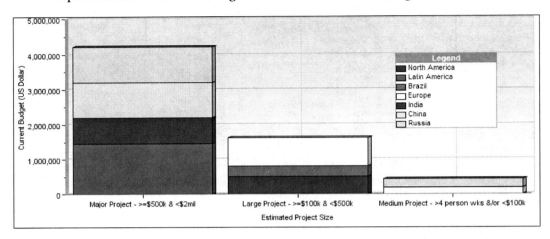

Scenarios

When you view a portfolio using the techniques above, all of the data displayed comes real-time from the P6 database. Sometimes you may wish to make a snapshot of a graph for display later on. This is where scenarios can help.

To make a scenario, simply open up a portfolio view and click **Save**. A new screen will appear as shown in this screenshot:

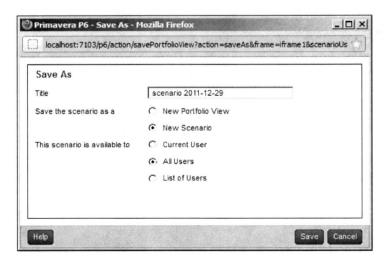

Enter a title for the scenario. It is a good practice to put the current date into the scenario name in a manner that sorts well by date. For example, the name can begin with YYYY-MM-DD, as in 2012-12-31.

Once you have made a scenario, you can use it when viewing portfolios. In the following screenshot, we are comparing the current budget data for the IT Portfolio with a scenario from 2011-12-29. You can see that the budget taken up by Brazil has grown since then.

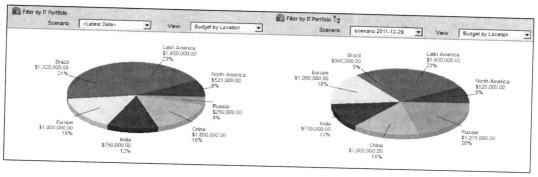

User Defined Fields (UDFs)

Earlier we mentioned that a portfolio filter could be based on user-defined fields. These fields are custom items you can add to P6 to hold special properties that are not natively included with P6. For example, you could add a date at the project level to represent the year in which a facility was commissioned. Or you could add a field to hold a project number to use on reports. Or you could add a cost field to represent the initial estimated cost of the project.

The fields that come with P6 are designed to meet the needs of the majority of users. UDFs allow you to provide additional input that is specifically tailored to your company and your industry. The risk of using a UDF instead of built-in fields is that UDF fields are easily overwritten and there are no controls in place to ensure appropriate spelling or other mistakes. UDFs often are used to bring in data from another system through an automated integration script.

UDFs are not limited to projects. They can be assigned to all of the following entities:

- Project
- WBS
- Activity
- Expense

- Step
- Assignment
- Resource
- Issue
- Risk
- Document

All UDFs are defined in a similar screen with similar options. In the following example we will show project-level UDFs.

To access UDF definitions, go to the upper right-hand corner and choose **Administer | Enterprise Data**.

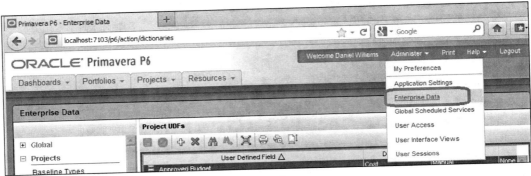

The screen that appears has a menu running down the left-hand side. Choose the item labeled **Project UDFs**:

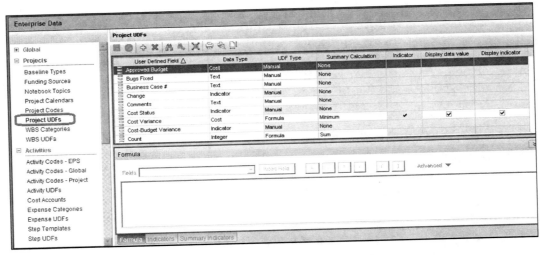

This shows all of the UDFs defined for projects. There are a number of types of UDF:

- Text is a text field that can hold about a thousand characters.
- Integer holds any positive or negative integer number.
- Number holds a decimal number which is shown to two decimal places.
- Cost holds a currency amount in the user's currency and displays the number of decimals specified in the global currency settings, or no decimals, if that has been specified in the user settings.
- Start Date lets you enter a start date.
- Finish Date lets you enter a finish date.
- Indicator lets the user choose a symbol to display.

A UDF may also have a formula, an indicator, and a summary indicator. A formula can be created from numerical values, and basic mathematical operators can be applied to the values. For example, a formula could be:

[Actual Labor Cost] * 1.20

This UDF would then show 1.20 times the Actual Labor Cost. These calculated UDFs are invaluable and are very similar to Excel. With the latest version of P6, the spreadsheet-like interface, coupled with these calculated fields will likely allow you to consolidate your project data in P6 and not use MS Excel as often, if at all.

An **indicator** will show an icon based on a formula. In the following example, we use ranges of cost amount to display circles of different colors. A variety of icons exist for you to choose including checks, flags, and even happy and sad faces.

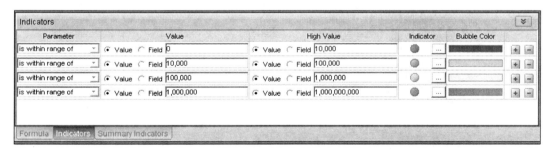

A summary indicator is similar to an indicator, but it determines which icons to be shown at the summary level. It is helpful to define the summary icons in the same way as the non-summary icons.

Summary

This chapter has introduced us to project portfolios. We have seen how to create and manage them and how to use them to analyze projects using views and scenarios. We have also discussed user-defined fields which can help when organizing and filtering projects within your portfolios. In the following chapters we will dive deeper into creating, customizing, and using portfolios and scenarios.

12
Portfolio Analysis

Now that we have seen how to create and maintain portfolios, let's take an in-depth look at how to use them. First, we will discuss how to use the main Portfolio Analysis screen. Then we will dive into the different kinds of analysis views, how to configure each kind, and what the various options and settings do.

In this chapter, we will cover:

- The Portfolio Analysis screen
- Scorecard screens
- Graphical displays

Note that all of the items and examples in this chapter are for the Web client, not P6 Professional. In our opinion, the Web client is superior for viewing and maintaining portfolios.

The Portfolio Analysis screen

To get to the Portfolio Analysis screen, click on **Portfolios**, then choose one of the available views that appears in the lower portion of the menu. If you would like to re-visit a previously-opened portfolio, the most recent ones appear at the bottom of the dropdown menu when you click the down arrow.

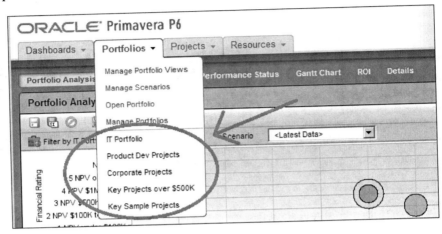

This drop-down menu of portfolios contains the last five portfolios that the user has most recently viewed.

 Be cautious about assigning a portfolio to another user account. The account you are logged into will no longer be able to view that specific portfolio, and if you choose such a portfolio from your most recently used list, you will get a warning that the portfolio "does not exist or you no longer have access to it."

When you choose or create a portfolio, it opens in an **analysis view**. P6 keeps track of which view you were last using with each portfolio and by default always opens that last view for each portfolio.

An analysis view consists of two screens showing portfolio data. The screens can be oriented horizontally or vertically. Use the radio buttons near the upper right side of the screen to choose either horizontal or vertical display. You may need to refresh your screen after changing orientation, as the screens do not always resize after the switch.

Also, note that in analysis view there are always exactly two screens displayed.

You may view the two screens horizontally, with one above the other:

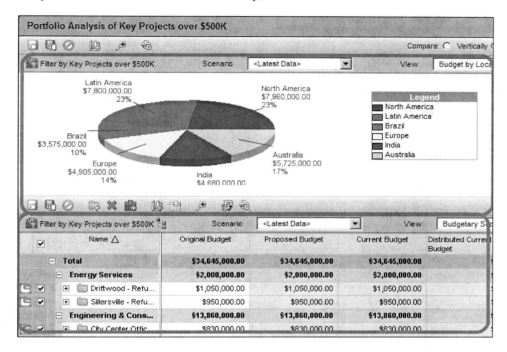

Or you may view the two screens vertically, or side-by-side:

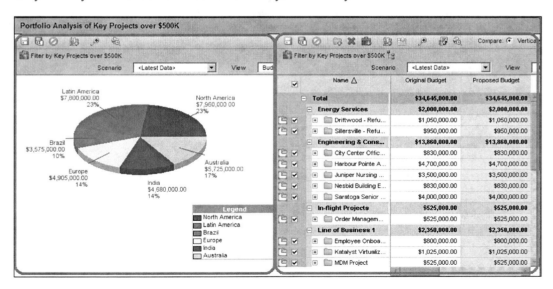

If you wish to look at only one of the views, you can click on the magnifying glass icon . This will change the screen to show only one view. Click on the magnifying glass again to return to the dual-view.

One idea behind Portfolio Analysis in P6 is that it gives you the ability to quickly make ad-hoc reports. You can quickly change the view and alter what data is displayed and in what form. There are two main kinds of views — scorecards and graphs. In the next sections we discuss these in detail, starting with scorecards.

Scorecards

A scorecard displays a grid of data in cells, much like you see in an EPS or WBS view, or in an Excel report. And also as with Excel, you can quickly choose what data to display, move columns around, and change the grouping and sorting of the data. Here is an example of a scorecard:

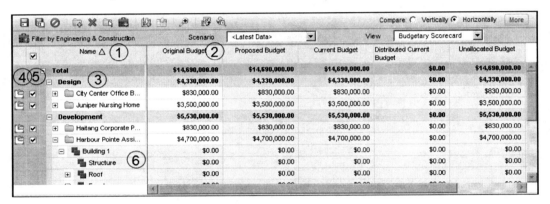

There are six features on the screen that deserve clarification:

1. The project name is always displayed as the leftmost column, and it is frozen or locked on screen.

2. The other columns are defined with the view.

3. Grouping can be performed at many levels, and subtotals are displayed with the groupings.

4. Clicking on the leftmost folder icon will open up the **Project** tab and take you immediately to the selected project.

5. If a graphical view is displayed alongside the scorecard view, then this checkbox determines whether the corresponding project is shown on the accompanying graph.

6. Under each project, data is shown down to the WBS level.

Choosing data to display

There are three areas that you can customize on a scorecard: **Columns**, **Group**, and **Waterline**.

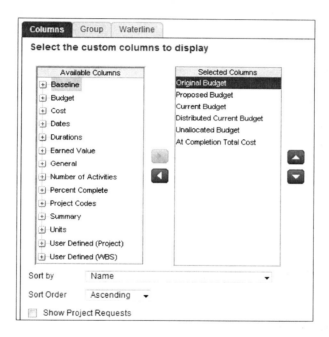

Columns

The columns available are a mixture of Project-level data as well as WBS-level data. You can choose any of these columns on the left-hand side and press the right-arrow to move them to the **Selected Columns**. On the right-hand side you may re-order the columns by selecting them and using the up and down arrows.

You can choose the default sorting of the data as well. Once on the scorecard screen, you can change the order by simply clicking on the column headers.

The option **Show Project Requests** determines whether potential projects should also be included in the scorecard.

One thing that differs from Excel is that you cannot edit formulas on a scorecard. However, you can achieve the same goal using formulas in User-Defined Fields. See the previous chapter for more information on creating formulas in UDFs.

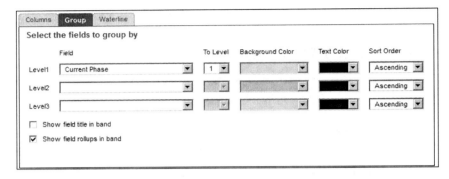

Sorting basically categorizes the data and then displays it in a hierarchy by the colors selected.

Up to ten **group levels** can be defined for a scorecard. Each of them can have a different color and you can choose how the group is displayed and how values are rolled up.

Waterline

A waterline can be set on the view. This will take the scorecard data and rank projects as either above or below the waterline threshold. Those projects below the waterline threshold (control limit) will have a blue background, while those above will not.

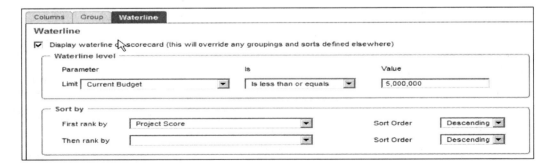

 When you choose to display a waterline in your scorecard, the waterline overrides any grouping and sorting you may have applied.

The waterline parameter determines what quantity you are measuring, and that quantity is viewed *cumulatively*. In this case we are looking at the current budget and sorting by project score. The waterline is drawn after the cumulative current budget of the top scoring projects exceeds $5,000,000.

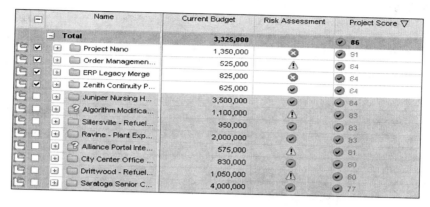

For example, if you needed to find what top-ranked projects you could fund with a total of $5,000,000, this chart clearly shows you the answer!

Excel Export: Scorecards can be exported to Excel by pressing the export icon ![icon] at the top of the display. Note that the generated file will go to a temporary location on your computer – you must click **Save As...** in order to save and make changes to it.

Graphical displays

In this section we will see the various graphical display option provided by the P6.

Pie charts

A pie chart is the simplest graph, displaying one dimension – the angle or "slice of the pie. There are only two things to select for the pie chart: the *data* to represent and the *grouping* of that data across projects in the portfolio, as shown in the following screenshot:

Color Theme can be Primary or Pastel colors.

Pie data label determines whether the data represented is labeled. For example, if the data is **Current Budget** then the pie data label will show the amount of the current budget in each grouping.

Group by label determines how and whether to label the groups. For example, when grouping by region, this determines whether the region names will be displayed.

Show Percentage determines whether the percentage of each grouping is displayed.

Show 3-D determines whether the pie is displayed face-on, or at an angle with a third dimension.

The following two images show the effect of these choices. The first image shows what the chart looks like using Primary Colors and none of the boxes checked.

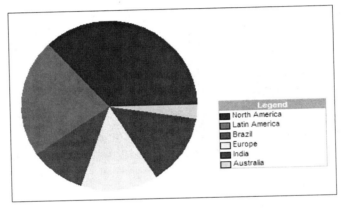

The next illustration shows a chart using the Pastel Color palette and all of the options checked:

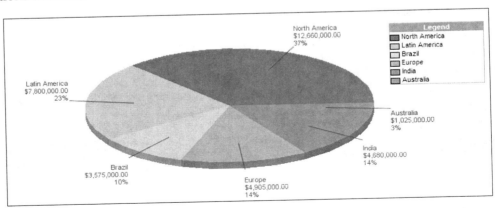

Note that in each illustration, there is a **Legend** displayed. All graphical views have such a legend. The legend shows the label which represents the coloring seen on the graphs.

Graphs cannot be exported to Excel as a Scorecard, but all graphs can be printed out. An example of a pie chart printout is shown in the following screenshot:

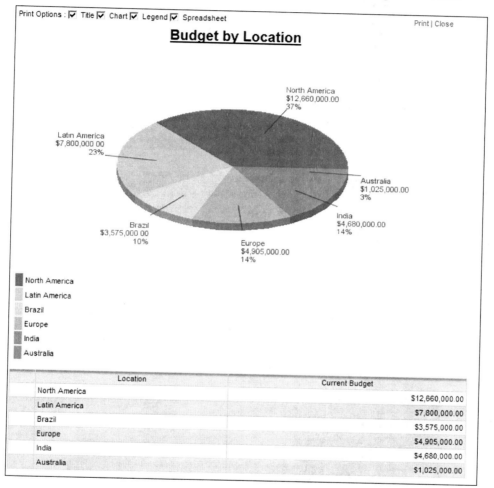

You can choose a number of options: whether to print the title, to show the chart, to show the legend, or to show the underlying values in a tabular form.

All of the other graphs can also be printed, and their options are identical.

Histograms

Next up after the pie chart is the histogram. Note that this is not a true histogram, which is a diagram representing a distribution of data. An example of a true histogram would be a chart showing the number of activities completed each month. Histograms in the Portfolio Analysis view are rather a "Relative order of Magnitude" chart presented as an X-Y chart.

There are two quantities to choose from — data on the x-axis and data on the y-axis. Note that the data to display on the x-axis can be any of the available project or WBS properties. However, the y-axis can only represent numeric data. For example, you cannot choose project codes.

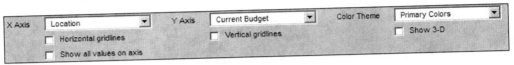

Like a pie chart, a histogram can be shown in primary or pastel colors, and can also be shown in 3D. It can also show horizontal and vertical grid lines. Note, however, that there is no Legend as each distinct color corresponds to an item on the x-axis.

The last option **Show all values on axis** determines whether to show all possible X-axis values, even if there are no projects representing each value. For example, here is a histogram showing the current budget by the project code **Location**. In the first screen none of the choices are selected.

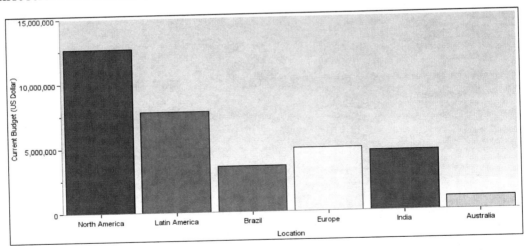

In the next screen, we choose all of the options for the same data.

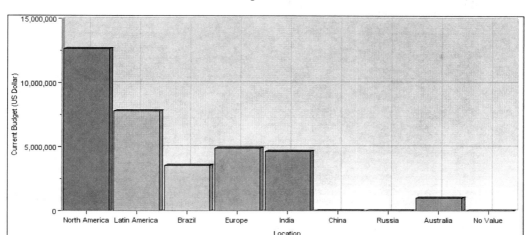

Notice that there are empty columns for **China, Russia** and **No Value**. These Project Codes are not represented in our current portfolio. But choosing **Show all values on axis** causes these to be displayed as well.

One question you may have is what determines the ordering of the locations in the screens above? The answer is that this is the order set when the project codes are defined. If you want your display to show in a different order, you must change the project code ordering. However, keep in mind that this will affect every screen where project codes are used.

Side-by-side histogram

Next up in complexity is the side-by-side histogram. As you can guess, it is very similar to the regular histogram, but with an added dimension — for each of the items along the x-axis, the data can be split out and grouped into additional bars.

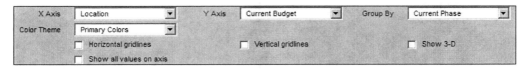

As you can see, the options are almost identical to the standard histogram, but with the addition of **Group By**. This is unfortunately named, and perhaps a better name would be "split out by". This value represents how each item on the X-axis will be split out into individual histograms. As such, it is best to choose a discrete value such as a project code for this grouping.

In the graph below we display location along the X-axis, current budget along Y, and then split out the locations by the project code "Current Phase".

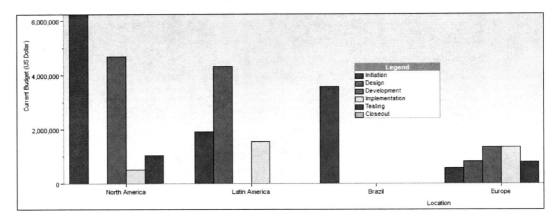

This is very similar to the histograms shown in the last section. However, each location is now broken down by Current Phase, and each phase receives a distinct color. Because of this further breakdown, the graph can become quite wide, and in the previous image we have cut off the display past **Europe** in order to fit it onto the page.

Below is the same chart, but in pastel with all of the options chosen.

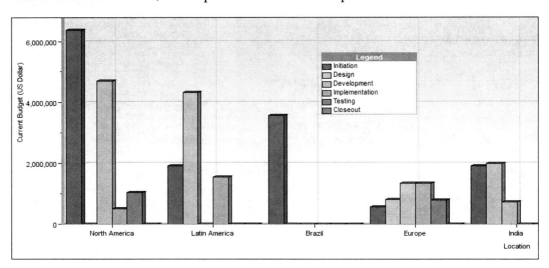

Note that with the side-by-side histogram, it is necessary to have a Legend. Otherwise you cannot know which colors correspond to which project phase. A Legend will appear whenever it is needed.

Stacked histogram

The side-by-side histogram is helpful, but as we saw, it can be rather wide. An alternative to the side-by-side, which yields a very similar analysis of the data, is the **stacked histogram**. As you can see in the following screenshot, the options are identical to those of the side-by-side histogram.

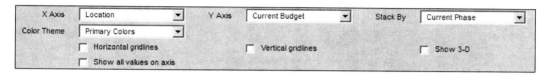

Here the **Group By** option is much more appropriately called **Stack By** for this is exactly what it does. Below is the stacked histogram equivalent of the example from the side-by-side. Note how the data all now completely fits onto the page. However, this representation does lose the easy visual comparison of the side-by-side. It is more difficult to tell which phase has a higher budget in each region.

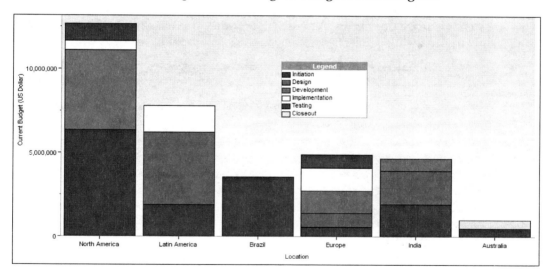

Here is the same data, but in pastel with all options checked:

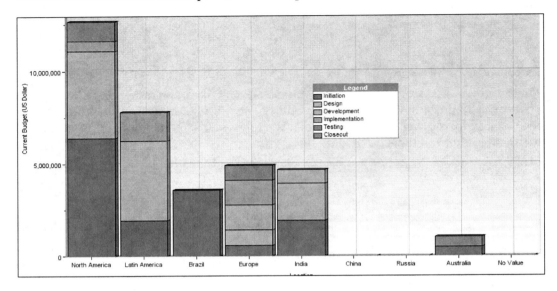

Bubble charts

We now come to the most complex and powerful portfolio view: the **bubble chart**. This view shows three quantities. As with histograms, there is an X and Y axis. There is also a grouping for the projects by color. In addition there is bubble size.

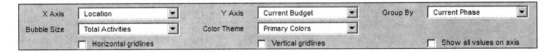

As these charts can be confusing, let's go through the chart represented by the options above and shown in the following graph. As before, the X-axis shows the Location set in the project codes. The Y-axis represents current budget and we are again grouping by current phase. But rather than showing this as a histogram, we represent each point with a circle, or bubble, whose size is proportional to the total number of activities in the project.

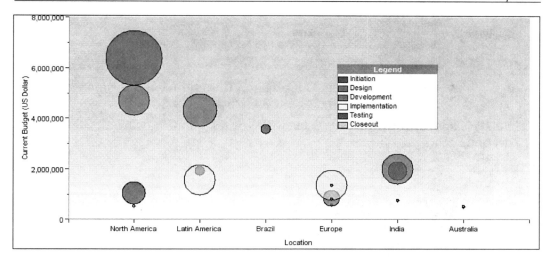

From this graph we can glean a few things quickly.

- Projects in North America have a:
    - Significant number of projects in the **Initiation Phase**.
    - **Current Budget** that contributes greatly to the overall value not only for North America, but for all Locations. It is considerably larger than any other **Phase** or **Location**
    - Similar number of **Testing** projects and a comparable number of projects to other locations.
    - Nominal numbers of projects in the **Implementation** phase; and those projects have a very small overall value.
    - Similar number of **Development** projects as compared to the **Design** or **Implementation** projects in Latin America, **Implementation** projects in Europe, or **Design** projects in India.
- Only Australia has any activities in **Closeout** and the value of those projects is small.
- India has a similar overall budget for **Initiation** and **Design**, and has more **Design** projects than **Initiation**.

- Latin America has a:
  - ° Similar number of projects in **Design** and **Testing**.
  - ° Design projects with approximately twice the budget as **Testing**.
  - ° A similar budget for **Testing** and **Initiation**, but the number of projects for **Testing** is quite a bit less.

Here is the same diagram, but in pastels with gridlines and showing all values of **Location**.

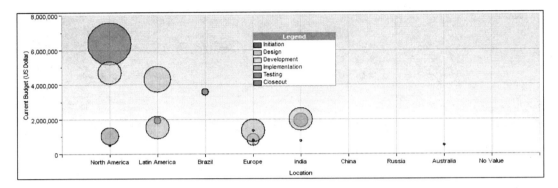

As you can see, a bubble chart provides a wealth of information at a glance!

Summary

In this chapter we have gone deep into the different kinds of Portfolio Analysis views that you can create and use. Each view has its strengths in representing different kinds of data, and you should now feel comfortable choosing and configuring the views you need.

But we have not yet discussed what data best represents meaningful metrics on projects. Nor have we discussed using historical data to compare portfolios over time. In the next chapter those two topics will be covered in depth.

13
Measuring and Scoring Projects

In the last chapter we surveyed the many charts, graphs, and tables available to use in analyzing projects. Armed with these tools we will now see how to use and learn more about them through the following topics:

- Scoring projects
- Creating and using scenarios
- Waterline Analysis

Scoring projects

When analyzing a portfolio, there are many criteria that you can use—budget versus actual costs, spend per month, production rates, and capital returns. All these data points can be daunting, and sometimes you want to use a single metric that captures the overall health of your projects. Primavera provides just such a metric in the project score. This can be the best of all worlds; one score representing all the items of importance to your organization, and chosen by you.

Name	Project Score	▽	Resource Rating	Technology Rating	Financial Rating	Strategic Rating
Total	✓ 78					
⊞ Juniper Nursing Home	✓ 84		4 Able to Shift	4 Innovative	5 NPV over $2M	3 Strong Alignment
⊞ City Center Office B...	✓ 80		2 Hire or Outsource	4 Innovative	5 NPV over $2M	3 Strong Alignment
⊞ Haitang Corporate P...	✓ 78		4 Able to Shift	2 Status Quo	5 NPV over $2M	3 Strong Alignment
Saratoga Senior Co...	✓ 77		3 Limited Resources	2 Status Quo	5 NPV over $2M	3 Strong Alignment
⊞ Nesbid Building Exp...	✓ 75		3 Limited Resources	3 Industry Standard	5 NPV over $2M	2 Moderate Alignment
⊞ Harbour Pointe Assi...	⚠ 72		2 Hire or Outsource	3 Industry Standard	5 NPV over $2M	2 Moderate Alignment

Expand All   Collapse All   Customize   Filter by Portfolio: Engineering & Constructic

Project Statistics

Expand   Collapse   Customize   Display ○ List ● Group

What is this project score, and where does it come from? This number is something that you can define and control so that it meets your organization's specific requirements. The score is set in the project codes. Unlike all other codes, such as activity and resource codes, project codes can be weighted. Each project code can be assigned a weight, and each value of the project code can be assigned a weight. The weighted values are then aggregated to form a score between 0 and 100.

To edit the project codes, go to **Administer | Enterprise Data | Project Codes**:

Project Codes

Name	Maximum Len...	Secure	Weight	Weight Percent	Maximum Code Value Weight
Priority	11	☐	0.0	0%	0.0
Strategic Rating	20	☐	30.0	30%	1.0
1 Weak Alignment			0.3		
2 Moderate Alignment			0.5		
3 Strong Alignment			0.7		
4 Mission Critical			0.8		
5 Legal - Reg			1.0		
Financial Rating	20	☐	35.0	35%	1.0
Technology Rating	20	☐	20.0	20%	1.0
Resource Rating	20	☐	15.0	15%	1.0

You will see many different project codes available. However, not all of them are used in scoring. Only those that are assigned a weight are used. Note that the weight you assign can be any value. The program will then convert the weights into a percentage of the overall score.

Within each project code, you can assign weights to each value. Again, these do not need to add up to 100 percent but can instead represent values that are meaningful to you. The system will then normalize them to 100 percent.

Let's take a very simple example with only two codes feeding into the project score—**Urgency**, which can be **High** with a value of **100**, and **Low** with a value of **0**, and **Importance**, with a **High** value of **100**, and a **Low** value of **0**.

Name	Description	Maximum Code Value Weight	Weight	Weight Percent
Importance		100.0	50.0	50%
High	High		100.0	
Low	Low		0.0	
Urgency		100.0	50.0	50%
High	High		100.0	
Low	Low		0.0	

First we create the two new project codes, and give each two values—**High** and **Low**. Next we assign equal values of **Maximum Code Value Weight**. We set them to **100.0**, but we could just as easily set them to **75** or some other value. As long as they are equal, the **Weight Percent** column will assign each **50%**.

Next we assign each **High** value to **100**, and each **Low** to 0. Again, the specific values do not matter. We could have assigned **25** and **0**, and the project score results would have been the same.

Note also that we have modified the **Project Codes** screen so that it shows us the columns that we want to see first.

In general, the project score is the weighted sum of the normalized project code values. In our simplified previous case this becomes:

Score = (Importance Value + Urgency Value) / 2

As we only have two project codes with two values the results should be:

Urgency/Importance	High	Low
High	100	50
Low	50	0

The following screenshot shows the actual results in P6:

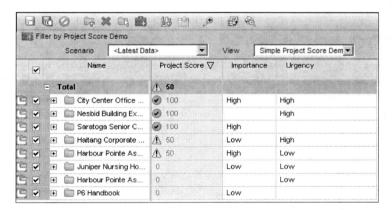

Note that to show these values, we first created a portfolio with these six projects. Then we made a portfolio analysis scorecard showing the project score and the two project codes.

One critical thing to point out here is that we have four projects where we only assign one project code. For example, the **Nesbid Building** has only a high urgency, and no importance assigned. You might expect that the importance would be treated as **0** in this case. Instead, that value is not even considered in the score, and so the project gets **100**. This can be misleading if you do not understand this fact. A good practice is to require that every project code that contributes to the project score be assigned a value.

Note the symbols shown in the **Project Score**. There are three symbols available, and these are set in **Administer | My Preferences**.

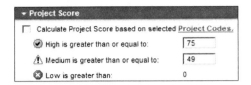

First note that you can check the checkbox **Calculate Project Score based on selected Project Codes**. This allows you to create the score based on whatever codes you like. Perhaps you want to use urgency, but not importance.

This should not be done lightly, you risk forgetting that the scores are calculated in a non-standard manner and analysis may be based on wrong calculations. Next you can choose which of the three symbols to use. Note that the low symbol will only be set for scores that are greater than zero, but not zero itself, which is not intuitive. In our example, the only possible values are 0, 50, and 100, so only the other two symbols are shown.

Creating and using scenarios

In the previous chapter we looked at Portfolio Analysis, and the tools we can use to measure our projects. The data we were looking at was real-time. If you want to show your Portfolio Analysis to someone else, it is possible that by the time the other person sees it, the data may have changed. Scenarios help to address this problem. A **scenario** is a snapshot in time of one or more projects. In this respect it is similar to a baseline.

Let's make a scenario for the project scoring we did in the previous section. Note that in earlier scorecard screen there is a box labelled **Scenario**, and the value says **<Latest Data>**. This means that the scorecard is showing live data for the projects. To make a new scenario click on the **Save As** icon in the upper left hand corner of the scenario.

The **Save As** screen looks something like the following screenshot:

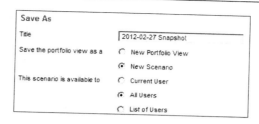

When you save a new scenario, make sure that you put something in the name, such as a date, that identifies what the scenario represents. A good practice is to prefix the title with the year, month, and date, so that it sorts well.

Now you can choose this scenario and compare it to the current data.

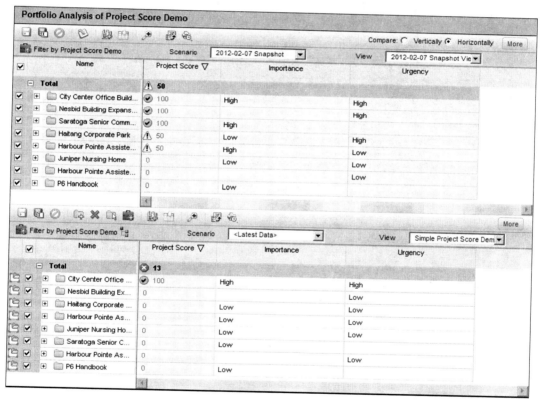

Here we are comparing the project scorecards from February 2012 to today. The scores have gone down! This is an excellent way to view changes in your projects over time.

Also, note that when you select a scenario, the view is set to a new view that has the same name as the scenario. This view is also a snapshot of the view that was showing when the portfolio was made. You can also choose to use any of the current Portfolio Analysis views as well, such as the one called **Simple Project Score Demo**.

Scenarios are easy to create and easy to use, and provide for powerful analysis. Therefore, you can incorporate creating scenarios into your periodic update process. Then, for example, you can view which data has changed in the update.

Waterline Analysis

When viewing tabular data on a Portfolio Analysis scorecard in **Capacity Planning**, you can assign a waterline to the table. The waterline will show which items are below the line by shading them blue, as though there were under water.

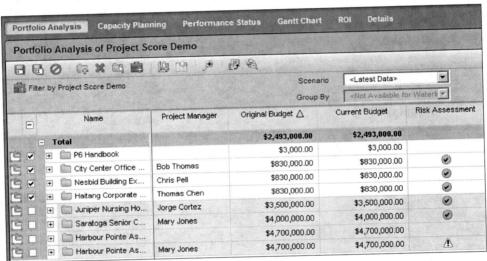

The waterline has two key properties—the parameter and the sort order.

The parameter is the quantity you will use to measure if a project is above or below the waterline. You choose the parameter, the comparison operator, and a value.

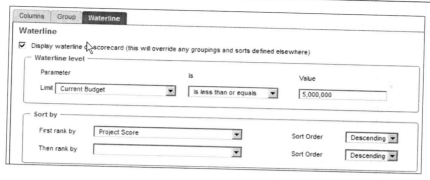

In our example, we use current budget as the parameter, and request that a waterline be drawn for all projects when the cumulative value is less than $5,000,000 and we sort by project score. Therefore, this will show the top-scoring projects whose cumulative value is at or below $5,000,000. All the other projects will show as under water.

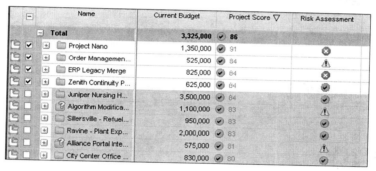

This view will show us the best-scoring projects we can afford for $5,000,000. Now let's ask the question—which are the worst-performing projects that we can get rid of in order to save $10,000,000? To get this information, we simply reverse the **Sort Order** to **Ascending** and change the limit to **$10,000,000**.

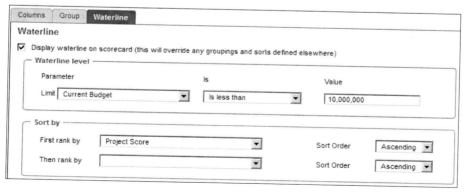

Now the poorest-performing projects are shown above water.

			Name	Current Budget	Project Score △	Risk Assessment
	⊟		**Total**	**6,835,000** ⚠ **68**		
	☑	⊞	📁 Employee Onboar...	800,000 ⚠ 62		✓
	☑	⊞	📁 Hemaform Program	1,500,000 ⚠ 63		✓
	☑	⊞	📁 Zepher Phase III	500,000 ⚠ 65		✓
	☑	⊞	📁 KRS3000 Replace...	500,000 ⚠ 70		✓
	☑	⊞	📁 3D Prototype Project	1,435,000 ⚠ 72		✓
	☑	⊞	📁 Cordova - Plant Ex...	1,350,000 ⚠ 72		✓
	☑	⊞	📁 ACH Integration Pr...	750,000 ⚠ 72		✓
	☐	⊞	📁 Harbour Pointe As...	4,700,000 ⚠ 72		⚠
	☐	⊞	📁 Nesbid Building Ex...	830,000 ✓ 75		✓
	☐	⊞	📁 MDM Project	525,000 ✓ 75		✓
	☐	⊞	📁 eBusiness Transf...	1,050,000 ✓ 76		✓

Scorecards can be exported to Excel by pressing the export icon at the top of the display.

Note that the generated file will go to a temporary location on your computer. You must click on **Save As...** in order to save and make changes to it.

Summary

We have seen how projects can be measured by creating a custom project score metric based on weighted project codes. This can be customized for the needs of your own particular company, and is quite flexible. We have also seen how to create snapshots of projects in time, called scenarios, and how to make quick visual analyses with waterlines.

In the next chapter we dive into an even more specialized tool for analysing the use of resources in our portfolios—**Capacity Planning**.

14

Capacity Planning and ROI

Capacity Planning and ROI are both tools that let you manage different features of a portfolio of projects. Capacity planning helps you to ensure that you have the resources to perform the project work, while ROI lets you calculate which projects will yield the best return on capital. In this chapter we introduce the capacity planning feature of P6 and review the following topics:

- Capacity Planning screens
- Customization
- **Return on Investment (ROI)**

Capacity Planning

The **Capacity Planning** screen of the **Portfolios** section is a very powerful feature that allows users to clearly see which skills or equipment will be needed to complete a group of projects. The feature gives the user a windscreen (forward facing) view of resource usage and the landscape ahead. If the analysis highlights the fact that more cranes are needed, users have data to support decisions, such as renting or purchasing more cranes or moving the project to different dates to avoid over-allocation. This feature is best used when planning or bidding on future projects by allowing a user to stack all project timelines onto a single Gantt chart and view the resources needed month-by-month or per quarter as each bid or project is moved.

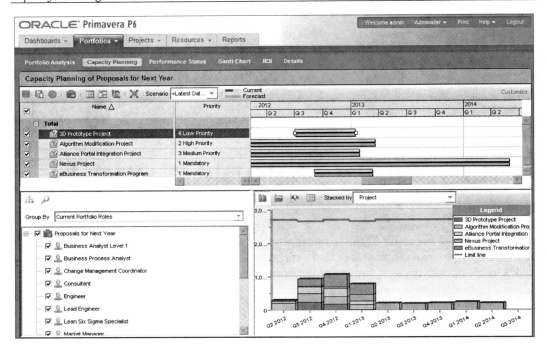

There is a lot going on in the previous screenshot! Let's break it down into more manageable sections.

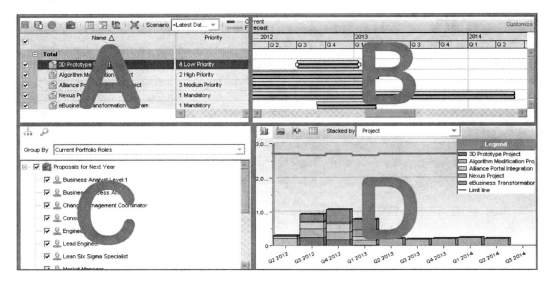

Frame A—scorecard

Frame A is a scorecard area with a list of all projects within the currently open portfolio. As with any scorecard, you may add columns to this view. To add columns, click on the **Customize** link at top right of frame A. In this customize screen, users can choose columns to show, select how the projects are grouped, set up a waterline analysis, and select a type of chart to view.

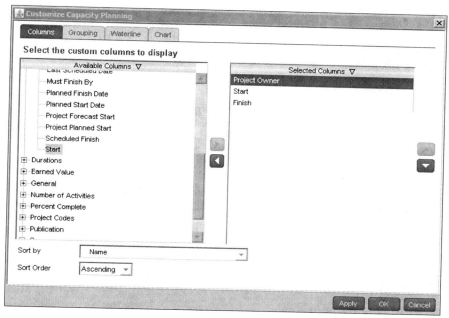

As in most areas of P6, to select a column to view, simply highlight it within the list on the left-hand side and use the arrow in the space between the two lists to send the selected column to the **Selected Columns** list on the right. Using the set of arrows at far right-hand side, users can re-order the columns in the view. In the web, all changes must be saved by clicking on the **OK** button.

In the following example, we have removed the **Project Owner** column and added the **Actual Total Cost** column. The projects in the portfolio can be grouped using the **Grouping** tab of the **Customize Capacity Planning** window. Here we have grouped them by **Project Planned Start**.

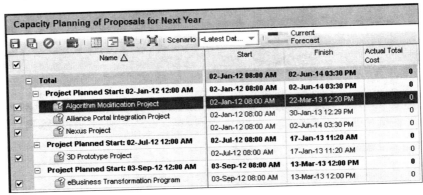

If the grouping is simple, the color of text or band and the sort order are the only other adjustments to be made. However, if the criteria are hierarchical, you may select the number of indentions or level of the hierarchy to consider when grouping.

For example, suppose you have a hierarchical project code for location grouped by country, region, and then state.

In this case if we choose to group by location, then all regions and states will be listed together. However, if we choose to group using the To Level feature and group to level 3, all countries would be grouped together, and within that grouping would be a sub-group for each region, and within that grouping will be a grouping by state.

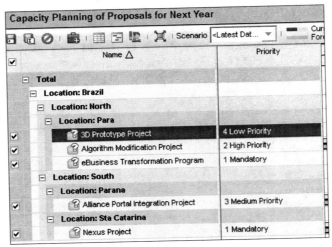

Using the **Chart** tab, users can change the **Capacity Planning** view to show **Units** or **Costs** in the Gantt chart, and can choose to display either only projects selected or the entire portfolio. Other adjustments can be made here to create a desired view.

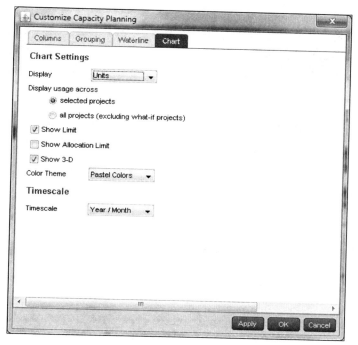

Frame B—Gantt chart

Frame B is the top-right quarter of the **Capacity Planning** screen. This is the Gantt area where projects are represented using scheduled dates on the green bar. The orange bar is only seen in P6 on this screen and represents the forecast. The forecast bar will be the same as the schedule/current dates bar unless forecast dates are specifically used (which is not typical). The purpose of the two bars is best used when viewing bids or projects in the future.

The best feature of this frame is that its timeline is shared by area D, the capacity chart area. As the project lines are stacked against time in the Gantt area, they affect the histograms or other charts in the area just under—showing the capacity or workers it would take to complete the projects as forecasted. Therefore, if I move the orange (forecast) bar to the right or left, the chart area (D) also rearranges to show the different work effort in the new time frame.

In the following sample, several projects are shown top right and the second project forecast bar has been moved to earlier dates—to create a scenario in which we can evaluate the capacity of resources required to complete all the projects if we move one earlier.

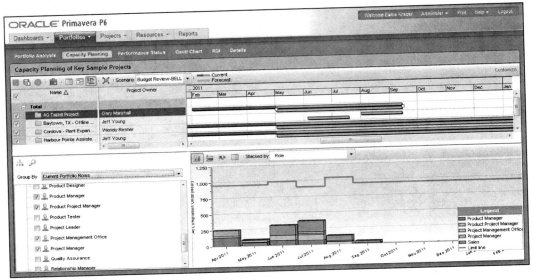

If you move the bars without saving, no changes are permanent. However, if you move a project forecast bar and then use the **Save** button, the project is moved to the forecast bar dates and all dates within the project are changed to the new time frame (except constraints—they are generally a bad practice). The proper usage of this feature is to move the forecast bars to the desired dates and save as a scenario until you are certain the projects should be moved permanently. Scenarios can be used for decision-making and analysis.

The value of area B is best explained in combination with area C and D in mind.

Frame C—resources and roles

The bottom-left frame C is a key element to capacity planning. This area is where the specific resources that we evaluate can be selected. This area has options to view resources in three ways:

- View only the roles assigned to projects in the currently selected portfolio
- View roles hierarchically as they are arranged in the system

- View roles by **Role Teams**. See more about **Role Teams** in *Chapter 6, Resources*

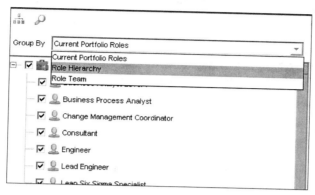

Another option in area C of **Capacity Planning** is the search feature where users may search for specific roles by name by using the first letter of the name or if the search criteria occur anywhere within the name.

Frame D—Resource and Role Usage

The bottom-right pane of the **Capacity Planning** screen is where the magic happens; this is the area that displays the effect of the choices made in the three areas (A, B, and C). area D—the **Capacity Planning Chart Work** area. Based on projects shown in area A (scorecard area) and time frames selected in area B (Gantt area), and using the selected roles in area C, the capacity planning chart will show resources needed to accomplish the work in those projects for those roles in that timeframe.

The limit line is set as the cumulative for all the selected roles and there are three types of charts for analysis. Look at each one for a full view of the situation.

For example, following are four specific roles related to sales and the project office (PM, Project Lead, Product lead, and Product PM). The limit line is the sum of hours for those roles available to the company (see *Chapter 6* for more on the limit line settings). The projects (as they are in the Gantt chart) have these roles assigned to them and the total hours required for those roles is charted.

The first view shown is the stacked histogram sorted by role. By using this chart, users can evaluate spikes in usage of certain roles (see pink sales team in June and July) as well as overall allocation. By rolling a cursor over each stack in the histogram, details about the layers are shown.

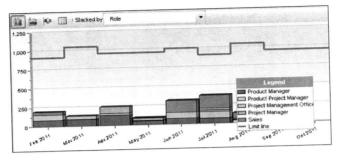

Closer examination of the details shows a need for 173.75 hours of sales activities on the selected projects during July. If your company has only 20 salespersons working for eight hour per day, then you can expect 13.75 hours of overtime that month or move some activity to another time to avoid hiring or retraining.

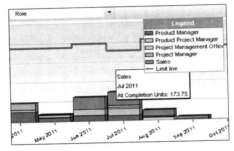

The second view choice is an area chart view. The area chart shows spikes in the overall portfolio. The selected portfolio of projects will create a spike of activity in April (mostly project managers) and another spike in June and July with sales being most active and product project managers being busy.

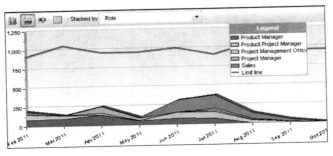

The third view option is the net availability chart view. This view allows a user to clearly see where the skill sets throughout the organization will be over allocated and by how many hours. This view is much like a waterline report where items under the line are over allocated:

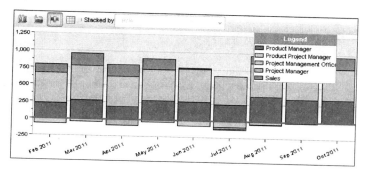

If a user scrolls over the items under the red line, it's clear which roles are over allocated for that time frame. In this example, the project managers group is over allocated by 87.01 hours in April, 30.14 in May, and 30.14 in July.

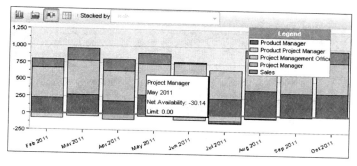

All the data behind the chart may be viewed by clicking on the spreadsheet icon next to the views:

	Apr	May	Jun	Jul	Aug	Sep	Oct
Total At Completion Units	**252.08h**	**105.20h**	**320.00h**	**381.10h**	**143.57h**	**50.63h**	**0....**
Product Manager	144.40h	53.13h	80.00h	73.75h	0.00h	0.00h	0....
Product Project Manager	0.00h	6.25h	80.00h	86.88h	40.00h	16.88h	0....
Project Management Office	20.66h	3.19h	0.00h	23.36h	11.79h	0.00h	0....
Project Manager	87.01h	30.14h	0.00h	23.36h	11.79h	0.00h	0....
Sales	0.00h	12.50h	160.00h	173.75h	80.00h	33.75h	0....
Limit	*966.00h*	*966.00h*	*1,012.00h*	*920.00h*	*1,058.00h*	*966.00h*	*96...*

Putting it all together

Dynamically as users move the forecast bars across the Gantt chart, the allocations change in the chart area for the selected roles. Entire role teams or individual roles may be selected as desired. Keep in mind, the allocations are only for the projects within the selected portfolio and will be different across all projects (likely a more severe over allocation than shown).

 Ensure all projects have been recently summarized so the assignments data is up-to-date in the database for the most accurate data.

Return on Investment (ROI)

ROI involves looking at a project and determining whether it will be profitable or not. The information in these screens comes from WBS and project-level information. In the planning stage this calculation can be straightforward. However, once a project is in progress, it is even more crucial to track if the project is trending toward profit or loss.

Portfolio Analysis	Capacity Planning	Performance Status	Gantt Chart	ROI	Details

ROI of Key Projects over $500K

Name	Annual Discount Rate	Total Benefit Plan (Present Value)	Payback Period	Total Spending Plan (Present Value)	Net Present Value	Return on Investment	
Key Projects over $500K		605,826,873		229,916,948	375,909,925	163.5%	View Chart
3D Prototype Project	7.00						View Chart
ACH Integration Project	7.00	2,749,355	322.5d	1,948,604	800,752	41.1%	View Chart
Algorithm Modification Project	7.00						View Chart
Alliance Portal Integration Project	7.00						View Chart
City Center Office Building Addition	10.00	0		0	0		View Chart
Cordova - Plant Expansion & Modernization	5.00						View Chart
Driftwood - Refuel Outage	5.00						View Chart
eBusiness Transformation Program	7.00						View Chart
Employee Onboarding Portal	7.00	927,175	279.5d	591,346	335,829	56.8%	View Chart
ERP Legacy Merge	7.00	2,639,664	473.0d	938,024	1,701,641	181.4%	View Chart
Harbour Pointe Assisted Living Center	5.00	195,798,648	344.0d	73,791,544	122,007,104	165.3%	View Chart
Hemaform Program	7.00						View Chart

To see what information goes into the calculations, click on the project's title.

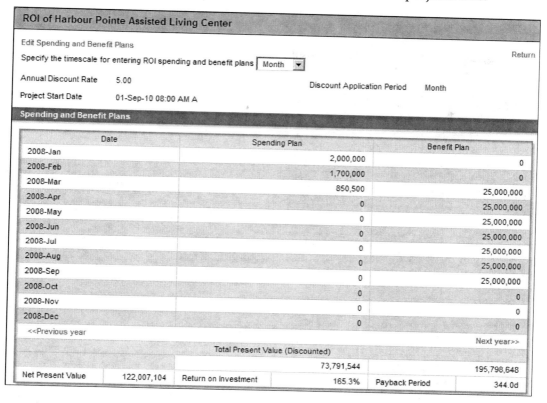

ROI of Harbour Pointe Assisted Living Center

Edit Spending and Benefit Plans

Specify the timescale for entering ROI spending and benefit plans [Month ▼]

			Return
Annual Discount Rate	5.00	Discount Application Period	Month
Project Start Date	01-Sep-10 08:00 AM A		

Spending and Benefit Plans

Date	Spending Plan	Benefit Plan
2008-Jan	2,000,000	0
2008-Feb	1,700,000	0
2008-Mar	850,500	25,000,000
2008-Apr	0	25,000,000
2008-May	0	25,000,000
2008-Jun	0	25,000,000
2008-Jul	0	25,000,000
2008-Aug	0	25,000,000
2008-Sep	0	25,000,000
2008-Oct	0	0
2008-Nov	0	0
2008-Dec	0	0
<<Previous year		Next year>>

Total Present Value (Discounted)		
	73,791,544	195,798,648

Net Present Value	122,007,104	Return on Investment	165.3%	Payback Period	344.0d

You can edit this information by clicking on **Edit Spending and Benefit Plans**.
This will also allow you to edit the **Annual Discount Rate** and **Discount Application Period**.

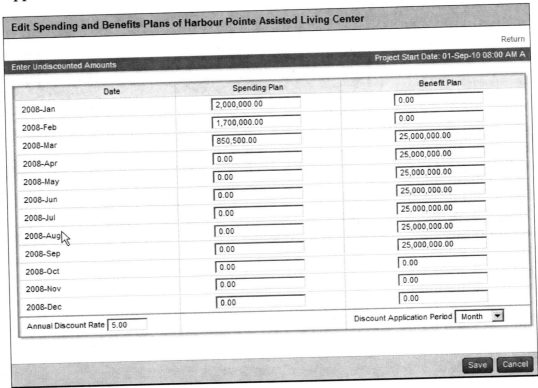

ROI calculations are valuable when you are planning future work. You can estimate
a spending plan to pay for the capital investment, along with a discount rate for that
money borrowed to make that investment. You can also create a benefit plan to see
how long it will take to make a return on that investment.

Summary

The capacity planning feature is one of P6's most valuable and it is one of the easiest to use. With most of P6's power coming from the schedule, inputting a high-level schedule with estimated hours and roles gives incredible power to an organization looking to plan for its future needs in terms of people and money. Simple, dynamic adjustments create immediate scenarios for analysis before committing to the changes. Users can pinpoint where rentals, overtime, cross training, or other solutions will be required, months and years in advance simply by moving a bar on a bar chart!

In the next chapter we look at how to bring together all of the tools we have covered in the book so far to create dashboards. These dashboards provide quick views into different aspects of projects and ultimately a complete 360 degree view of the organization's projects. This feature truly allows users to turn around in the driver's seat away from the rear view and look ahead into the windscreen to plan best where to turn.

15
Dashboards

The value of P6 is that all data stems from the core: the detailed project schedule. However, the data that best supports strategic organizational decision-making needs to be visible at a higher level. In earlier chapters, we showed how portfolios are used to analyze groups of projects with intuitive graphics and scorecards. Dashboards build upon those analysis tools and present project and portfolio information in a way that is easy to set up and use. These dashboards can be customized and assigned so that specific users or groups of users can see the same information when they log into the system. Dashboards can be configured to suit individual needs or literally get everyone on the same page.

In this chapter, we will cover:

- Dashboard examples
- Managing dashboards
- Customizing a dashboard
- Dashboard layout
- Dashboard security access

Dashboard examples:

If you install a new instance of P6, there will be no dashboards present, so you will be starting with a blank slate. This can be a daunting task. However, you can also use the P6 installer to set up a P6 database, which is pre-loaded with sample data. The P6 sample database contains eight dashboard layouts that you can study as examples of how you may wish to set up dashboards at your own company.

The sample dashboards include:

- **Corporate**: Emphasizes project schedule, resource teams, budgets, project scoring, and prioritization
- **IT**: Highlights project value metrics, resource analysis, project issues, and investment spending
- **Product R&D**: Emphasizes project gate progression, a New Product Introduction (NPI) weighted scorecard, and capital costs
- **Construction**: Highlights budgets, spending, and earned value
- **Energy**: Shows costs by region, earned value, and project schedules on a quarterly timescale
- **Manufacturing**: Highlights a performance scorecard and project health
- **Workflow**: Focuses on proposals and communication
- **Strategic Programs**: Emphasizes capital costs, strategic objectives, and the project pipeline

Shown in the following screenshot is a portion of the **Corporate** dashboard:

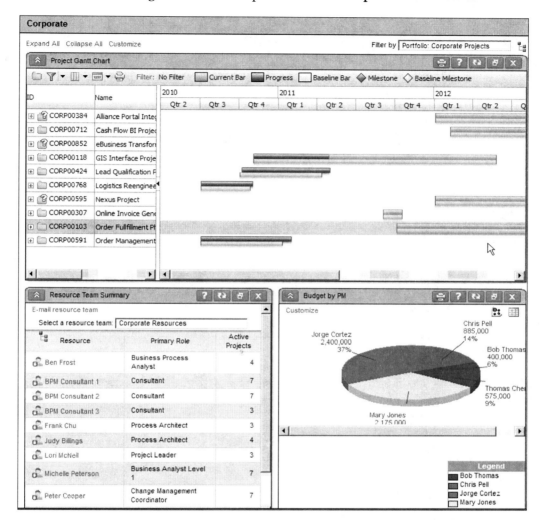

Dashboards are not only configured for industries, but also for user roles. An HR manager may need a dashboard emphasizing resource allocation and availability. A scheduler may need one emphasizing project risks, issues, and a two-week look-ahead. A cost analyst may be interested in seeing the overall budget, actual costs, and earned value.

Managing dashboards

Dashboards are created with up to 12 windows of data called **Portlets**. A variety of pre-defined portlets come with P6. Users are assigned dashboards as a part of adding a new user to a user-group profile. Some organizations allow users to create dashboards, too. Simply choose up to 12 portlets, arrange them in a pleasing view, and then indicate who gets to see your new dashboard. An example portlet is shown in the following screenshot:

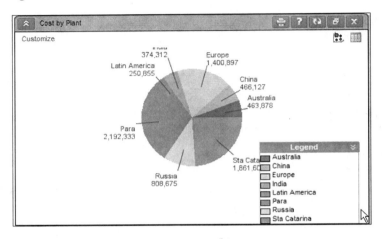

Portlets all have a set of common buttons, such as, **Print**, **Help**, **Close**, **Expand/ Minimize** and a special button to refresh the data within the window using up-to-the-minute data from all users in the system.

Clicking on the epaulets on the right of each portlet header will collapse or expand the portlet.

To grant a user the ability to manage dashboards, go to **Administer | User Interface Views,** and check the box next to **Dashboards | Menu Items | Manage Dashboards**:

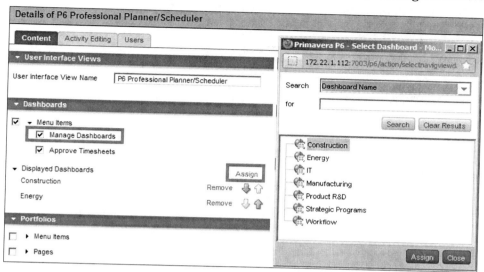

You can also use this screen to assign a default list of dashboards available to a given set of users.

Any P6 user who has the ability to customize dashboards can click on the triangle on the **Dashboards** tab to get to the dashboard management screen:

The main headings — **Dashboards**, **Portfolios**, **Projects**, **Resources**, and **Reports**, are all shown according to your security. The name of each section is actually a link to that section of P6. When in a drop-down feature, simply click on the section name to return to that section or use the **Save and Close** function at the bottom of the screen.

Dashboards also allow a user to focus attention on specific groups of projects. The criteria used to determine which projects are represented on the dashboards are called **filters**. Each dashboard is filtered using the **Filter by** field at the top right of the dashboard.

Users can filter a dashboard by **Portfolios**, **Project Codes**, or by individual projects which you manually select.

Click on the link on the dashboards section drop-down list to manage dashboards. This is where all user specific dashboards within the system can be added to your dashboards toolbar. See how the following displayed dashboards relate to the items available on the dashboard toolbar:

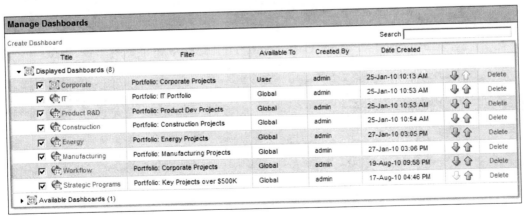

Customizing a dashboard

To customize or alter a dashboard, click on the **Customize** link at the top-right section of the dashboard. A pop-up window of selections will appear as shown in the following screenshot. (Your screen may have each grey area expanded to show selections). Three tabs are featured: **Content, Layout**, and **Access.** By default, up to 12 portlets may be displayed in a dashboard. Note that this limit can be changed by your system administrator.

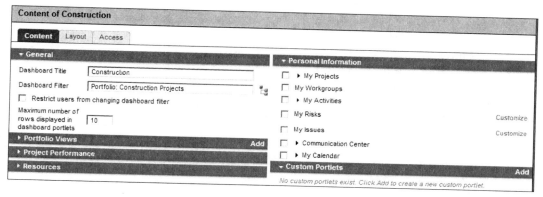

 When customizing a dashboard, be sure to save often! Otherwise, your dashboard customizations could be lost.

Content tab

The **Content** tab contains six sections:

- **General**
- **Portfolio Views**
- **Project Performance**
- **Resources**
- **Personal Information**
- **Custom Portlets**

General

This is where you name the dashboard. Keep the name short and simple, so that it will fit well on the **Dashboard** tab.

Choose a filter to set the default project information to display for this dashboard. You can filter by portfolios, specific project codes, or projects.

You may choose to restrict users from changing the dashboard by checking the checkbox. Without this checked, any user can alter this dashboard.

Special 8.2 feature — a user may select a sub-filter for his personal perspective of the dashboards, if desired.

To minimize the screen size and time to display, select a lower number of rows to display in each portlet.

Portfolio Views

A list of available portfolio views can be chosen from the **Portfolio Views** portlet. If none are shown, then you must create a portfolio view in the **Portfolios** section. See *Chapter 11, Portfolios* of this book for more information.

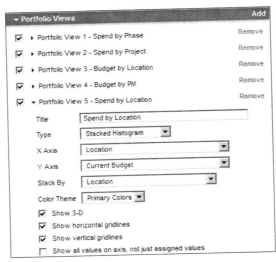

Check the checkbox to display a portfolio view, click the **Add** link or the **Remove** link to add or remove portfolio views from this dashboard.

If you are adding a portfolio view to the dashboard, check the box next to the portfolio name. An unchecked box leaves the view available, but not visible.

You can also customize the portfolio view using the same settings as explained in earlier chapters.

Project Performance

This set of portlets is concerned with a range of project properties such as schedule performance, earned value, and key performance indicators (KPIs).

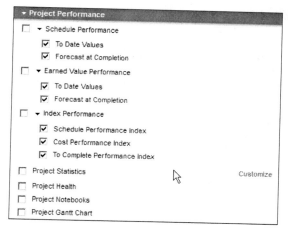

Three main performance portlets are available with choices to each one:

1. **Schedule Performance**
2. **Earned Value Performance**
3. **Index Performance**

The **Schedule Performance** portlet shows progress from a schedule perspective with columns for data that is To Date and/or Forecast at Completion data. To choose which ones to show, simply check the checkbox with a double-click. The **Earned Value Performance** portlet has the same two choices on columns.

The **Index Performance** portlet can show earned value standard indexes for each project such as **Schedule Performance Index (SPI)**, **Cost Performance Index (CPI)**, and **To Complete Performance Index (TCPI)**.

Choose the data you wish to show by double-clicking on the attendant checkbox. These values follow standard numeric values as recommended by the project management institute where 1.00 is a perfect score indicating that all items were executed as planned for both time and cost data. Subsequently, score of 0.85 states that only 85 percent of what was planned to be done or spent was actually completed or spent. A score greater than 1.00 indicates that you did more than planned or spent more than planned. The planned value for these calculations is the baseline and the actual values are in **Actual Cost** and **Actual Units** fields on the project.

The **Project Statistics** portlet is a popular portlet to use on dashboards because it allows a user to choose the columns of data as desired. Dozens of data columns are available to select and show in this portlet.

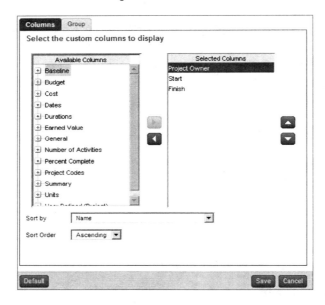

The **Project Health** portlet is also popular as a very high-level summary of the project. The data is not editable or customizable but it is generated from **Global** settings in the administrative menu. The portlet displays a short paragraph about the progress of the project.

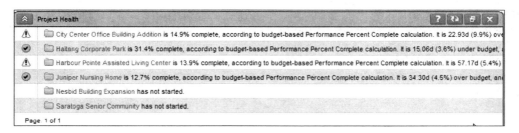

The **Project Notebooks** portlet is where all the project level notebook topics are shown in one location. This is especially helpful if your business process is consistently used to show reasons for delays, reasons for change orders, or other significant project communications:

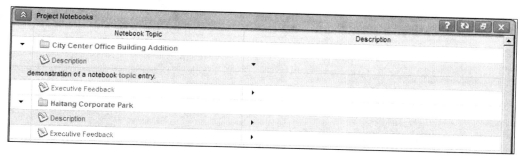

The **Project Gantt Chart** portlet is a great way to view the entire group of projects (those matching filter criteria for this dashboard) on a single Gantt-styled chart.

There are two frames in this portlet. The left-hand side frame is a table listing of projects that are typically collapsed to the project level. By clicking on the plus sign next to the project folder icon, the project is expanded to show its milestone activities.

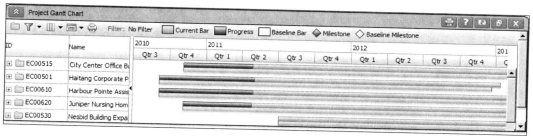

In the right-hand side frame, each group of bars represents each project and is shown along a timeline so that you can evaluate each project against the others in terms of overall timing. Just as in other parts of P6, the blue bar represents completed activities, the green bar represents planned activities, and the yellow bar represents the baseline activities. Ideally the blue/green bars should align perfectly with the yellow to indicate all is progressing as planned. If the yellow bar is separated from the blue/green bar, then work is not progressing as planned in the baseline. If the project is expanded to show milestone activities, planned dates are charted using a black diamond and the baseline dates are charted using a yellow diamond.

In the following example, the first project **Arcadia** finished later than planned. A milestone in first quarter 2011 was missed by a small margin, which delayed the final milestone by a larger margin—pushing it into the next quarter.

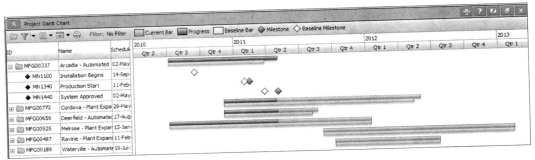

The **Melrose** project is progressing as planned. The **Waterville** project shows to be planned in the future with no progress. This chart shows progress as of mid-Q2 according to the imaginary vertical line along the blue part of the bars.

Resources

The resources section of the dashboard customization is shown next and has some of the best features in the web-based part of P6. There are three main options to show in portlets for resource information:

1. **Resource Team Summary**
2. **Open Requests for Resources**
3. **Resource Analysis Chart**

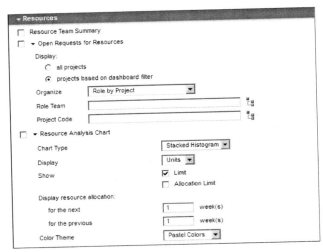

The **Resource Team Summary** portlet shows a list of resources that are assigned to the projects within dashboard filter and which belongs to the team shown in the **Resource Team Summary** portlet filter at the top-right corner of the portlet.

Resources are listed on the far left-hand side. Over-allocated resources will have a red spot on their icon. In the following example, all resources are over-allocated except **Harry Shaw** and **Robert Lincoln**.

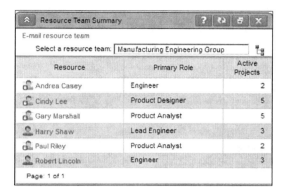

The primary role is the designation given to that resource in the resource pool and may or may not be the role they are assigned to perform on the project. The number of active projects to which each resource listed is assigned is in the last column on the right.

When the number of lines in the portlet exceeds the set limit of lines for that portlet, the bottom of the portlet shows the current page number and total number of pages. A **Next>>** link takes the user to subsequent pages when clicked.

A favorite feature of this portlet is the **E-mail resource team** link at the top-right corner of the portlet. Users can click on this link and an e-mail is auto-populated with the team members' e-mail addresses in the **TO** field. The login used to access the system must have its own e-mail address assigned for this feature to operate. Additionally the e-mail exchange protocols must be set up by your administrator. See the P6 Admin Guide for more information or contact your administrator.

The **E-mail resource team** feature does not use Outlook or other e-mail clients to send the e-mail. The e-mail is sent from the P6 e-mail feature within the P6 system. If you want a copy of the e-mail, add your own e-mail address into the **CC** field.

The **Open Requests for Resources** portlet allows users to show which activities on projects have only a role (that is, engineer) assigned and need a resource (that is, David Jackson) assigned by their Manager.

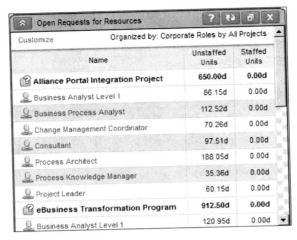

The portlet has a number of customizations. The first choice to be made is to show open assignments on all projects or just those within the filter for this dashboard. The **Organize** field allows a user to define how the listed open assignments are sorted and shown. The drop-down list offers views where open assignments are shown as:

- Roles with open assignments project by project
- Projects with open assignments role by role
- Roles with open assignments, sorted by project, and sub-sorted by project codes

If you select the **Role by Project by Project Codes** feature, then you must select a code before saving this customized dashboard.

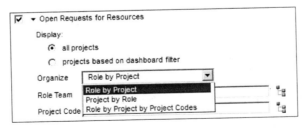

  You must select a **Role Team** (and therefore must have role teams created) in order to use the **Organize** feature.

The following example shows the **Open Request for Resources** portlet set to organize by **Role by Project by Project Codes**, with **Location** as the selected **Project Code**. The project **Alliance...** is under the **Project Code** location **Parana**. The project code icon is a file folder with a tag on it.

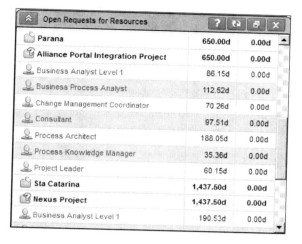

To learn how to fulfill an open request, see *Chapter 6, Resources*, and the scheduling/ creating a project discussions in this book.

The **Resource Analysis** portlet is the last one in the **Resources** section of the **Dashboard customization** screen. Here several types of graphs can be selected to show resources that are assigned to the projects within the filtered portfolio for this dashboard in terms of usage. Each graph will show a different perspective of resource usage, availability, and assignments.

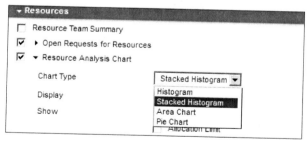

These charts are similar to the ones shown in *Chapter 14, Capacity Planning and ROI.*

Personal Information

The next section of the dashboard portlets is the **Personal Information** section. This section is used to identify you (the user you have logged in as) as a specific resource assigned to project work. The portlets available in this section for viewing on the dashboard will display information as it relates to you (logged-in user) and your assignments (resource on activities and projects). For example, the first portlet is **My Projects** and this portlet requires that the user is associated with a resource and/or the OBS.

Keep in mind that choosing to display items in the **Personal Information** portlets will show items selected for the currently logged-in user. David Flintstone signing in will see all of his personal items on this dashboard, but when Wilma signs in, she will see hers in that portlet. These portlets display user-based information.

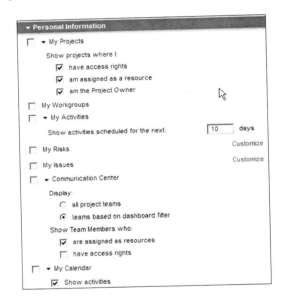

To use the **My Projects** portlet, select one or more of these three options:

- The **have access rights** checkbox will display only those projects that your security profile allows—the OBS element you have been assigned to.

- The **am assigned as a resource** checkbox will display any project on which your associated resource has been assigned to activities. (Resource associated with your login is a setting managed in your security profile and also in the resource administration area).

- The **am the Project Owner** checkbox will display any project on which you have been deemed the project owner in the **Project Owner** field of the **General** tab of **Project Details**.

The next area of the **Personal Information** set of portlets options is where you can choose to show workgroups your user ID is associated with, the activities your associated resource is assigned to (and you can indicate how far into the future P6 looks for those activities) and where your assigned risks and issues can be displayed in the portlet. The risks and issues you entered will also show in this portlet.

Remember, these are individually personal and user-based. Each user sees their own information in these portlets.

The next portlet is the **Communication Center**. This is where you can choose to show all project teams or teams that relate to the projects matching the filter criteria for this dashboard. The **Communication Center** is where a user can send e-mail to one or more team members who are also assigned to the project, or they can view and send to everyone assigned to the project. The **Project association** column shows how each team member is associated with the project. For example, as an assigned resource, project owner, and so on. Select the person or full team at the project level to send e-mails by checking the appropriate checkbox.

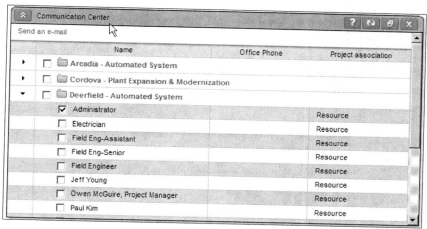

My Calendar is the last portlet available under **Personal Information** section of the dashboard customization. Check this checkbox to display the **My Calendar** portlet in which all assignments scheduled for you can be shown week by week as you click on that timeframe in the calendar provided. The colors shown have the same meaning throughout P6 where blue represents work completed, green is work planned, and red is for critical path activities. Blue and green activities represent work currently in progress.

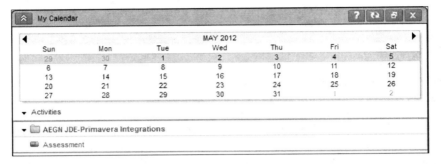

This simple portlet displays useful information so that a user can quickly see activities for the highlighted week.

Custom Portlets

The final section of the customizing dashboards screen is where users can add a custom portlet to this dashboard. Custom portlets are acually a place to insert any website address or URL. Several websites can be added using the **Add** button at the top-right corner in the grey title bar for **Custom Portlets**.

The information that will appear at the top of the portlet is whatever is typed in the **Title** field. Make the title short so it appears on screen easily and make it very descriptive for the user. Good ideas for this area are to insert your SharePoint site, extranet project area, or other Primavera modules, such as, contract or risk management.

If the URL you enter here is actually a web-served app, the username and password for P6 must match the username and password for the app. If they do not match, some software will not load and cause an error message to appear in this portlet. Not all apps will allow the first screen to be the actual app as it may bypass a login screen. In these cases, make sure the URL is for the login screen.

The goal for dashboards is to place all relevant project information on one screen and one location so the team members can literally be on the same page. Make sure the custom portlet URL leads users to pertinent information.

We have described every feature that allows a user to define the content of dashboards and now the next step is to work on how that content looks on screen. For this function, we will use the **Layout** tab.

Dashboard Layout

The **Layout** tab allows a user to order the portlets to show on screen as desired. Typically the most important portlets are at the top of the dashboard. Each portlet can be displayed using the entire width of the screen or as a half-width portlet:

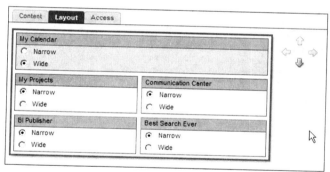

To change the size of the portlet, choose the **Narrow** (half-width) radio button or the **Wide** (full-screen width) radio button. Height is not alterable except to change the size of the application window.

To change the position of the portlets, simply drag-and-drop or use the arrow buttons to move the portlets up, down, or sideways.

Access

The **Access** tab is the final barrier for security on this dashboard. To allow users to access this dashboard, they must be granted access on the **Access** tab. This can be a manual process or can be automated.

To make the dashboard automatically available to the users, without manually adding their name to the list; choose one of the top two options:

1. **Current User**
2. **All Users**

To make the dashboard available to specific users only, they must be added manually to the list of selected users. Locate their name in the users listed in the **Available Users** column and throw them over to the **Selected Users** column using the arrow in between columns as shown. If the list of users is lengthy, you can use the search icon to locate the username.

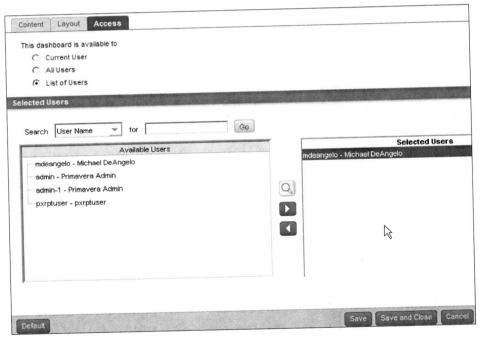

When you are done, click on the **Save and Close** button to create the dashboard.

Summary

Dashboards provide quick insight into project information. About four to fifteen dashboards can fit across a view, depending on monitor size. By naming dashboards in a meaningful manner, you can convey to users what is important and most useful to them. Dashboards also allow team members to view information both in a common manner, and also in a highly customized manner. Use dashboards at your next meeting instead of paper printouts— they are more dynamic and timely as well as impressive and environmentally friendly. Dashboards are a good feature to use to ensure project information is in one place, and your team is literally on the same page.

16
Resource Management

Implementing good resource management is fundamental for running successful projects. In a fully-developed schedule, specific people, equipment, and materials will be assigned to activities in order to get the work done. When activities are assigned resources, the schedule is said to be **resource-loaded**. However, in order to use such a schedule, you must have a firm grip on your resources. The **Resources** tab contains a number of screens that help you to do just that. We covered the basics of resource and role administration in *Chapter 6, Resources.* In this chapter, we will cover three other main functionalities associated with resources and roles:

- Planning allows you to put resource place-holders into projects without having to assign your resources to specific activities
- Assignments helps you to assign resources where they are needed
- Analysis shows you what resources you are currently using and where

Planning

Sometimes you know you need certain people or roles for a project, but you are not yet ready to assign them to specific tasks. Through the **Resources** tab, you can assign resources to a project at the project and **Work Breakdown Structure (WBS)** level. Note that this planning assignment does not necessarily prevent the resources from being used elsewhere. Instead, the **Resources** tab lets you add resources to your project during the early planning phase, without removing them from the general resource pool. You may later on choose to assign these resources to actual activities once the project is approved and underway. You can also prevent a planned resource from being used in other projects by checking the **Committed** box in the specific assignment. This is one way to securely reserve a resource for a project.

The following screenshot shows the **Resources** tab:

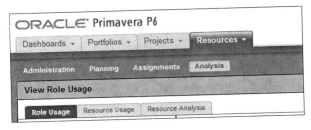

The planning resources feature is similar to top-down budgeting, in that the planned resource assignments do not tie directly to the actual assignments made to activities. Instead, you can think of this as a wish list to refer to when assigning resources to projects. Ideally, once you have created all your activities and made all of the assignments, your assignments will somewhat match what is planned, though this is not strictly necessary.

There are two main modes when planning resources. In the first mode, you choose from **Portfolios**, **Project Codes**, or **Projects**. The screen will then show you a list of selected projects and, beneath them, their WBS and resources (see the left screen in the following screenshot). In the second view, you choose from among **Resources**, **Teams**, **Resource Codes**, **Roles** and **Role Teams**. In this second view, you see first the resources, and then the projects beneath them (see the right-hand side screen in the following screenshot):

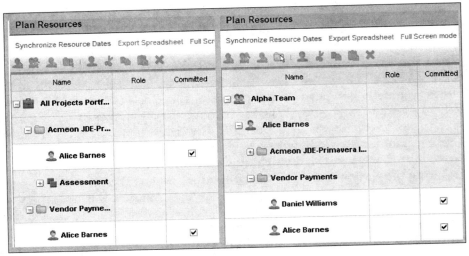

To open resource planning, go to **Resources | Planning**. If you do not see your projects, do not panic! You simply need to choose some criteria to determine which projects and/or resources to view. Click on the icon to the right of the text box after the words **Filter and group by**.

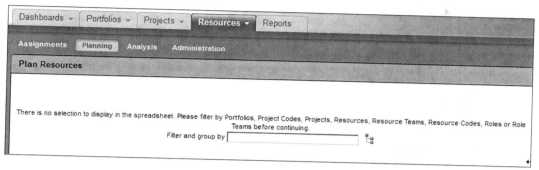

This will open up a familiar screen that lets you select from a number of criteria, including projects, portfolios, and various resource and role properties. Note here that you can also select **Resource Teams** and **Role Teams**, as described in *Chapter 6*.

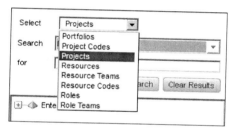

Choose the filtering criteria, and now you are able to begin planning.

Planning by project

When you are in project-based mode and you choose a project or a WBS element, the following three icons are enabled:

The **Activity Resource Assignment** icon lets you choose a resource to assign using the standard resource selection screen.

The **Role** icon lets you assign a role to the Project or WBS element.

The Search icon is new. This one lets you search and locate resources using a sophisticated filter. You can search on a wide range of criteria, including date range, role, proficiency.

For example, in the following screenshot we are searching for all resources with **Developer** as the **Primary Role** with **Proficiency** of **Master**:

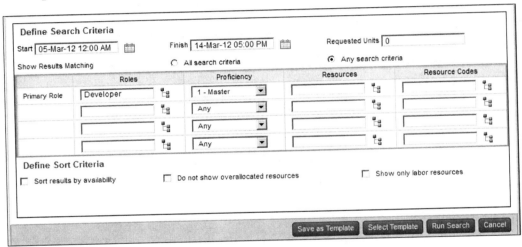

Once you have created a search criterion you can save it by pressing the **Save as Template** button. When you want to use a template in the future, choose it using the **Select Template** button. When you press the **Run Search** button, the search criteria are used to find all the resources that match.

Planning by resource

When you are viewing and planning by resource, the three icons are grayed out. Instead, the folder icon is enabled, as shown in the following screenshot. If you click on a resource, and then the folder icon, you will be able to choose a project. You can assign the resource to the project, or choose to assign the resource to a WBS element within the project.

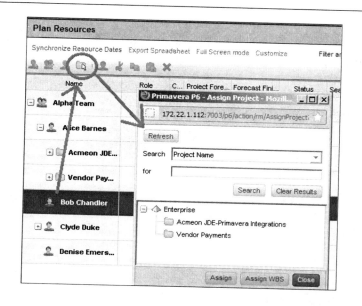

Splitting

You may want to split resource planning within a project or WBS element. One example would be that you need to have one architect resource dedicated 75 percent of the time and an engineer dedicated the other 25 percent. Or, you may want to have two architect roles and one engineer assigned. At the planning phase, it is not necessary to know which specific architect will be needed, but it may be very helpful to see that there are two roles to fill.

In another situation, you may want to split the planning by time. For example, one project manager might fill the role from February through April, while another one might fill the role for the remainder of the project.

To split a resource, you should be in the project-based planning view. Select a resource and notice that the split icon is now enabled. Click on the icon circled in the the following screenshot, and the splitting window appears, as shown as follows. There now are a few choices to make.

First, select a resource to split. There are a number of search criteria to choose from, including resource ID and name, timesheet login, e-mail, and resource codes.

Next, choose by what percentage to split the work. As in the examples mentioned previously, you can split the work by 75 percent and 25 percent or by some other breakdown. By default, the splitting is 50 percent.

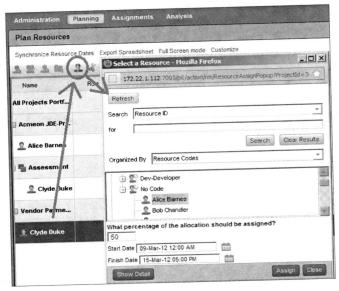

If you would rather split by time, leave the percentage alone and choose a start and a finish date. In the example given earlier, you would take one resource and assign it from February 1 through April 30, then let the other resource cover the rest of the project's duration.

Assignments

The **Assignments** tab shows you all of the assignments in your projects. The results can be quite large, so this is a good place to use a filter. For example, the following screenshot illustrates using a filter to show only unassigned roles. These are the activities that need specific resources assigned to them.

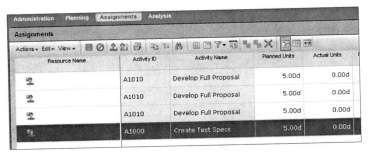

On this same screen you can assign and alter resources. If you double-click on the **A1000** activity as shown in the previous screenshot, the resource selection screen is displayed. You may then select a resource, which then assigns it to that activity.

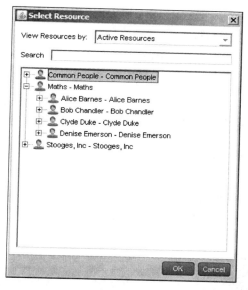

There are a number of standard filters that come with P6 right out of the box. In the preceding example we have chosen **All unstaffed assignments**, but you can choose from other helpful filters, such as **My assignments** to see all activities assigned to you. Another helpful filter is **Assignments occurring in the next 10 days**, which lets you see the upcoming assignments. You can of course alter the number of look-ahead days as needed.

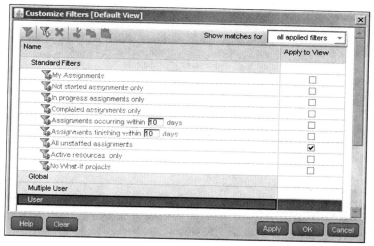

Now that you have seen how to assign resources quickly, let's look at the resource analysis tools. The screens here will help you to see the impact of all those assignments you have made.

Resource analysis

Resource analysis lets you see how resources and roles are assigned in your projects. This will show you what roles need to be filled and how your people are assigned, whether they are under or over allocated. One thing to note is that before you can analyze resources, you must summarize the projects. Go into **Projects | EPS**, choose your project, and choose **Actions | Summarize**. Depending on the size and speed of your database, this may take a few seconds to a few minutes. In some organizations, summarization of projects may be run as a scheduled job, so that all projects are summarized on a daily basis.

Once your job is summarized, you can analyze resources by going to the **Resources** tab choosing **Analysis**, then the **Resource Analysis** tab, as shown in the following screenshot:

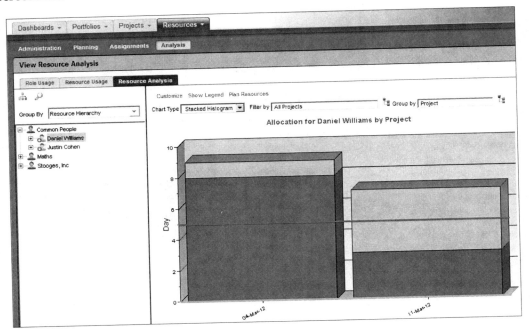

To see how a specific resource is being used, select the resource. There are a number of chart types from which to choose. By default, you will see the stacked histogram that in many cases is the most useful chart. Other options include side-by-side histogram, pie chart, and area chart.

For a given resource you may also filter by projects, project codes, and portfolios. You may also group by project or project code.

The **Resource Usage** tab shows how specific resources are being used. The spreadsheet view shows a breakdown of a resource's allocated hours for each project assigned. In the following screenshot you can see that for the week of March 4, **Daniel Williams** has been assigned to work on two projects with a total of nine days of work, and is therefore, over allocated by four days:

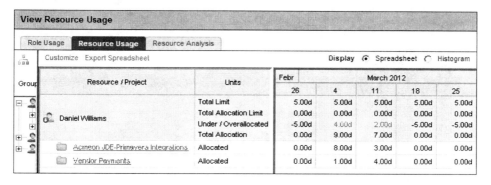

Besides the spreadsheet view, you can also view usage as a histogram. In the next screen we look at **Role Usage**. As you can see, we need to staff some developer roles. You know what to do—go to the **Assignments** screen, find those unassigned roles, and assign them.

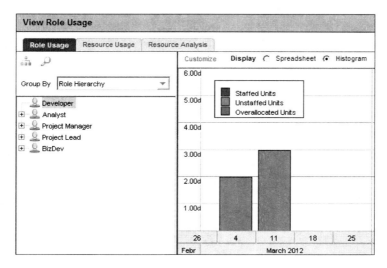

For the role usage, the histogram shows over allocated units, staffed units, and unstaffed units, all in different colors for easy identification.

Summary

In this chapter we have gone through the tools available to help you manage resources across all of your projects. You have seen how to reserve resources through resource planning, how to assign resource through the assignment screens, and how to view the allocation and use of resources in the analysis screens. With these tools in your arsenal you can master resource management in a number of ways.

In the appendices you will learn how Primavera P6 can be integrated with ERP systems. One commonly desired touch point between P6 and ERP is to tie together employee resources in ERP and labor resources in P6. Once this is done, the powerful resource management tools of P6 can feed right back into the ERP system, and across the enterprise.

A
Integrations

Oracle owns a wide variety of software products, many of which, such as Primavera, were created by independent companies and then acquired by Oracle. Yet it is strategically important to Oracle that these products work together. There are a number of approaches to unify these disparate systems. The core technology behind this unification is implementing a standards-based web-services API. This API series of interfaces allow virtually any software—from Java, to .NET, to Ruby, to Excel—to communicate with Oracle software using an HTTP client that passes SOAP messages.

On top of these interfaces, Oracle implements specific integrations between its products. These integrations may vary in their underlying architecture, but at a high level, Oracle has implemented a set of standard integrations between P6 and a number of its ERP systems. In this appendix we start with a general overview of integration, and then discuss the standard integrations between P6 and the following key Oracle products:

- JD Edwards
- PeopleSoft
- Oracle E-Business Suite

Integration overview

Integration is one of those words that means different things to different people, and therefore usually winds up with a bad reputation. In this appendix, we have a very specific meaning of integration. It is the set of processes that exchange data between P6 and one of the three Oracle ERP systems.

ERP stands for **Enterprise Resource Planning**. If you think this sounds a lot like P6, you are right. But P6 and ERP systems have different origins and end-goals. P6 grew out of construction and engineering scheduling, while ERP systems generally grew out of accounting and other processes and systems used to run a business. Such systems include components for:

- Accounts Payable for paying vendors, suppliers, and subcontractors
- Accounts Receivable for being paid by customers
- Human Resources for managing employees
- Payroll for paying employees
- Address Book Management for tracking other people and businesses
- Contract Management for managing the terms and deliverables of contracts

These systems are fairly generic across companies. Your corner bakery needs Accounts Payable, as does your neighborhood bank and your national rail line. There are many such systems out in the world, each being popular in some subset of industries. Among the top ERP systems worldwide are the *Oracle Big Three*: *JD Edwards*, *PeopleSoft*, and *E-Business Suite*. Their main competitor at the top tier is SAP. These are the ERP systems used by most Fortune 500 companies and by many governments. These systems are designed to handle massive amounts of data with thousands of simultaneous users.

Below this level are a plethora of ERP systems, including Timberline, Lawson, MRI, and Microsoft Dynamics, all the way down to Quickbooks. And of course, many companies, large and small, run their businesses with a disparate set of *home grown* systems.

Besides the ERP systems, there are also domain-specific applications that perform some of the functionality of ERP systems, but in a more focused manner. One example would be Maximo, which is a widely used Work Order management system, or Hard Dollar, used in project estimation.

Integration benefits

For integrations between P6 and ERP there are often two points of view involved:

- **Project Management** sees things at the project level, in terms of delivering the full scope of the project on time and within budget
- **Accounting** sees the project as a cost center, where the dollars allocated and spent need to be accounted for accurately, often in compliance with government regulations and **Generally Accepted Accounting Principles (GAAP)**

A few of the concerns of Project Management versus Accounting are listed in the following table:

Project Management	Accounting
• Completing project scope	• Appropriate project expenditures
• Meeting the schedule	• Reduced financial risk
• Avoiding claims	• Regulatory compliance
• Managing crews, equipment, and materials	• Meeting payment terms on invoices
• More progress, less paperwork	• Accurate recognition of revenue

Often, companies may treat their Project Management and ERP systems as two completely independent entities. And given the level of a specific company's process maturity, this may be the right approach. However, integrating systems can bring about a number of benefits, including:

- Enforcing best practices
- Ensuring data integrity
- Scaling to a large volume of projects

Enforcing best practices

In order to integrate data between two or more systems, the people working in those systems must use the systems in a consistent manner. You cannot have schedules on one project updated biweekly, and on another project updated at the whim of the manager, and expect to have meaningful ways to compare progress on both jobs. In order to have working integrations, you must establish how projects will be managed in a consistent manner. This is not to say that you must manage a $30,000 project in exactly the same way as a $30,000,000 project, but you do need to have all interested parties first sit down and talk face-to-face about how the company wants to manage projects. In many ways, the plan to integrate data is successful before it even begins, simply by requiring that these conversations take place.

Ensuring data integrity

You know the old adage, *garbage in, garbage out*. When you integrate systems, the integration processes themselves require that certain rules be enforced before any data can be exchanged. For example, your committed costs should not exceed your budgeted dollars. Cost accounts and vendor identification in one system must match those in the other system.

Calendars must be consistent so that, for example, the P6 calendar does not have one day as a working day while the same day is a holiday in the ERP system. These requirements need not be onerous. In a well-designed set of integrations, any discrepancies are quickly identified and flagged, and the appropriate parties are notified. This tight feedback loop ensures that current people learn how to use the system consistently, and that new people can quickly learn the rules of the system.

Fewer people handling more projects

Integrated data systems ultimately remove information silos, as well as duplication of effort and other manual activities that keep people doing "busy work" rather than pushing projects to completion and profitability. Rather than waiting until project completion to learn whether you've made or lost money, you know in real time. Rather than fighting claims after the fact, you can see problems arising before they become an issue. As project personnel are moved from one project to another, there is a consistent, professional approach to handling project information. And because projects are managed consistently, you can measure results and improve your project management processes.

Integration pitfalls

Integration is not trivial, and there are a number of pitfalls to avoid.

Over-analysis

The first item is **over-analysis**. As with any endeavor, you should aim first to solve the easy situations. For example, we can all agree that the budgets in P6 should reflect the budgeted project costs in ERP. And fortunately, project-level budgeting in P6 is fairly simple so that this is easy to accomplish. However, mapping budgets down to the WBS-level can quickly become a quagmire, as different projects with different WBS structures can generate lively debate. As you will see later, in the Oracle integrations if you can agree that WBS will match at a fairly high level, you can integrate budgets easily. This is because budgeting is a general concept that is handled pretty consistently across a wide range of companies.

Work orders, on the other hand, can mean many things to many people, and can vary widely among industries. Do you mean a work order to fertilize an oak tree the next time your crew is in the area during regular maintenance, or do you mean a work order to bring in an emergency team to replace a leaking vessel? To integrate work orders, you need to evaluate carefully all the ways they are used in your company, and then come up with some common rules that handle 80 percent of the most common situations.

For the small percentage of work orders that will not simply flow between ERP and P6, just let these go, and resolve that you will continue to use manual and redundant processes in these situations. You will find that by handling the majority with integrated processes, the remaining "squeaky wheels" are much less of an issue.

To this same point, evaluate the cost benefits of integration. In one recent integration consulting project, the client was treating subcontracts and purchase orders at the same level. The subcontract integration was fairly simple, while the purchase order integration rules were quickly running out of control. When one of the project sponsors was asked what percentage of project costs were purchase orders, he replied, "Less than one percent." That settled the matter: energy was put into integrating subcontracts while leaving purchase orders alone.

Imposing external culture

Often a company will bring in a well-known consultancy to *tell them what to do*. And the consultants will do just that, showing how the company is currently doing so many things wrong, not following the latest management theories, and not using the latest technologies. They will then lay out how the company should alter its work flows, change its project management structure, and apply integration technology as a silver bullet to solve all their woes.

What people in this situation do not realize is that the company that hired them obviously knows what they are doing or else they would not have a budget to hire a team of expensive consultants. Also, that no one knows their own business better than the people running the business day-to-day. When companies look to integration, they are not actually looking to fundamentally change how they work. They are looking for help in identifying inefficiencies that can be solved by automating certain processes and replacing manual, duplicate data-entry with reliable, automated processes. The non-automated processes that are currently in place are not in and of themselves terrible, but they could be improved if someone who knew integration asked the right questions.

To this same end, the integration team needs to understand that the integrations are not only about communications between data systems, but are first and foremost about communications between individuals. It is true that an accountant should not be making decisions about project scheduling, and that a project scheduler should not be making decisions about the chart of accounts. However, each should understand and respect the point of view of the other. In this respect, the role of integration consultant is less that of a dictator, and more that of a marriage counselor, or an orchestra conductor.

In a well-run integration project, all stakeholders involved in a project should feel that their needs and concerns are being met, and that the integrations are helping them all to make the company and its projects successful.

Underestimating technical skillset

P6 and ERP integration is not rocket science. Yet if you expect to hire top-notch business gurus, take their advice, and then hire a kid off the street, or your brother-in-law working out of his garage to implement your business-critical integrations, then you do not appreciate the complexities involved, and are in for a world of suffering. The relatively accessible APIs of both P6 and the Oracle ERP systems make it technically fairly simple to integrate data. Yet this also makes it quite simple for the insufficiently careful person to completely ruin the systems upon which your company relies. Anyone who has the power to send data into your systems should also have experience doing such work and a healthy professional background working with both systems.

Make sure that the person who is ultimately responsible for your integrations is in constant in-depth communication with both your ERP and P6 system owners. Make sure that they understand how the integrations work, and the possible impacts the integrations will have on both ERP and P6 systems.

We mention these cautionary tales not because we believe that integrations are problematic, but because we know that properly implemented integrations can have a tremendously positive impact on a company.

Integration possibilities

As mentioned, Oracle has taken to heart the idea of establishing well-defined, easily accessible APIs for all of their products. The integrations to be discussed in the next sections show the standard integration between P6 and the main three Oracle ERP systems. These integrations are pretty basic, but are also useful to the majority of companies. If you want to create your own system to be built upon the Oracle integration fundamentals, you can do so using the Oracle APIs. For example, work orders are not addressed in the standard integrations, but once a company can define proper scope, it is quite possible to integrate work orders between systems. And of course, as Oracle makes advancements in the products, more integration points and capabilities are expected to come with every new release.

Integration technology

The integrations from Oracle for JD Edwards and E-Business Suite are based on a set of technologies developed by Oracle.

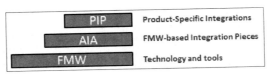

At the base of this technology is **Oracle Fusion Middleware (FMW)**. This is a set of software components such as WebLogic Server, Java Enterprise Edition, and SOA Suite. They are fairly generic tools that can be used to develop other applications. Many Oracle products are moving towards using Fusion Middleware as their foundation, and this can easily be seen in the latest releases of Primavera P6, where WebLogic Server and BI Publisher are now core components.

The **Application Integration Architecture (AIA)** is a set of tools built on top of FMW. These tools are designed to facilitate integrating data among systems. Components include definitions of standard business objects, a messaging and orchestration system, connectors to read and write data, security, versioning, and process flows, to name just a few.

The **Process Integration Packs (PIP)** are product-specific formalizations of integration data flows and processes. For example, the integrations between EBS and P6 are implemented in a PIP.

This may sound confusing and complicated. Perhaps this analogy will help. Pretend that you are five years old and are going to have a tea party with your friend. You will make the tea party set out of Lego bricks. If integrations were a Lego tea-party, then Fusion Middleware is the Lego brick itself. They are the preformed, yet generic items that you can use to build whatever you like, such as a set of tea cups. Application Integration Architecture is the cups and plates that you build with the Lego bricks, as well as the rules of etiquette when pouring tea. The Process Integration Pack is the specific tea party between you and your friend, with Chamomile tea and Madeline cookies. It's not so complicated when viewed that way, is it?

JD Edwards

JD Edwards is widely used in a number of industries, including manufacturing, distribution, and asset-intensive industries. It is in these asset-intensive industries where capital projects are a major concern that P6 and JDE meet.

The standard integrations from Oracle are based on a Process Integration Pack. In order to use the PIP, it and the underlying technology must be purchased and installed separately from the JDE install. JD Edwards has two main code branches: EnterpriseOne and World. The integrations work with EnterpriseOne, not with World, and with EnterpriseOne versions 9.0 and above.

The integration points between JDE and P6 can be broken into two components, global data and project data. As you will see, this pattern is true with EBS and PeopleSoft as well.

Global data exchanged between P6 and JDE is oriented around the management of resources. Resources in P6 can tie to three different entities in JDE:

- Assets in JDE map into non-labor resources in P6
- Materials in JDE map into material resources in P6
- Address Book employees in JDE map into labor resources in P6

In JDE, assets can be managed from a number of modules, including **Capital Asset Management** and **Service Management**. No matter which JDE modules are used to manage the assets, the integration pulls equipment data from the F1201 family of tables and rates from the F1301 family of tables.

Materials in JDE are managed through a number of modules such as **Materials Management**. The integration pulls materials from the F4101 family of tables and the item rates from F4106.

In JD Edwards, all individuals and corporations are stored in the **address book**, which revolves around the F0101 set of tables. Items in the address book include suppliers, customers, and subcontractors, as well as employees. These entities can be pulled into P6 as global labor resources.

Global roles from JDE are stored in the job tasks table F08001. These roles are brought into P6 as global roles.

Calendars from the F13 system of JDE are brought in as global calendars.

The supplemental job table F5109 brings JDE chart types into P6 as WBS Project Phase categories.

In all of this, JDE is considered the master of the data. Changes in JDE will flow into P6, but changes in P6 are not sent back into JDE. For this reason, these global resources should not be altered in P6.

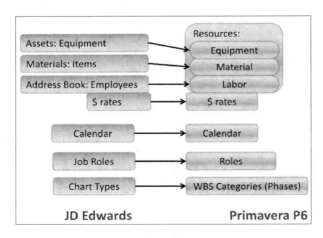

Project-level data exchanged between JDE and P6 is oriented around synchronizing budgets, forecasts, and dates at the WBS level.

Projects may originate in either P6 or in JDE. In practice, it is best to choose one system or the other as the origination point of projects.

When a project originates in JDE and is sent into P6, the JDE chart of accounts (F0901) and cost code schedule (F51901) are used to create top-level WBS elements in the P6 project, which correspond to the project phase. Account balances and forecasts are brought into these same WBS elements from the JDE account balances table, F0902. When a project originates in P6 and is sent to JDE, the reverse of this process happens.

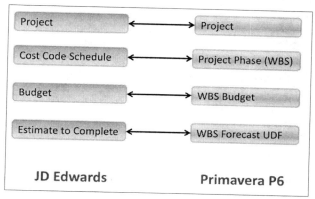

As the project is scheduled in P6, the dates at the WBS level are updated. These dates then flow back into JDE on the **Cost Code Schedule**.

E-Business Suite

The **E-Business Suite** (EBS) integration with P6 is similar to the one for JDE. It too uses the Application Integration Architecture, Fusion Middleware, and a process Integration Pack. The integrations require Oracle Project Foundation 11.5.10.2 or later.

One difference is that EBS has built-in project functionality quite similar to P6. This is implemented in its **Project Costing** and **Project Management** modules. But the ideas are similar: resource definitions and financial costs are owned by EBS, and resource assignment and scheduling are owned by Primavera.

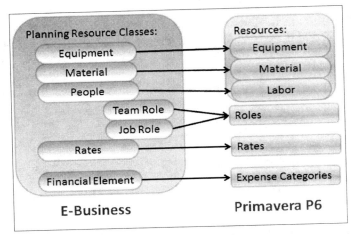

As in the JDE integration, resources and roles are defined in EBS and then sent into P6.

The integration at the project level does differ, however. Shown in the following screenshot are some of the project-level integration settings in EBS.

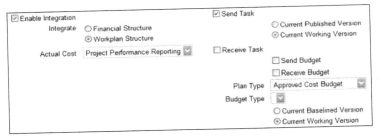

Projects can be integrated in two fundamentally different manners, by **workplan** or by **financial structure**. In EBS, the concept of a **workplan** is analogous to a WBS element. You can choose to integrate at the workplan level, which means that activities are exchanged between EBS and P6, and actual costs are sent from EBS to P6 at the resource level.

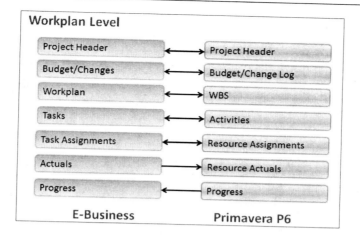

If you choose to integrate by **financial plan**, then data is synchronized at a higher level. For example, actual costs are placed into a user-defined field at the WBS level. The level of WBS mapping can be set to only map data at a number of levels. So you may just map at the top-level WBS, or at all levels, depending on your needs.

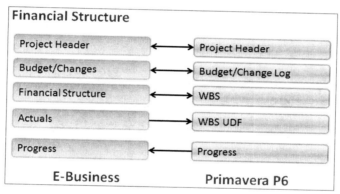

In both situations, the project header is synchronized, and the project header integration will allow you to create and close projects. Budgets are handled similarly in both situations as well.

PeopleSoft

PeopleSoft is widely used in local government, healthcare, and education. As the name implies, PeopleSoft's origins rise from managing groups of people.

Unlike the JDE and EBS integrations, the PeopleSoft integration with P6 comes *out of the box* at no additional cost, and with very little configuration required. The integration technology used is not FMW and AIA, but is instead based on PeopleSoft's Integration Broker technology.

The P6 integration first appeared in PeopleSoft version 9.0 in 2011 and has been improved and expanded for PeopleSoft 9.1 in 2012. Both the **PeopleSoft Program Management** and **Project Costing** modules are required for the integration.

As with JDE and EBS, the global data exchanged between P6 and PeopleSoft center around the three kinds of P6 resources: people, materials, and equipment (labor, materials, and nonlabor).

You can only have materials in PeopleSoft if you have installed the **Order Management** and **Purchasing** modules.

Similarly, you must have **Asset Management** installed in order to set up Equipment.

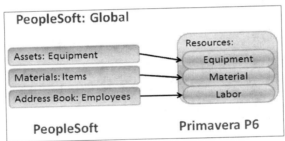

[The global integrations will not send over calendars, roles, or rates. These items must be entered manually in each system.]

In PeopleSoft, there is no distinction between activities and WBS elements. Activities are simply WBS elements that do not have any other elements beneath them. These two entities are very distinct in P6, and so when sending data such as resource assignments back to PeopleSoft, you must be careful that the activities and WBS elements map properly between the two systems. The installation guide from Oracle covers how to manage these properly and avoid common pitfalls.

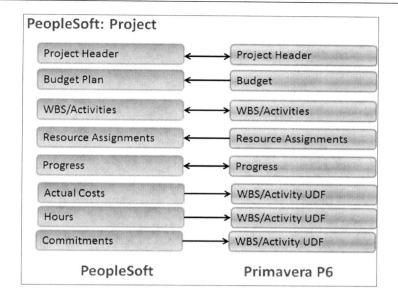

Actual Costs, Hours, and Commitments are sent from PeopleSoft into user-defined fields at the WBS or activity level, depending on how the data is rolled up.

 PeopleSoft 9.1 also allows integration between its own internal timesheets application and P6's timesheet application, **Progress Reporter**.

Summary

In this appendix we have touched lightly upon the topic of integration, and given an overview of the standard P6 integrations provided by Oracle for PeopleSoft, E-Business Suite, and JD Edwards. Oracle has put much effort into making sure that its products are accessible through standards-based APIs. They have also created an integration framework and applied it to integrating P6 with two of their ERP systems.

Integration of data is a powerful way to streamline your work processes. But it should be done in a thoughtful manner. If done properly, it can bring great advantages to your project management processes.

B
Reporting

Reporting is getting data from the system into a format where you can share it with others. Usually this report is a printout, a PDF file, or an Excel workbook. With P6, there are many ways by which you can retrieve and view data. In this appendix we will cover the following reporting options:

- P6 Professional
  - Screen Printing
  - Reports
- P6 Web Client
  - Screen Export
  - BI Publisher

Reporting from Professional

The simplest way to report data from P6 Professional is to choose **File | Print** and follow the onscreen options. You may also press *Ctrl + P* or click on the printer icon. However, you will want to choose **Print Preview** so that you can edit the formatting of the reports.

Screen printing

Choose **File | Print Preview**. This brings up a screen showing what the output would look like on your printer. In the following screenshot we have chosen a small envelops size in order for it to fit well into this book:

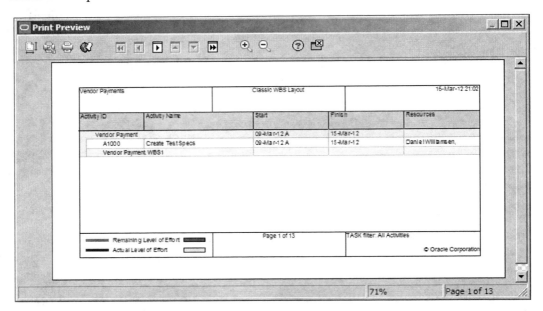

The main things to notice here are the page navigation buttons, the boxes with arrows at the top, and the text in the lower right-hand corner of the screen, **Page 1 of 13**. This printout would go for 13 pages! Specifically, this report includes a Gantt chart that extends from project's start to end. You can adjust this by clicking on the icon at the upper-left of the screen (the paper icon with the up/down and left/right arrow). There are a number of tabs which will be familiar for Excel users. The first page lets you adjust the scale of the report so that it will fit into a set number of pages. Here is also where you would be able to adjust the paper size to something a little more reasonable than a DL Envelope!

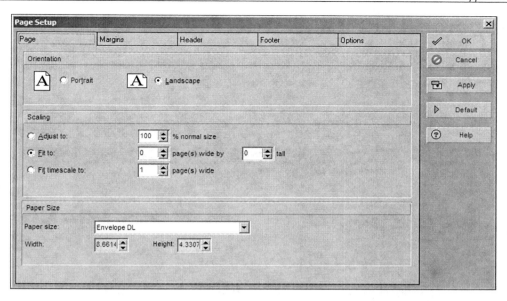

The **Margins**, **Header**, and **Footer** tabs are helpful and were discussed in *Chapter 2, Getting Around: Understanding and Customizing the P6 Interface*. The unique tab is **Options**. This lets you choose what will be printed. If you don't need the Gantt chart, deselect it.

If you must show the chart, you can choose a date range to display.

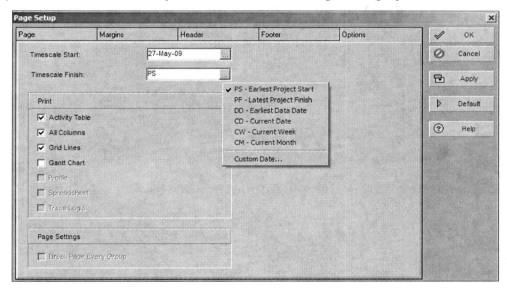

Once the preview looks reasonable, you may print it out from your favorite device.

Reports

P6 comes with a reporting engine and a set of preconfigured reports. You can see these reports by clicking on **Tools | Reports | Reports**. This brings up a tab showing a number of reports grouped by area of functionality:

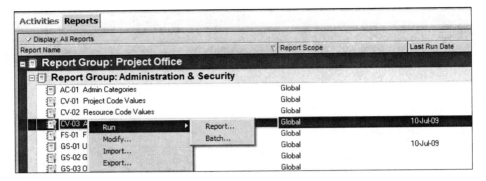

If you right-click a report and click on **Run | Report…**, you will be able to run the report and then view and save it in a number of formats and with a number of options.

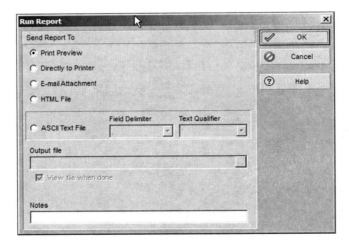

If you choose **Print Preview**, you will see preview of the report:

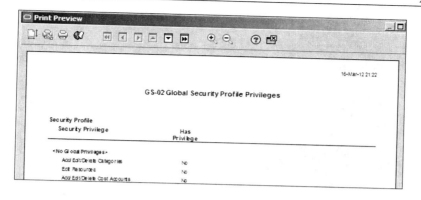

 In the main reports listing the reports are grouped together in bands and levels. You can edit this organization and move reports around by clicking on **Tools | Reports | Report Groups**.

Sometimes you want to print a collection of reports all together at once. This is called a **batch**. You can view and manage batch reports by clicking on **Tools | Reports | Batch**.

There are **Global Batches** that show data that is not specific to one project, and **Project Batches** that will show report data designed on the currently opened project. Create a new batch by pressing **Add**. Give it a name, and then assign existing reports to the batch.

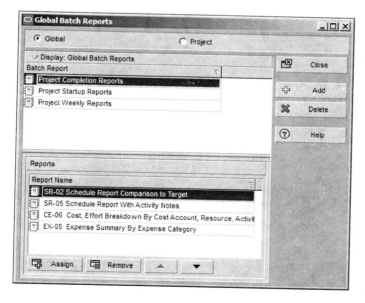

Editing reports

You are not limited to the reports that come with P6. You can copy and modify them as needed, or create your own reports anew. To do this, click on **Tools** | **Reports** | **Report Wizard…**.

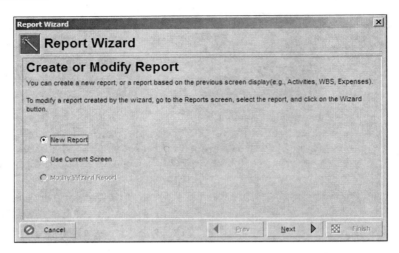

When you run the wizard you can create a new report, or base it on an existing screen. If a report was originally created by the wizard, you can also modify it. The wizard walks you through selecting data to show, and then lets you sort, group, and filter as needed.

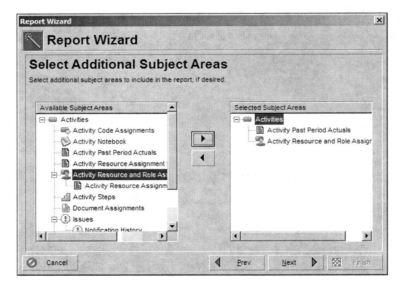

This is a very handy way to create straightforward reports for showing your data.

You may also use the report editor to create your report at a finer level of detail. To enter the editor, go to the **Reports** screen, right-click on a report and click on **Modify...**.

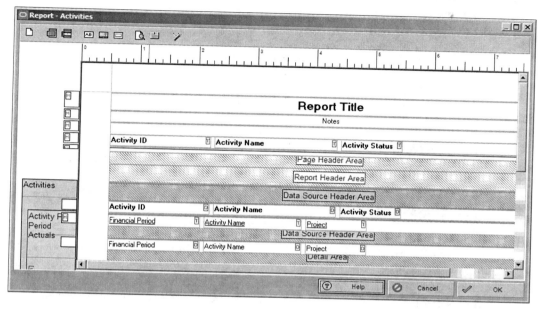

You can use the report to generate far more sophisticated reports than the wizard can produce. Such reports can be optimized for HTML viewing, and can include hyperlinks. You can also access fields and create combinations of fields that are not available through the wizard. A full discussion of this powerful tool is beyond the scope of this book.

The report editor has been around for many years, and is loathed by some, loved by others. Although it does the job, the technology behind it has not advanced much over the past few years. The reporting engine behind the P6 Web client, however, is quite advanced. We invite the reader to experiment with the reporting tool in P6 and to consult the built-in help documentation.

Reporting from the web client

The web client has two main ways to report data. The first is to export screen data to Excel, and the second is to use BI Publisher.

Screen printing

Many screens have the option to export to Excel. First create a screen showing exactly the data you need, and then choose the export button (shown in the following screenshot) in the toolbar. Once you have the data in Excel you can modify it to display exactly what you need to show.

This can be convenient, but can also become tedious if the same data is required again and again. A far better solution is to show the report as a BI Publisher report.

BI Publisher

BI Publisher is a key part of the Oracle Fusion Middleware stack. The technology for BI Publisher was originally developed for Oracle E-Business suite, but it is now used in a wide range of systems, including Primavera Contract Manager, JD Edwards, and PeopleSoft. From a user's point-of-view, it is very convenient to learn one well-designed reporting tool that is also used in many other systems. BI Publisher has many users, and many resources available to help with reporting needs.

BI Publisher is designed such that the data being reported on is completely separated from the layout of the report, and the layout of the report is completely separated from the report output format.

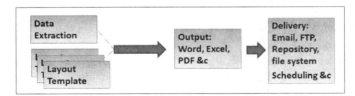

This has a number of advantages. Data is extracted into XML format, which means that you can design a report using sample XML data stored in a plain-text file. The data itself can originate from a database, from multiple databases, from a CSV file, from a web service, or a mixture of these. You can design your layout using a template builder for MS Word or for MS Excel. And with BI Publisher 11g, there is now a very convenient web interface for editing reports, which means there is no software to install on your local machine.

The report is generated by the BI Publisher engine and rendered into a desired format. The same report can be rendered as PDF, MS Word, MS Excel, HTML, or even in an interactive web view. This rendered output can then be sent on demand or on a schedule to many destinations including e-mail, content repository, a file system, and more. The possibilities available for reporting from BI Publisher are quite amazing.

When reports are set up properly, P6 will show a fifth tab called **Reports**. The list of reports is similar to the ones for P6 Professional.

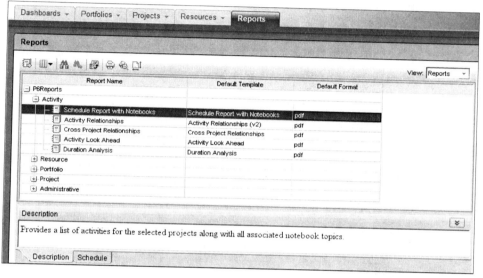

Reports can be run on the spot or scheduled. If you run a report on the spot you can choose to have P6 e-mail the report, or save it locally. The default output formats of the reports are PDF, RTF, and XML. RTF is readable by MS Word, and XML is a data-storage format that is easy for computers to read.

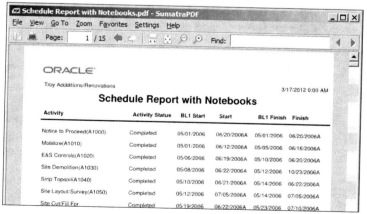

The XML format has one great advantage – it can be used as a data set to design more BI Publisher reports!

Reports may be set to run on a schedule. This is very handy if you need a set of reports all generated at the same time. For example, you may need reports showing data as of the 25th of the month available for a review meeting the following day. You can schedule a set of reports to run at 11:59 pm on the 25th. They can then be automatically e-mailed to all meeting participants. In this sense, scheduled reports are similar to the batch reports of P6 Professional, but with the added bonus that you can schedule the delivery.

When you set up a schedule you can choose the format and the e-mail recipients.

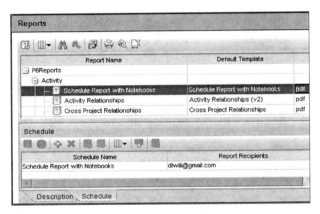

To view and change the detailed information about the the schedule, right-click on it to bring up the **Options** and **Schedule** screen. In the screen shown, we are making a new schedule for a report. Choose the format and the e-mail recipients.

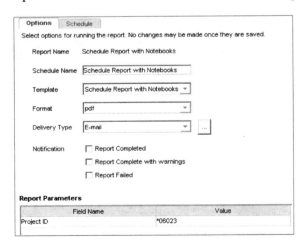

You can edit the e-mail subject line and message, and may CC and BCC recipients as desired:

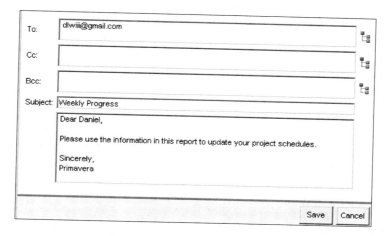

The scheduling tab lets you choose to run the report once, daily, weekly, or monthly:

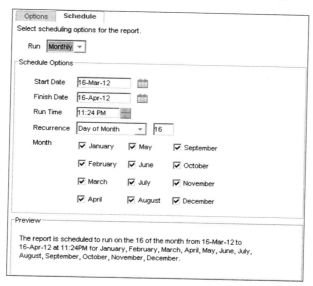

These are only the features of BI Publisher that come with P6 *out of the box*. The full BI Publisher product will allow you to modify reports and create new ones. You can generate output in more formats, such as Excel and HTML, and have more delivery options beyond e-mail, such as saving reports into a document repository such as Oracle Universal Content Management or even to send reports to an FTP site.

Summary

You have now seen the myriad ways in which you can get reports in both P6 Professional and in the Web Client. In P6 Professional the options include screen printing and using the built-in report tools. In the web client, the main reporting tool is BI Publisher. Both systems come with a number of reports that should serve many of your common needs. You can use the reports to share information with your team as you successfully plan and execute your projects.

While BI Publisher is a powerful tool, its just the tip of the iceberg, one part of a larger application called **Oracle Business Intelligence, Enterprise Edition**, or **OBIEE**. This large application is a framework of tools and technologies for creating data warehouses, transforming and storing data, and generating a wide variety of reports for a range of devices, including mobile. There is a specific implementation of **OBIEE** dedicated to reporting on P6, which is called P6 Analytics. This is sold separately from P6, and serves to grant far greater reporting capability than is found in P6 itself (which is saying quite alot!). Using P6 Analytics, users can drill down into the data and create sophisticated ad-hoc reports. A full discussion of P6 Analytics is beyond the scope of this book, but we invite interested readers to learn more online.

Index

Return on Investment (ROI) 256-258
Risk entity 220
risk management 184
risks
about 175, 176
managing, in P6 Enterprise 183, 184
managing, in P6 Professional 180-183
Risks tab 120
roles
about 137, 138
General tab 138
Limits tab 140
Prices tab 139, 140
Resources tab 139
Roles tab, resources 137
Role Team
creating 141, 142
root node 65

S

scenarios
about 242
creating 218, 219
using 242-244
schedule 112
Schedule Performance Index (SPI) 269
Schedule Performance portlet 269
schedule, visualizing ways
about 128
activity network 129
Gantt chart 128
table view 129
scheduling
with CPM and P6 155, 156
scheduling algorithm
about 155, 156
formula for start and finish 157
scheduling engine 155
Scorecard
about 217, 226
columns 227, 228
data, selecting for display 227
waterline 228, 229
screen overview, P6 Web Client
about 30, 31
activities 32

Floating Toolbar 31
Project Expenses 32
Project Issues 32
projects 32
Project Thresholds 32
reports 32
Resource Assignments 32
resources 32
Risks 32
tracking 32
WBS 32
WP & Docs 32
screen printing
P6 Professional reporting 308, 309
web client reporting 314
screens, P6 Web Client
customizing 56
layouts, saving 56
Select Threshold Parameter window 176
Service Management 300
shared calendars 135
shifts 137
Side-by-Side Histogram 217, 233-235
sorting 227
Stacked Histogram 218, 235, 236
Start Date, UDFs 221
start milestone activity
about 121
example 121
start to finish relationship 127
start to start relationship 126
Step entity 220
steps 112
Successors tab 119
summary indicator, UDFs 221

T

tab actions, P6 Web Client 25
table view 129
tabs, P6 Web Client
about 24
dashboards 24
portfolios 24
projects 24
reports 25
resources 24

task 112
task-dependent activity 122, 150
teams 140
technical skillset
  underestimating 298
template
  about 203
  creating, from existing project 206
  new project, creating from 207, 208
Text, UDFs 221
threat 181
thresholds
  about 175-178
  viewing 176
Timescaled Logic Diagrams 52
To Complete Performance Index (TCPI) 269
Tools menu, P6 Web Client
  about 50
  Auto-Reorganization 50
  Global Change 51
  Issues Navigator 52
  Monitor Thresholds 52
  Timescaled Logic Diagrams 52
total float 128
Trace Logic tab 120
Tracking Layout 179

U

UDF definitions
  accessing 220
UDFs
  about 219
  cost 221
  entities 219
  finish date 221
  formula 221

indicator 221
integer 221
number 221
start date 221
summary indicator 221
text 221
types 221
units per time (U/T) 135
Units & Prices tab, resources 136, 137
User Baseline
  about 193
  examples, for comparison 193
User Defined Fields. *See* UDFs
user level settings 158, 159

V

variance 128
View menu, P6 Web Client
  about 48
  Lock All Toolbars 48
  Reset All Toolbars 48

W

waterline 228, 229
Waterline Analysis 244-246
Waterville project 272
WBS entity 219
WBS Summary activity 124
Work Breakdown Structure (WBS)
  about 68
  example, for software development
    project 69-71
  inserting, into existing project 208-210
workplan 302

Thank you for buying
Oracle Primavera P6 Version 8: Project and Portfolio Management

About Packt Publishing

Packt, pronounced 'packed', published its first book "Mastering phpMyAdmin for Effective MySQL Management" in April 2004 and subsequently continued to specialize in publishing highly focused books on specific technologies and solutions.

Our books and publications share the experiences of your fellow IT professionals in adapting and customizing today's systems, applications, and frameworks. Our solution based books give you the knowledge and power to customize the software and technologies you're using to get the job done. Packt books are more specific and less general than the IT books you have seen in the past. Our unique business model allows us to bring you more focused information, giving you more of what you need to know, and less of what you don't.

Packt is a modern, yet unique publishing company, which focuses on producing quality, cutting-edge books for communities of developers, administrators, and newbies alike. For more information, please visit our website: www.packtpub.com.

About Packt Enterprise

In 2010, Packt launched two new brands, Packt Enterprise and Packt Open Source, in order to continue its focus on specialization. This book is part of the Packt Enterprise brand, home to books published on enterprise software – software created by major vendors, including (but not limited to) IBM, Microsoft and Oracle, often for use in other corporations. Its titles will offer information relevant to a range of users of this software, including administrators, developers, architects, and end users.

Writing for Packt

We welcome all inquiries from people who are interested in authoring. Book proposals should be sent to author@packtpub.com. If your book idea is still at an early stage and you would like to discuss it first before writing a formal book proposal, contact us; one of our commissioning editors will get in touch with you.

We're not just looking for published authors; if you have strong technical skills but no writing experience, our experienced editors can help you develop a writing career, or simply get some additional reward for your expertise.

Oracle Advanced PL/SQL
Developer Professional Guide

ISBN: 978-1-84968-722-5   Paperback: 440 pages

Master advanced PL/SQL Concepts along with
plenty of example questions for 1Z0-146 examination

1. Blitz the 1Z0-146 exam

2. Master the advanced features of PL/SQL to
   design and optimize code using real-time
   demonstrations

3. Efficiently design PL/SQL code with cursor
   design and subtypes

Oracle Service Bus 11g
Development Cookbook

ISBN: 978-1-84968-444-6   Paperback: 522 pages

Over 80 practical recipes to develop service and
message-oriented solution on the Oracle Service Bus

1. Develop service and message-oriented
   solutions on the Oracle Service Bus following
   best practices using this book and ebook

2. Extend your practical knowledge of building
   solutions on the Oracle Service Bus

3. Packed with hands-on cookbook recipes,
   with the complete and finished solution as an
   OSB and SOA Suite project, made available
   electronically for download

Please check **www.PacktPub.com** for information on our titles

Getting Started with Oracle Data Integrator 11g: A Hands-On Tutorial

Getting Started with Oracle Data Integrator 11g: A Hands-On Tutorial

ISBN: 978-1-84968-068-4   Paperback: 384 pages

Combine high volume data movement, complex transformations and real-time integration with robust capabilities of ODI in the practical guide

1. Discover the comprehensive and sophisticated orchestration of data integration tasks made possible with ODI, including monitoring and error-management

2. Get to grips with the product architecture and building data integration processes with technologies including Oracle, Microsoft SQL Server and XML files

3. A comprehensive tutorial packed with tips, images and best practices

Oracle JDeveloper 11gR2 Cookbook

Oracle JDeveloper 11gR2 Cookbook

ISBN: 978-1-84968-476-7   Paperback: 406 pages

Over 85 simple but incredibly effective recipes for using Oracle jDeveloper 11gR2 to build ADF applications

1. Encounter a myriad of ADF tasks to help you enhance the practical application of JDeveloper 11gR2

2. Get to grips with deploying, debugging, testing, profiling and optimizing Fusion Web ADF Applications with JDeveloper 11gR2

3. A high level development cookbook with immediately applicable recipes for extending your practical knowledge of building ADF applications

Please check **www.PacktPub.com** for information on our titles

CPSIA information can be obtained at www.ICGtesting.com
Printed in the USA
BVOW061628110912

300031BV00002B/3/P